LESSONS FOR LEADERS AND GOVERNING BOARDS

GARRY MCGIBONEY

ANAPHORA LITERARY PRESS

TUCSON, ARIZONA

ANAPHORA LITERARY PRESS
5755 E. River Rd., #2201
Tucson, AZ 85750
http://anaphoraliterary.com

Book design by Anna Faktorovich, Ph.D.

Cover Image: "A Cotton Office in New Orleans" by Edgar Degas. 1873.

Published in 2014 by Anaphora Literary Press

Lessons for Leaders and Governing Boards
Garry McGiboney—1st edition.

ISBN-13: 978-1-937536-61-9
ISBN-10: 1-937536-61-0

Library of Congress Control Number: 2014932469

LESSONS FOR LEADERS AND GOVERNING BOARDS

———————————

GARRY MCGIBONEY

CONTENTS

I would much prefer to suffer from the clean incision of an honest lancet than from a sweetened poison.
—Mark Twain

Men become accustomed to poison by degrees.
—Victor Hugo

Poison is in everything, and nothing is without poison.
—Paracelsus

INTRODUCTION

The Roman writer Titus Lucretius wrote, "*What is food to one man is bitter poison to others.*" King George III of Great Britain was notorious for his outrageous and unpredictable leadership ideas and practices. A recent study in *The Lancet* revealed that King George III was receiving liberal doses of medicine to improve his behavior, but the medicine he consumed was emetic tartar which contains arsenic. Emetic tartar taken in small doses is fairly innocuous, but there is a fine line that was crossed, turning the medicine into a destructive dose for King George III. This altered his behavior, turning him into a tyrant. In a perverse way, the same could be said about leadership and governance; because like medicine, they can both make an organization effective or poison it. Leadership is in everything, from the small family store business to large Fortune 500 companies, from a local community non-profit agency to a worldwide philanthropic organization, from the smallest private or public school classroom to the largest lecture halls on university campuses. And in many if not most of these organizations a governing board has been created to be a steward of the organization's best interests.

In her book *Bad Leadership*, Barbara Kellerman identified several types of leadership that could be considered poisonous: incompetence, rigidity, intemperance (lack of control), callousness, corruption, insularity, and evil. Rising to a level of incompetence is not so readily apparent to a leader or a governing board simply because most incompetent leaders are somewhat delusional about their own level of ability and because many of them have quality skills that seem impressive and are not clearly discernable from the bad leadership types Kellerman describes. Some leaders are blinded by their ambition, and some governing board members are easily duped by seemingly competent leaders and true believers. In *The Smartest Guys in the Room: Management Lessons from Enron's Leaders*, the authors chronicle one of the largest corporate failures in history. Enron's leadership destroyed a corporation, but more importantly, the failure of leadership and the ineptitude of the board of directors damaged the lives and reputations of employees and depleted the investments of thousands of individuals. The leadership at the top of the company and in the board room became poison to the organization. According to the authors, Enron leaders radiated so much charisma and dogmatic loyalty that they induced blind obedience in followers. This blindness to principles compromised the integrity and legitimacy of Enron's corporate practices.

Some leaders view rigidity as an asset and as a leadership function with the encouragement (intentionally or unintentionally) of the organization's governing board. It is an extension of the military model of leadership and is reinforced typically at the beginning of a leader's time at the helm of an organization as a clear message to everyone that "a new sheriff is in town." This behavior is oftentimes encouraged by the governing board, up to a certain point. This type of leader is determined to be the boss and everyone must follow blindly or leave immediately. Any employee that disagrees with the rigid leader is branded a trouble maker and poisonous to the organization. The poison that seeps from a leader who has a callous disregard for employees is often the same leadership type that lacks self-control, but the lack of self-control is not necessarily manifest in verbal outbursts and/or verbal threats. Instead, many poisonous leaders contrive to embarrass, control, demean and discourage employees in a variety of ways - through other employees or the governing board, through sarcasm in front of others, by marginalizing the duties of employees, or by demoting employees. There are many examples of how these poisonous traits take a leader to a point where self-importance either weakens an organization or leads to the destruction of the leader. In these situations, the spiraling pattern of leadership corruption leads to insularity and isolation and even to what Kellerman called "evil".

An article in *Psychology Today* titled "*A Toxic Leader Manifesto*" by Alan Goldman, describes the role and outcome of poisonous leadership and how that type of leadership style devalues organizations and crushes employee morale. Goldman challenges leaders. If a leader is determined to be poisonous, Goldman wants, with tongue-in-cheek, to make sure that type of leader does it "right." Although Goldman is having some fun with this topic, there are many essential points to gleam from his "manifesto."

It is essential to bypass dialogue and question and answers; the leader must attack, deflate or discard employees who are identified as lacking in any way or who dare challenge the leader; bullying must be cultivated and perfected; the leader must yell at and demean employees who fall short, error or are deemed annoying; the leader must stifle any workplace conversation that questions the leader; all attacks against employees must be brought forth into public forums for all to witness; it is mandatory to yell at employees in an effort to promote fear, humiliation and sufficient loss of face; when criticizing employees the leader must carry this forth harshly and publicly without any opportunity for the offending employee to respond; and the poisonous leader must remember that civilized and substantive feedback is his mortal enemy.

Goldman mentions other features of this type of leader in his manifesto, but suffice it to say that the others follow the same negative pattern. Additional research on poisonous leadership can be found in *The Allure of Toxic Leaders*. The book notes that many employees follow the toxic or poisonous leader from a basic need to survive. Employee behavior gives the leader the false impression that she is a good leader and virtually everything she does is appropriate, so the caustic style of leadership appears to be working in the organization, or so the leader and governing board believes, because employees are compliant and perhaps afraid to be anything other than compliant. The leader observes employees implementing her policies without question, and hears no criticism of her leadership style. Many times the internal poisoning of the organization is hidden by a temporary boost in productivity or the allusion of productivity or the impression to the governing board that the new leader is really "shaking things up" and, consequently, it appears that improvement, success and prestige cannot be far away. To some employees a strong, dominating, overbearing, cruel leader has a certain attraction. Typically, employees who fall into this category are those that had very little respect for the previous leader and think a new hard-driving intimidating leader will bring back past glory. Employees that have little self-respect think they deserve someone that is cruel and insensitive; yet, some aspire to be a leader of the same type, so they view the totalitarian leader as a role model. Of course, there are many talented employees who simply leave the organization because of the behavior of the leader and the governing board. They do not want to work in that type of workplace climate.

It seems that a poisonous leader would be easy to identify; therefore, it is puzzling why so many exist and equally curious as to why so many continue for years in an organization before their brand of destructive leadership is fully realized. However, poisonous leaders can be smart, strategic, manipulative, skilled, observant, instinctive, perceptive, articulate, and very persuasive. These are the same skills that many successful leaders possess, so it is not surprising that poisonous leaders continue to find work at significant levels of influence and control in organizations. A quick look at the resumes of some National Basketball Association and many CEOs will confirm this point. Governing boards that select this type of leader are naturally very defensive about their selection and are quick to point out the qualities of the leader that first made the person attractive for the position. This is a vague and weak excuse, for seldom does a poisonous leader first show signs of venomous behavior when he becomes the leader of an organization. There is usually a telling work history or behavior of the prospective leader that the governing board ignored or for some reason thought was just the type of behavior and attitude needed in the organization.

The powerfully negative impact of poisonous leadership and untrained or irresponsible governing boards in the business world can reduce profits and weaken a company's competitive edge in the market. According to an article in *Chief Executive* by Pamela Mendels, the estimated cost of a failed executive business CEO, one who is fired within 18 to 24 months of employment, ranges from $1 million to $2.7 million. By using a formula that includes the cost of recruiting and hiring the CEO, cost of a severance package, cost of finding a temporary replacement and then a permanent replacement, cost of the CEO's decisions, cost of unraveling and repositioning the company's strategic plan, and the cost of the executive's decisions and performance on the company's stock all add up to a substantial cost of failed leadership. This type of leadership takes a toll on morale and productivity, also. As reported by CDC's National Institute for Occupational Safety and Health studies show that over 40 percent of American employees classified their jobs as stressful and 75 percent of employees said the most stressful part of their job was related to the behavior of the organization's leadership. A study in the *Journal of Business and Finance* indicates that most employees prefer a more conducive, healthy, and positive working environment over a higher salary. These same studies point to workplace climate as a reflection of leadership.

Ineffective leadership from a leader and a governing board in non-profit organizations can negatively impact donations, reduce the volunteer workforce, and cause a reduction in services to the community. Moreover, poisonous leadership in educational organizations, such as private and public schools and colleges, can be equally devastating. Careers can be destroyed, of course, but more tragically the critically important quality of education for students that determines their quality of life and, over time, becomes a significant factor in economic development is compromised by poor leadership and ineffective governance. This cannot and should not be tolerated for any reason.

The danger is, as stated before, that the qualities of good leadership and poisonous leadership are so closely aligned that it is not simple to discern the two. However, it can become clearer when components of ineffective leadership and interfering governance are revealed in organizations by descriptions of behavior and subsequent results of such behavior. That is the purpose of this book. The descriptions of leaders and governing board members and their behaviors are central to better understanding why governing boards cannot misstep when choosing a leader and why governing boards must understand their role in organizational leadership and leadership evaluation.

Any discussion about poisonous leadership and governance would not be complete without including remedies or antidotes. By definition, an antidote is a substance that counteracts poison. Ineffective leaders and governing boards are not necessarily lost causes. Training and awareness can work. Sometimes the antidote has to be administered steadily over a long period of time in order to counteract ineffective leadership; for example, it takes a steady dose of supportive leadership to counteract the poisonous effects and aftereffects of dictatorial leadership.

The examples of leadership and governance, including ineffective and effective leadership, in this book come from the non-profit sector, business and industry, colleges and universities, and private and public K-12 education. Some of the stories are troubling and some are reassuring. Other stories are puzzling and yet revealing. The message should become clear after reading case studies and research that governing boards and leaders should be held accountable for allowing poisonous atmospheres to contaminate what otherwise could or should be a healthy organizations. Research shows that two-thirds of people currently in leadership positions will fail, primarily due their inability or unwillingness to build and maintain good communication practices, develop a productive management team, create a positive work climate, and work with the governing board, or due to the failures of a governing board, but it does not have to be that way.

CHAPTER 1

LEADERSHIP, HUMILITY AND CRITICISM

If you can keep your head while those around you are losing theirs,
perhaps you don't understand the situation.

—Nelson Boswell

Poison: *Effective leaders have the ability to handle criticism while ineffective leaders take any criticism as attempts to limit their power or persuasion. Additionally, effective leaders and governing boards let subordinates make hard decisions and support those decisions even during difficult times. There is a belief among ineffective leaders making difficult decisions that they must above all else protect themselves from governing board criticism. The leader believes he will become the target of criticism and thereafter work in a climate of mistrust and blame. The ineffective leader is defensive when the implementation of one of his concepts, projects, or initiatives runs into obstacles. He will not concede that his idea was flawed in design or was doomed by a lack of resources or ineffective strategies; instead, the leader blames others and may convince the governing board that he is not responsible.*

A small college was well known for its many innovative ideas and programs. The president was a gregarious, energetic and ambitious leader who enjoyed the full support of the college's governing board. He was constantly pushing his staff to implement his latest ideas, even if the staff members lacked specific details and even if they were still working on the president's previous ideas and how to put them into practice. Most staff members agreed that the president was very innovative and many of his ideas had merit. However, trying to translate ideas into practice and paying for the cost of those practices was anything but simple. The president's response to those concerns was simply, *"Make it work."* It was clear to the staff that the president did not want to hear any reason why his ideas could not be implemented, and he certainly did not want to hear that the college could not afford the cost of implementing and sustaining his projects and strategies. All he wanted to hear was, "*Yes, sir.*"

Developing an international center for innovative ideas at the college was one of the president's projects, and he had noble ideas of what it should look like and what it should do. He hired a director to lead the effort who had a stellar reputation for making such projects work. However, after arriving at the college, the person soon realized that there was no budget for any of the projects that had to be completed to make the concept work. The president heard from staff members and a few local politicians who were present at one of the international center's community events that the international center was not making much progress in bringing in new international businesses or even promoting dialogue that might lead some day to an international business and cultural center at the college. The president, while brilliant and innovative, was not a leader that could handle criticism well at all. Additionally, he viewed any delay in implementing his projects as a deliberate effort to circumvent or even sabotage his ideas. He did not want the person responsible for implementing his project to express concerns about the project, and he certainly would not tolerate the idea of a different way to develop the project. He was indifferent about the budget and operational issues.

In an article on leadership, *Five Wrong Ways to Respond to Criticism*, Ron Edmondson discusses how misinformed or misdirected leaders respond to criticism: (1) finding fault with the critic; (2) blaming others; (3) throwing back criticism; (4) ignoring an opportunity to learn; and (5) appeasing. This college president covered many of the five in his response to criticism. Instead of admitting that there were implementation challenges and issues that needed to be addressed before the international center could thrive, including those that he failed to plan for, he instead attempted to discredit the persons offering the criticism, with public comments like, "*They are not realistic with their expectations.*" "*They don't understand the complexity of the projects.*" "*They don't want it to work.*" "*They are jealous of our efforts.*" When that approach backfired, he criticized and blamed the international center staff members, particularly the director. He said publicly that the director of the international center did not possess the wherewithal to handle the job. In fact, at one point he said the director did not handle the budget well. He failed to acknowledge that there was no budget for the director to mishandle.

As is often the case with this type of leader, a leader who blames staff members from a dictatorial mindset, his failure to handle criticism made the situation worse. He poisoned the workplace climate with his reaction to criticism, which made any hope of salvaging the project unlikely. The criticism shifted from the international center's failure to meet expectations to the president's reaction to the criticism. In similar situations where his ideas were rich in verbosity and creativity and poor in execution and practicality, he also blamed others, found fault with the critics and in almost every situation failed to learn in order to avoid the same mistakes again. Over time, his good, effective ideas were overshadowed by his egocentric, abrasive leadership style and fiscal disinterest. He refused to learn from his errors, refused to listen to this staff, and refused to accept responsibility for anything that failed or fell short of his expectations. The morale of the college staff members declined, and some of them left the college to take positions in other colleges. The governing board continued to support the president even though the reputation of the college was tarnished by his actions and attitude.

This poison of conceit was his downfall. In a relatively short period of time, he brought the entire college to the brink of bankruptcy and lost his job because state auditors found that the college was millions of dollars over budget and had been for a few years. To put that deficit in perspective, after the president was removed by the chancellor of the university system the interim president had to terminate over 300 employees to balance the budget. When this story became headlines in local and state news, the displaced president blamed the financial chaos on the chief financial officer. He never acknowledged any responsibility.

In his highly respected book on leadership, *The Enemies of Leadership*, Grady Bogue, former chancellor of Louisiana State University, wrote that arrogance is one of the main enemies of leadership and circumvents a leader's ability to handle criticism. In an article by Mortimer Feinberg and Jack Tarrant, *Why Smart People Do Dumb Things*, they agree with Bogue that arrogance and overconfidence can diminish a promising and even once effective leader. It negatively impacts the ability to appropriately handle criticism of any type. Fienberg and Tarrant state that when arrogance and overconfidence are combined with high intelligence a poisonous element is produced and criticism is simply not accepted by the leader. They referred to this as "Self Destructive Intelligence Syndrome (SDIS)." Leaders with SDIS, according to Fienberg and Tarrant, are isolated from criticism and are compromised by their own arrogance, narcissism, brilliance and a sense of entitlement. They state that this attitude is not only toxic for the leader; it also damages the organization and can take down the governing board.

In their book, *Presidential Derailment in Higher Education*, authors Grady Brogue, Stephen Trachtenberg, and Gerry Kauvar wrote:

Four University of Tennessee doctoral students and two colleagues explored derailment among college presidents. The students studied 12 presidents who were shown the exit shortly after they were appointed. The presidents worked in four different organizational types — research universities, comprehensive universities, liberal arts colleges and community colleges. They have found some overlap in factors associated with non-voluntary departures between corporate and collegiate leaders. These include poor interpersonal skills, inability to lead teams and key constituents, and failure to achieve goals. Among the distinctive factors found with college presidents were ethical breaches on the part of both presidents and board of trustees, and the failure to accept criticism, difficulty in adapting to organizational cultures, and flaws in the boards of trustees such as dysfunctional board dynamics, conflicts of interests, and manipulation of search processes by the board and/or an external actor such as governors.

One of the middle schools in the school district in which I worked was clearly in trouble and had been for a few years. Student standardized tests scores were very low and showing no signs of improvement. Also, there were growing student discipline problems in the school, to the point that the school was no longer safe. A change had to be made.

The process for selecting the school leader to replace the existing principal at this unfortunate middle school sadly followed a process that was dubious at best and destructive at worst. The school was in a low income area with a lot of street-smart students whose behavior was unchecked. Additionally, there were few limitations imposed on their behavior and low behavioral and academic expectations. This was a school where the teachers were afraid of the students and where the word "chaos" best described class changes, school lunch time, school dismissal and leadership. It was an unhealthy environment. The school district's principal selection committee paid scant attention to the ten most qualified candidates for the principal position. Instead, the committee selected a person who ranked in the bottom quartile of prospective school administrator rankings, based on peer reviews, work performance, supervisor evaluations and education credentials. He was selected because he was a friend of a friend who was on the selection committee and because a governing board member advocated for him, which in turn made him a darling of the school district's CEO, since he wanted to curry favor with the governing board. The selection was not fair to the students; it was not fair to the community; and it was not fair to the new principal. Equally naive was the charge to him to make the school "*an academic powerhouse*," in the words of the CEO. At the time, the person who was selected to be the new principal was a vice principal in a school located in a high income, high student achievement area. The newly appointed school leader had no experience with student discipline, daily operations of a school, or working with street-smart kids. He had been a vice principal for only two years and his only experience was in classroom instruction and academic testing.

Within two weeks of the new principal's first year at the middle school the students were mocking him unmercifully and calling him "pretty boy." He was always impeccably dressed, not just in a professional sense, but in a *GQ* style. His voice was so soft that no one could hear what he was saying in the best of circumstances, but in a crowded, noisy hallway with middle school kids screaming, pushing, yelling, bumping, slamming lockers, cussing, throwing whatever was availability, including each other, and all together creating a scene from Dante's *Divine Comedy*, he was simply inaudible. When he realized that none of the students were paying attention to him, the principal thought it would be useful to wave his hands in the air. The students viewed that as more of distress signal than as an effort to get their attention, so they felt compelled, as students that age are wont to do, to make the principal more distressed by ignoring him.

Student behavior became worse than ever before. Less than halfway through the school year, parents were very vocal about safety at the school and so were several faculty members – academics took a backseat to safety concerns. Comments from many parents, both verbal and written, were along the lines of, *"My child is afraid to attend school there."* Additionally, teachers were asking for transfers to other schools because of the safety issues. The principal simply ignored the criticism and concerns.

I received a call one day from the school district CEO's office. He instructed me to, *"Go to the school and find out what the hell is going on. Tell me what you see. I want a report this afternoon."* When I pulled into the parking lot at the school I saw trash on the school grounds and students out of class and out of the building during school hours. This was not a good sign at all. Additionally, no adults were visible, a certain sign of trouble. Inside the school was dirty, noisy, and clearly out of control. Teachers had given up trying to discipline the students and there was a line of parents checking their children out of school.

In a typical school when students move from one class to another class, it is common to see teachers in the hallway or in the doorway of their classrooms monitoring students as they move to the next classes. Not in this school. The teachers took refuge in their classrooms during class change, and understandably so, because the hallways were in total chaos. When I asked a couple of teachers about this, one of them told me that she was literally trampled when she stood in the hallway one day trying to maintain order. She said, *"I'm not doing that again."* Another teacher said she was pushed so hard from behind by a student that she stumbled against a wall and broke her glasses. I remained at the school for the day. That is all the time I needed to see that the school was in serious trouble. There clearly was a leadership issue. The principal was ineffective and defensive about criticism, and he blamed everyone – students, staff and parents.

My report to the CEO was essentially this: "*Get some help in that school before somebody gets killed!*" I did not, of course, use those exact words, but when I described the scene at the school to him the description was almost as compelling. A few weeks later the principal was replaced with a no-nonsense leader to restore order in the school. The replacement principal was hand-picked by the CEO because he wanted a leader who could quickly take control of the situation. And it worked, but not because the new leader was tough. The replacement principal was a mountain of a man with a heart just as large and a leadership style that encouraged respect. He had a voice like a trumpet and a commanding presence. He was self-confident and he communicated clearly what he expected of staff and students. Also, he was not afraid of the students, and he knew how to effectively interact with everyone. He grew up in a similar community so he understood all of the dynamics of the community. He told the students, staff, and parents that the first order of business was to make the school safe and orderly. Most important, he was an effective leader. He encouraged feedback and responded well to criticism; he learned from it and made changes, accordingly. He possessed several qualities and habits of an effective leader; consequently, he was the antidote to the poison created by the previous administrator and those who put him in that difficult position.

The number of discipline referrals skyrocketed for one semester after the new principal's arrival and then they dropped each semester thereafter. He had to make believers out of everyone and this included the students, teachers and the parents. He told teachers that he expected to see them in the hallway during class change and he wanted them to close and lock their classroom doors when the bell rang for class to begin. Tardy students would be left in the hallway. He added that he would deal with those students, and he did.

As soon as the teachers saw that he was determined to make the school safe and he was open to their ideas, they pitched in and took on more responsibilities. Teacher transfer requests stopped and parents were no longer worried about the safety of their children. The principal met with every school employee and listed his expectations. The school grounds were cleaned up, the hallways and restrooms were cleaned, and the smell of fresh paint was noticeable throughout the building as the principal made a concentrated effort to improve the physical appearance and climate of the school. The principal also tried to make the school better for students. He formed after-school student clubs and activities for students who had nothing to do when the school day ended. The students enjoyed the after-school activities, but they had to behave and make passing grades in order to participate. If they misbehaved in the after-school programs they were removed until they could earn their way back in. This reinforced appropriate student behavior. When asked about his strategy, the principal said,

The worse thing I could have done would have been to march into the school and act like the tough guy. The next worse thing would have been to start making changes without first listening to the students and the staff about what was good and what was bad. Also, I could not carry a chip on my shoulder and ignore criticism. I saw immediately that many things needed to change; that was obvious, but making changes without being thoughtful and inclusive, as much as possible, could just make things worse. You know another thing I avoided was criticizing the previous principal, because you know there will always be some that liked the previous principal for whatever reasons.

The school's climate was transformed by its new leader. For three straight years the number of student discipline problems and suspensions declined while student attendance improved significantly. Additionally, teacher retention improved; teachers wanted to work at the school. However, it was not easy, and student standardized achievement test scores did not improve much. But note this - research shows that school climate, student attendance and student achievement are all related. In fact, research sponsored by the National School Climate Center indicates that school climate must improve before student achievement improves. Some student achievement improvement was made, but not enough for some of the critics. A few vocal parents started to complain to a governing board member about the achievement test scores. That governing board member visited the school on several occasions. In fact, he interfered with the principal's efforts to run the school. The governing board member expected the principal to stop whatever he was doing to accommodate him, as did the few parents who claimed the board member as a friend and therefore thought they should be treated the same way.

The principal was always cordial and respectful, but he told the governing board member that he was taking care of running the school and it would be helpful if the governing board member could let him know when he planned to visit the school, especially if he expected the school staff members to escort him around the school. If the governing board member wanted to visit the school and just walk around, he was always welcome to do that. But that was not enough for the governing board member, who was one of the first to complain about the safety issues during the previous principal's tenure.

The governing board member told the CEO that the principal was being disrespectful and "*hiding things*," even though he never explained or delineated what the principal was supposedly hiding. The principal met with the governing board member and assured him that he was working hard at the school and the school was making progress, and with his cooperation they could work together. He shared data with him that showed improvements in student discipline, student attendance, and teacher retention. The principal also described the school's strategy for improving student achievement. But, that was not enough. The principal did not grovel, as the other principals before him did, and that offended the governing board member. He wanted and expected the principal and the school to stop everything and treat him like royalty. A member of a governing board cannot and should not have this type of interaction with an employee. The leader of the organization is delegated with this responsibility by the governing board, so that members of the governing board do not cross over into administration and operations. A responsible and effective CEO would not allow a governing board member this much authority or even opportunity to interact with an employee in this manner, whether the organization is a school, business or non-profit.

Perhaps the principal could have been more diplomatic at times, but why should he? He was trying to run the school while the governing board member was trying to exert his influence (which he does not technically have except during governing board meetings). The principal was effectively managing criticism and in fact used the feedback to improve school operations. Governing board members cannot distract employees from their duties and cannot make employees change how the organization operates. This particular governing board member had fallen into a position of self-importance that all members of a governing board must avoid. This type of undue and inappropriate influence can poison the work climate in any organization. Plus, the interference in a personnel matter based on unfounded criticism of an employee is clearly inappropriate for any governing board member.

Eventually the CEO succumbed to the constant badgering by the governing board member and removed the principal. The message was clear throughout the organization and among governing board members: the governing board is the operations center. Subsequently, the poison seeped into the school climate and the school declined. Since then there has been a parade of principals in and out of the school. The principal who should have been allowed to stay survived his removal. In his new assignment at a non-traditional high school he was an excellent principal. Left alone, he would have made that long-troubled middle school a success story by now. Instead, even to this day that middle school struggles, due to the poison of ineffective top leadership, the interference of a governing board member, and a paranoid way of responding to criticism.

Case studies have found that top management and governing boards responsible for making decisions that ultimately prove to be wrongheaded often sink into a defensive, self-preservation mode highlighted by the most basic of desperate strategies – blame someone or something else. Leadership expert, Scott Adams, said sarcastically, *"Informed decision-making comes from a long tradition of guessing and then blaming others for inadequate results."* How governing boards and ultimately organizational leadership handles criticism, particularly with personnel situations, is essential to the health of an organization, because so many issues can arise from those decisions. Personnel decisions that are generated primarily by governing board members can negatively affect morale, operations, retention of quality staff, and undermine the authority of top leadership. Additionally, governing board behavior and capitulation by the organization's leader invites criticism from many sectors. This then generates another set of issues on how the governing board and the leader handle and respond to criticism. Often times, governing board members and the top leaders in many organizations handle criticism by blaming others and thus ignoring an opportunity to see what worked and what did not.

A company that had a chain of daycare centers in a large metropolitan city decided that the company needed to decentralize by putting more responsibility on the directors of each daycare center. Two years later, the company was facing a serious decline in enrollment at several of its daycare centers. Rather than taking the time to conduct an extensive study of causation, the CEO privately and later publicly blamed the company's management team for pressuring her into the decentralization strategy that was not strategically sound. In reality, the CEO was a driving force in the decentralization decision. Her transfer of blame in response to criticism created a very unstable work climate; consequently, the company began to lose talented staff. Before the loss of talent reached a critical mass, the governing board ousted the CEO and promoted a senior staff member from within the company. She contracted with an outside source and found that the decline in enrollment was not unique to their daycare centers. Every other daycare center in the region was experiencing declining enrollment because of demographic changes. So, the company expanded its advertisement and provided more transportation options. Over time, the enrollment numbers stabilized. The new CEO and the governing board worked together.

Some organizational leaders try to insulate themselves from criticism through self-isolation. Psychologists remind us that the inability to accept criticism is linked to self-importance, the lack of humility, and a dogged determination that if anything goes awry it must be due to factors other than a person's own decisions. The lack of humility and the destructiveness of it are captured by the famous English writer C.S. Lewis, who wrote the following in his book, *Mere Christianity*:

There is no fault which makes a man more unpopular, and no fault which we are more unconscious of in ourselves. And the more we have it in ourselves, the more we dislike it in others. The vice I am talking of is pride, or self-conceit. Nearly all those evils in the world which people put down to greed or selfishness are really far more the result of a lack of humility, of pride. It is pride and self-importance which has been the chief cause of misery in every nation and every family since the world began. The virtue opposite to it is called humility. If anyone would like to acquire humility, I can, I think, tell him the first step. The first step is to realize that one is proud. And a biggish step, too. At least, nothing whatever can be done before it. If you think you are not conceited, it means you are very conceited indeed.

Antidote

There are effective governing boards that understand their role in the organization and do not try to influence the organizational leader's decision regarding personnel and other operational matters. This understanding is an essential antidote to the poison of governing board interference. Unchecked, governing board interference not only compromises the effectiveness of the leader, it also jeopardizes the outcomes of the organization. Strict attention to the development and implementation of governing board by-laws can counteract the poison of interference and unhealthy responses to criticism. This is not to minimize the role of the governing board, but instead to clarify their role and thus create a climate whereby criticism can lead to constructive change. The organization's leader can share information with the governing board in appropriate ways to keep them informed in order to enhance trust through communications and also to manage expectations. For example, it is appropriate for governing boards to monitor organizational risk through regular, formal reports from the leadership team, but not to the point that the reports interfere with the operations of the organization.

One of the biggest challenges for organizational leaders and governing boards is handling criticism. This is linked directly to the appropriate roles of each, and the failure to handle criticism in constructive ways can damage the relationship between the leader and the governing board.

Leaders and members of governing boards can benefit from training on how to handle criticism in constructive ways. Ron Edmondson, an expert in leadership and communications, offers ways to handle criticism that can be an antidote to the poison of criticism-reaction failure:

1. *Consider the source.* If the source of the criticism is from a person or group that never sees anything positive and is a constant source of criticism then that source would be viewed differently than criticism from an individual or group that shares the good with the bad. Also, a source that has facts, figures, etc. instead of rumor should be carefully considered. Too often, a leader or governing board treats any type of criticism the same way; they ignore it or shift the blame, especially if they have been guilty of interference or role confusion in the first place.

2. *Listen.* Leaders and governing boards should carefully and thoughtfully listen to criticism in order to understand and discern possible underlying issues. Leaders sometimes expect the worse, especially if they have made ill-advised decisions, and that's what they hear, even if the critic is offering constructive criticism. It is also possible that the critic has effective ideas on how to remedy the situation or prevent similar poor decisions in the future.

3. *Analyze.* Is the criticism accurate? Is it possible the criticism that leaders are quick to attribute to a subordinate is actually a criticism of top leadership and the vehicle or target of that criticism is the subordinate? Think of the ramifications if this is true. The leader's misanalysis results in a reprimand of the subordinate when the criticism of the subordinate is only an example of the failure of leadership at the top of the organization.

4. *Common themes.* Criticism can be widespread and vague or it can be narrow and specific. An effective leader will look for consistent criticism and thematic criticism, where the same type of criticism comes from different quarters with some of the same specific information. Governing board members who do not think their participation in the operations of the organization is inappropriate may discover, through an honest appraisal of criticism, how disruptive their actions are to the effectiveness of the organization. Leaders and particularly the governing board should look for trends in the criticism, so information can be gathered in order for the leader to help subordinates adjust accordingly to correct problems. Additionally, he needs to share trends with the governing board in case a policy needs to be revisited or if an honest discussion about the behavior of the governing board is necessary to avoid further

organization problems.

5. *Give an answer.* Edmondson states that a criticism is best viewed as someone asking a question; therefore, it deserves a response. Such as, "Why does the governing board participate in personnel decisions when they have selected the CEO to make those decisions?"It is okay to agree to disagree. A leader should not be hasty to agree or disagree and should not give an answer that commits him or the governing board to a certain course of action before he has the chance to analyze the criticism. The leader may want and need a change in the makeup of the governing board, for example, but he cannot and must not state that to subordinates who may be rightfully upset with ongoing governing board interference.

Leaders and governing board members should refrain from openly criticizing each other. There are many antidotes to that type of poison, including working together to improve communications and understanding each person's role through training. This open communication can generate a more open-minded reaction to criticism and a constructive use of criticism.

CHAPTER 2

THE GOOD AND BAD OF UGLY NEWS

If they expect us to expect the unexpected, don't the unexpected become the expected?

—*Diane Ackerman*

Poison: An ineffective leader hides bad news or tries to discredit the source of the bad news. The failure to address bad news typically makes matters worse, sometimes much worse than the original problem. A leader who strives to give the impression that everything is operating fine when in fact it is not has unleashed a poison that will be difficult to contain and counteract. Bad things happen in any organization. Some bad outcomes are self-inflicted through poor decision-making; some are self-inflicted because circumstances were not right or a decision was implemented at the wrong time; and some bad things happen because of circumstances beyond the control of the organization. Regardless of the cause or circumstance, every organization must be prepared for bad news and have a thoughtful and considered way of receiving and managing bad news. Ignoring the symptoms does not make the consequences anything but worse. The same is true with bad news. Leaders have to expect the unexpected, and many times the success or failure of a leader is determined by his reaction to the unexpected. So much depends on the leader's decision-making acumen. Some are known for making quick decisions, and are praised for their decisive response in difficult situations. Other leaders are more deliberate and inquisitive when a decision has to be made, and are admired for taking time to make the best decision. Depending on the situation, a quick decision maker can make a bad situation worse by not collecting all of the facts, elements, and contemplating possible consequences before making a decision. Yet, there are times when a leader can be paralyzed by indecision when a timely decision is essential. The poison of leadership

is manifest when a leader either approaches all decisions the same way,
with haste or hesitation, or misreads situations with haste when it needs
deliberation or with hesitation when expediency is necessary.

In Terence's *Comedies*, it was said that, "*Bad news always fly faster than good.*" That certainly was the case when the CEO of a non-profit organization heard that a major donor was withdrawing his substantial financial support of the organization because an audit finding indicated that the organization was mismanaging funds. The CEO was shocked the donor was withdrawing support, and he could not understand how the word of a minor audit recommendation had become public knowledge and how it could have concurrently been so exaggerated, too. There was an audit finding of a minor control weakness in an annual financial report of this small but influential non-profit organization. Even the outside auditor, author of the report, said that it was not serious enough to be considered a major financial control weakness, and it could be easily corrected. However, the audit company did warn the organizational leadership that they needed to be more diligent when managing and controlling accounts for expenditures. The CEO dismissed the audit recommendation as inconsequential when in fact it could be considered bad news. He later reflected on how poorly he handled the bad news. He went through the "SARA" stages: *Shock, Anger, Rationalization,* and *Acceptance.* He was initially shocked that the auditors found anything untoward. Then he was angry that they put it in the audit report and upset that his staff "allowed" this to happen. Soon, however, he rationalized that the audit report was not that bad and that the indiscretions were not serious; besides, he thought, the auditors were being too picky and just looking for anything negative to report. The audit report was posted on the organization's website, which was required by its internal policy. That is how the major donor learned of the audit recommendation. He did not hear about the audit from the organization's CEO, because the CEO did not contemplate sharing the audit report to anyone except the governing board. Consequently, the donor believed that the organization was "hiding" bad news and, therefore, must have either little respect for his contributions to the organization at best, or at worst thought he was a faithful contributor who paid little attention to the organization's operations. Whichever was the case, the major contributor was so distraught about the organization's failure to talk to him that he threatened to withdraw his current and all future contributions. The CEO failed to contact the donor to explain the situation and the specific components of the audit recommendations.

The Center for Community Engagement sponsored a dialogue entitled, *Managing Bad News*, which featured Carol Love from Planned Parenthood,

Jim Redmond from BlueCross BlueShield, and Rick Ammen a consultant to Fortune 500 companies who specializes in managing bad news at the corporate level. It was stated during this dialogue that managing bad news is not an issue limited to corporations.

Dealing with a crisis or bad news is not limited to a Fortune 500 company. Small nonprofit organizations are just as likely as multinational corporations to appear on the front page of the local newspaper with allegations of misconduct, conflicts of interest or regulatory inquiries. These nonprofits may be in much greater jeopardy if the bad news is not managed effectively. Not only is the crisis embarrassing to the organization, its board of directors and employees, it may also lose the trust and support of other stakeholders and donors, which places the very survival of the organization at risk.

Citing examples from their own experiences, dialogue participants all agreed that bad news is a management issue that cannot be dismissed by leaders of any type of organization. They all agreed that every organization will at some time have to manage bad news. They also revealed that many negative situations, if not most, are caused by internal problems, as one said, "*self-inflicted.*" That can be due to lack of prevention and intervention planning, poor management of bad news, or both.

There has been some research that's done every year by a group in Kentucky named the Institute for Crisis Management and one of the things that they point out is crisis in the public eye to see what the common denominators are. What they find, although the percentages vary slightly from year to year, it's basically two-thirds to three-fourths of crisis, regardless where they happen, were smoldering before they blew up. And 58 percent involved management. So what that says is that two-thirds to three-fourths of crisis are self-inflicted wounds, meaning that the organizations had some reason to believe or someone within the organization had some reason to believe that the train was coming down the track and was going to hit them and they didn't do anything to stop it. That is really significant because it says that, contrary to the kinds of things that we often think about - crisis such as fires, and shootings and that sort of thing - self-inflicted wounds really are what we need to worry about and respond to.

Delivering bad news can be one of the worst parts of a leader's job. It is a double dilemma, because the leader has the bad news to contend with and he has to be concerned with how he handles the bad news. Careers have been enhanced and some damaged not so much by the bad news itself as by how well or poorly the leader managed the crisis. British Petroleum

(BP) learned the hard way by delaying news of the oil spill in the Gulf of Mexico. Then to make matters even worse, BP falsely minimized the seriousness of the oil spill. It is a commonly held belief now that had BP been more forthright and accurate, some of the damage from the oil spill could have been avoided or at least better contained.

David Javitch, an organizational psychologist, said of leaders delivering bad news, *"Often times their intention is good, but they dig a grave for themselves when they deliver bad news. Those aren't easy topics to deal with. Unfortunately, a lot of people don't have a very good idea of how to do it and they mess it up."*

One of the most fatal flaws in managing bad news is procrastination. Seldom does delaying bad news make the bad news better. Dana Britol-Smith, author of *Overcome Your Fear of Public Speaking*, said, *"I think it just comes down to people are uncomfortable with confronting any sort of negative behavior or situation."* She advises, *"Try to address the bad news while it's as small as it's going to get rather than let something fester longer and longer."*

Trying to handle bad news is not a linear process, because many times there are factors that lead to the circumstances that created the crisis. A complex and interesting example is a case study from a school district.

In the 1980s and into the 1990s, gangs developed rapidly in my community and then in our schools, but this was not unique to our district. By the early 1980s, gangs had sprung up in most of the large cities across the nation, especially in the poorer inner-city and ring-city areas. By 1989, delinquent gangs were located in all 50 States, and they were beginning to appear more frequently in schools. The presence of gangs was a totally new experience for many communities that had a checkerboard of wealth and low income housing. Gangs were a new challenge for suburban communities; this was definitely bad news, a different type of bad news and evolving crisis. This was bad news for students, schools, parents, communities and a potential crisis for businesses and economic development.

A few students with a history of gang behavior transferred into our school district from Los Angeles, Chicago, Detroit, and New York, and they brought the gang culture with them. Descriptions and the graffiti of *Crips, Bloods, Down-by-Law, 5 Percent Nation, Gangster Disciples*, and other gangs began showing up in school restrooms, on student notebooks and clothes, on outside school walls, on neighborhood traffic signs and walls, on business walls and windows, and other places. Other students moving into the community brought a different type of gang activity. It was White Supremacist groups such as *Arian Nation, Skinheads*, and *2ndKKK* that brought their own brand of hate, disruption and crime to the schools. The clashes between and among the minority groups for control and between the minority gangs and White gangs for influence created the perfect storm of disruption and danger in our schools and in our communities, and it brought the challenge of managing bad news to a different level. This was bad news at all levels in the organization and community, including the business community.

My first direct encounter with gang violence in a school happened when I, as a school psychologist, was in a high school to work with a student. This high school was in a low-to-middle income area. It had its share of fights and other disruptions, but it was considered overall to be a safe school. I had just walked a student back to class after a counseling session and I was on my way back to the front office when suddenly the quiet hallways were filled with screams and shouts and the sound of people running. By the time I determined the direction of the noise, several students streamed past me in a desperate attempt to flee. Staff members were trying to weave their way through the stream of students toward the problem. I joined in their efforts to see if I could assist. It was obvious that students were very frightened as they panicked to get out of the school. When I turned the corner where the commotion was centered, I saw a student on the floor bleeding profusely from several wounds. I could not tell if they were knife wounds because the student was covered in blood. Three staff members were attending to him while others were attempting to restrain another student. We had to apply makeshift tourniquets to stem the bleeding for fear that the student would bleed to death.

The investigation of the assault found that both students were new to the high school. One was a *Crip* gang member and the other one was a *Bloods* gang member. *Crips* and *Bloods* do not tolerate each other. The attacker had put small nails in a bolo paddle and he used it as a weapon to slash the victim across his face and neck. The victim was seriously injured. Without the quick and skilled response of the school staff, the student could have bled to death in the hallway. The victim was transported to a hospital for emergency surgery. He survived, but he was covered with scars. The victim of the physical attack was not the only one with scars. Students who witnessed gang violence for the first time were traumatized by the shear violence of the attack. The dilemma for leadership at that point was deciding the best way to deliver the bad news without downplaying the circumstances and yet without also frightening students, parents and the community.

Because there was a delay in deciding how to best manage the bad news, some students refused to come back to school and parents were outraged at the school for "allowing" such violence and for failing to communicate with them immediately. In the article, *Good News About Bad News*, by James Lukaszewski, he states that *hesitation* creates a public perception of confusion, lack of preparation, incompetence, and perhaps even callousness. Something had to be done about this very worst of bad news and done quickly. It was becoming very apparent that the delay in sharing and managing the bad news could have long-term negative consequences.

I was called into the CEO's office shortly after the incident with a few other administrators. By this time I had participated in hundreds of student discipline hearings as the hearing officer and had worked in several schools with students and staff members on very difficult situations – bad news and crisis situations. Plus, it was common knowledge now that I had witnessed a few incidents of gang-related violence in our schools.

The CEO came to the school district only a few years before these series of violent incidents occurred. He was a highly intelligent, sincere, energetic, and resourceful CEO. He would serve as CEO for several years. His long tenure was attributed to the fact that he was an effective, decisive and thoughtful leader. Though he did not always make the right decisions, he tried to learn from his mistakes going forward, and in this situation he was trying to discern the best way to handle the bad news of gangs in the schools and community. In addition to discussing how to handle the growing crisis, the purpose of the meeting with the CEO was to discuss the growing gang problems in the schools and to discuss the recent taunts from members of the White Supremacist groups like *Arian Nation* and *Skinheads* threatening to disrupt the school district's efforts to encourage and support integration by offering minority students the choice to attend a majority White school with transportation provided by the school district.

At the same time gang-related incidents were increasing in the schools and in the community even though the local county police chief made a public statement that there were no gangs in the county. The business community was beginning to worry. The county commissioners were afraid that news of gangs would dampen business and economic growth in the county, so they pressured the police chief to deny the undeniable. The police chief and the commissioners were determined to deny that there was a gang problem in the community, and they encouraged the school district to do the same. This was a very ineffective and even dangerous manner to handle the situation. This was hesitation and deception at its worse.

The CEO was aware that I knew several police officers and of course he knew I was the student discipline committee hearing officer, so he began the meeting by asking me to respond to the police chief's press release about gangs or the lack of gangs in the schools and community. At the time I did not know how the CEO felt about the situation, or frankly if he even knew about the growing gang problem, and I certainly was not sure how he responded to bad news, so I was somewhat tepid in my response. In his deceptively charming and powerful manner, he leaned forward and quietly said, *"Please, tell us what's really going on. Tell us the truth. Tell us what you see and hear. I need to know everything, because frankly I don't know whether or not to believe some of what I'm hearing and because I will not know how best to handle this if I don't know the facts. Tell me so I'll know what we're up against, what we can do about it and what we need to tell the public."* I told him and the other central office staff members that school violence related to gangs was escalating rapidly to the point that the safety in some of our schools and communities was in danger of being compromised. I gave examples of violent incidents and how they related directly or indirectly to gangs, both in schools and in the community. I also told him that it was not confined to minority gangs. The White Supremacist gangs were growing in number and they were inciting violent incidents. Additionally, they were threatening to disrupt and stop the school district's integration efforts by intimidating minority students who were transferring to predominantly White schools. One of the administrators in the meeting read aloud an anonymous letter the central office had received from someone claiming to represent the *Aryan Nation* threatening to *"disrupt and grind to a halt"* the school district's plans to allow minority students to transfer to majority White schools. It was also noted that gang behavior was being observed in some communities and businesses.

I did not mention anything about the police chief's recent statement that the community did not have gangs, but the CEO circled back around to that issue. I told him that some gang experts had listed 15 different gangs in our community. Some of the gangs had national links, like the *Crips, Bloods,* and *Arian Nation* and some where locally developed, like *Down-by-Law, Kirkwood Boys,* etc. An internal police investigative report included names of suspected leaders of the various gangs. Some of them were students in our schools. The CEO stood up slowly from his chair, walked around his office in silence for a moment, and said, *"We are not going to hide from this and pretend like it does not exist. We have a problem that can be managed now, but if we wait it may not be so easily managed later. We owe it to our students, staff and the public to be open with them about this situation, and we're not going to give it to them with a spoon full of sugar either – we'll tell them what we're up against."*

Lukaszewski, in his article about bad news, said, *"Prevarication is perhaps the greatest error when managing bad news. There is no substitute for the absolute truth."* In addition to hesitation and prevarication, Lukaszewski lists several things that leaders and governing boards need to consider when trying to manage bad news that could escalate into a crisis: obfuscation; pontification; revelation; egos; downplaying the situation; arrogance; use of jargon; and unpreparedness.

1. *Obfuscation is the failure – deliberate or foolishly – to recognize that when time and understanding are critical, simplicity is a must.* Otherwise, the perception is of dishonesty and insensitivity, if not downright obstruction.

2. *Pontification is dangerous. While a leader's nose is in the air, he or she gets hit in another part of the anatomy.* Such a tactic is detrimental to controlling the situation. Additionally, no one likes the arrogance that pontification suggests. In fact, a message's meaning can get lost in an air of arrogance and the perception that pontification is a form of deception.

3. *Revelation is inevitable. If an organization is hiding information, that and the facts will be revealed in time, probably by a victim, employee or news reporter.* The fallout from this is certain to damage a leader's reputation, as well as that of the organization. In almost all case studies where an organization tried to hide significant bad news the outcome for the organization was negative. It is very difficult for an organization to recover from this type of situation with its reputation intact.

4. *Egos can be lethal.* Here is an example, "*I don't care what people say, we're not going to admit that we have a problem. We run this place and we have control of the messages, too.*" In his article, *You Should Beware the Dangers of the Ego Trap*, Robert Staub wrote, "*The ego trap has captured executives, religious leaders, therapists, lobbyists and politicians…it is easy to rationalize taking advantage of a person or situation when the action brings pleasure or avoids pain, and it makes [the leader] feel important or special.*" In a situation where bad news can evolve into a crisis, all leaders and governing board members must check their egos at the door.

5. *Downplaying the incident is misleading.* There are many examples of a leader minimizing a bad situation, "*It was only an isolated incident. This is not a widespread problem. We have it contained, and we are on top of it.*" A disturbing recent example of this was the misleading public comments made by Japanese leaders when the nuclear reactors were damaged by a tsunami. It is certainly advisable to manage expectations in response to bad news, but to downplay its importance can insult clients or employees, and can be dangerously misleading to the public. They may initially find some comfort when the situation is downplayed, more out of relief than anything else, but the full impact will eventually be revealed through some means, so ultimately there is no benefit to downplaying or misrepresenting bad news.

6. *Arrogance is unforgiveable.* For the most part, people are forgiving; people understand that people make mistakes, but it is also human nature to be less forgiving of leaders whose mistakes are shrouded with arrogance from defensiveness and denial. An arrogant response to bad news goes something like this, *"Why are they always looking for something to go wrong; why don't they talk about the good stuff I'm doing. It's really not their business how we run things; they don't know what we have to contend with, and we can't let our employees talk about it."* An Arab proverb states, *"Arrogance diminishes wisdom."*

7. *Jargon doesn't fool anyone.* Do leaders trying to cope with bad news really think organizational jargon will be accepted by the public as anything other than a poor attempt to downplay the bad news? This is an example of jargon. *"They are no gangs, just some groups of kids. We have a collection of students with commonalities that meet sometimes and those infrequent meetings sometimes cause them to try to ascertain different ways of communicating or seek different means of expression."* Leaders that think jargon will temper bad news can expect the following questions: *"So, what does that really mean? Why didn't you do more to prevent the situation from escalating?"*

8. *Unpreparedness is not an excuse.* Trying to cover up for bad news that stemmed from unpreparedness sounds like this: *"We have had a few problems over the last few years, but nothing that would indicate that this would happen to this degree."* Being unprepared for events that no one could realistically anticipate can be excused, but being unprepared for the possible is not acceptable to the public, clients or employees. In sharing bad news a leader must anticipate questions of preparedness; it cannot be avoided for very long.

Regarding the bad news of the aforementioned gangs, the CEO decided to take the full message to the public about gangs, despite what others advised him to do. He held a number of brainstorming sessions with senior staff members and immediately created a straight-forward message to students, parents, employees, community leaders and businesses. The CEO first briefed the governing board members, who reluctantly agreed that full disclosure was the best course of action. The CEO had faith that the community would respond to his call for action as a community. That was the good news about the bad news. The bad news was that it was not over.

We learned that the presence of gangs in a school creates another set of issues, not just the direct problems with gangs. This is often the case with bad news; it is not limited to one set of facts or issues. The school district now had non-gang related firearms being brought to school by non-gang related students because of gang-related fear. There was no doubt that the school district had to expand its intervention and communication strategy and had to redouble its anti-gang efforts as well as add a firearm reduction strategy. There was no doubt; this could not be hidden any longer in statements of denial. A decision was made to take the concern about firearms to the public, as well. Instead of suppressing the data about firearms like some school districts may do, the school district went public with a clarion call for the public and particularly for parents to help the school district address the growing number of firearms in the schools and communities.

In an 18 month period of time, school district staff members made over 60 speeches to PTAs, community groups, religious groups, parent groups, community agency groups - to any group of people who would listen. Community advocates were recruited, too, in an all-out effort to inform the community about gangs and firearms. They were shocked to hear that 90 percent of the firearms confiscated at school were brought from the homes of the students or from the homes of relatives and were not possessed by gang members, but by other students. This was a way of sharing bad news that readily admitted that the organization needed help from others.

Experts on managing bad news often warn leaders that they need to be aware of the nuances of those who will receive the message. Being in the Deep South we did run into some who said we were intruding on the rights of individuals to have firearms in their homes. So, we addressed that in our speeches. We did not get into an argument, capitulate or dismiss their comments, but we told them this: *"If you have a firearm in your home, that's your right to do so and it is your decision. However, if you think your child does not know you have a firearm in your house, you are kidding yourself and if you think your child does not know where you keep that firearm you are sadly mistaken. So, if you have chosen to have a firearm in your house, be responsible. Safely secure your firearms."* That was as direct and as honest as we could be. The bad news was that guns were coming to school, but the good news was that we collectively could do something about it. We also went to community leaders for assistance. The local chapter of the NAACP developed an incentive program to reward students for informing school administrators about the presence of a firearm at school. The tips were anonymous. The program was very effective and played a key role in reducing the number of firearms at school.

The message and efforts were picked up by the local press. The public's reaction was not about gangs and firearms, but about parental and community responsibility. The school district's message was often quoted, *"If the community of parents will take care of the 90 percent of the firearms, the schools will take care of the ten percent."* After the Littleton, Colorado massacre at Columbine High School, *Time* magazine used the school district's efforts to curb firearms at school as an example of what school districts can do, or try to do, to reduce the presence of firearms and appropriately handle bad news.

Reducing firearms and gangs became a community effort and it is an example of how a school district or any organization being honest about bad news with its consumers, clients or community can lead to positive changes. Within just two years, the number of firearms in the school district dropped from 76 to 21. Obviously even one firearm in a school district is bad news, but for an urban/suburban school district with over 100,000 students to reduce the number from 76 to 21 in two years and later to less than 10 is a success story - the success story of a community, not just schools. At the same time, the number of gangs and gang-related incidents declined significantly. This was also a success story of how to manage bad news and transform it into positive, united action. And it was handled this way because of the school district's CEO with support from the governing board.

Of course, the reduction in firearms and gangs was not only related to community efforts, it was also related to the school district's continuous efforts to curtail and prevent gang activity. It may seem overly dramatic to say so, but I am convinced that these efforts, which included the community, saved the school district and its students and staff from being in a dangerous environment. Had the decision been made to hide and deny the bad news, the schools would have spiraled down into a state of decline and danger. Too often leaders underestimate the power of successfully and thoughtfully managing bad news.

The courage of the CEO to address the gang and firearms issue shows the importance of governing boards selecting the right person to lead the organization and then allowing him to lead. The governing board was under enormous pressure during this time from the commissioners and business executives and business owners to deny gangs and firearms were in the schools, and they were shocked to hear that the school district was asking for the public's assistance in addressing the firearms and gang problem. Nevertheless, the governing board stood strong in support of the CEO. The managing of bad news started with the CEO, but without the support of the governing board, the efforts of the CEO would have been compromised.

The case for sharing bad news in an efficient and thoughtful way applies to any organization. A mid-size company that manufactured tiny segments of a device that was used in the telecommunications world received news that the raw materials essential to making the segments was no longer available. The company was unprepared for this situation and top management came to the CEO panicked about the crisis. One of the managers said to the CEO, *"If our clients hear about this, we're finished and our Board of Directors will fire all of us."* The CEO asked each of his managers to report their version of the crisis and what each of them thought the company should do about the situation. He encouraged everyone, even the most reluctant managers, to comment on the situation and suggest a course of action. They all encouraged the CEO to keep the situation quiet until they could figure out how to manage the crisis. A manager offered, *"People don't know what it takes to run this place and how complicated it is to secure the raw materials to make the segments; they don't know how difficult this can be. They won't understand. Our clients will dump us before we have the chance to do something."* The CEO noticed that one manager appeared to be thoughtfully and intensely listening to everyone but he had not offered a comment, so he asked him if he had anything he would like to say. The manager sheepishly looked away and then around at the others and said quietly,

This is a tough situation, but the only way to let our clients know that they can trust us is to tell them the truth and reassure them that we're doing everything we can to manage the situation. Think of it from their perspective. They depend on us and they have been loyal to us. How will they feel if we hide the bad news and cause them to possibly lose business from their point in the supply chain? They will find out. I think the trust would be gone and they would dump us for the long run. It's a risk, I guess, to be honest with them; they may dump us immediately and never return. That's why I was debating within myself before saying anything. And it seems like everyone else here, and I respect everyone here, feels differently.

There was a long quiet moment before anyone said anything, but had they been paying close attention to the CEO they could have detected a slight smile developing at the corners of his mouth. The CEO said,

This is what we will do. We will continue our dialogue with our raw materials supplier while looking for another way of obtaining the raw materials. This will allow us to do two things, manage this situation and plan better against this happening again. I will personally call each board member and inform them of the situation – and not downplay the crisis. We need to maintain their trust, also. Immediately after that I will call our clients and let them know what is happening, including our strategies to get the raw materials, as well as our long-term strategy to keep this from happening again. They may panic and drop us and cuss me out for not informing them sooner and ridicule me for not having a backup plan. So be it. The news will leak out anyway and perhaps they will appreciate knowing that we informed them with the truth as soon as we learned about the dilemma. Now, let's get to work and we'll reconvene this afternoon at 2:00 to get an update from everyone. At that time, I'll let you know what our clients are saying.

It cannot be reported that all of the clients appreciated the honest and timely delivery of the bad news. Some were upset and threatened to move their accounts to other companies. However, the core of the clients appreciated the honesty and the personal contact from the CEO and maintained their business relationship. And in a stroke of luck that derived from how the situation was managed, one of the clients informed the CEO that he could possibly help with finding another source for the raw materials. As it turned out, that source could not meet the company's full raw materials needs, but later became a secondary supplier and at the same time emerged as part of the CEO's new backup plan.

The news of the Tylenol poisoning in 1982 reached the CEO shortly after a lunch meeting. At that time, the makers of Tylenol, Johnson & Johnson, claimed 35 percent of the United States over-the-counter analgesic market, which was 15 percent of the company's profits. A million possibilities went through the CEO's mind at the same time this unexpected event took place – the safety issues, the public's confidence in all of the company's products, his board's reaction, the impact on the company's stock market performance and standing, the attitude of employees, and many other thoughts. Some observers of leadership behavior and many business analysts predicted that he would take a cautious approach as he contemplated a reaction to the crisis. They were correct in the prediction that the CEO would move mountains to get the facts and determine what happened. However, they did not accurately forecast that the CEO's first thoughts were his concern and grief for the victims and the safety of consumers. To him there could be no hesitation in removing all Tylenol products from the shelves. He let it be known around the world that his company was first and foremost concerned about the safety of the public, and his company could not and would not hesitate or respond in measured strategies. His decision was based on a basic principle that was at the heart of his company but mostly at the heart of his attitude about his company's mission. The focus was on the safety of its customers. Had he hesitated; had he taken a defensive posture; had he taken a wait-and-see attitude, the safety of many customers could have been compromised, and the future of the company would have been at risk. Instead, his decision making during the crisis and his follow-up decisions regarding the bad news were applauded by the business world and the public. He had so many choices and decisions to make, he could have fallen victim to the "centipede syndrome" where he did not know which foot to put down next. That is the weakness of some leaders and governing boards, who are efficient and effective when difficult decisions do not have to be made, but sink into what Michael Cohen and James March in their book *Leadership and Ambiguity* called "ambiguous decision" making during difficult times when tough decisions have to be made during a crisis and when confronting bad news.

In the article, *How a Good Leader Reacts to a Crisis*, about decision-making during a crisis, John Baldoni said that effective and efficient leaders have to be thoughtful about the situation and their reaction to it:

1. *Take a moment to figure out what's going on.* In many unexpected situations the first meeting of pertinent staff is often dominated by nervous chatter, where everyone is talking at once. This is seldom constructive chatter. Under these circumstances, it may be wise for the leader to delegate responsibilities and direct staff members to reconvene in one hour. According to Baldoni, "*This helps impose order on a chaotic situation.*"

2. *Act promptly, not hurriedly.* A leader must provide direction and respond to the situation in a timely fashion. But acting hurriedly only makes people nervous. A leader can act with deliberateness as well as speed. Legendary coach John Wooden advised, "*Be quick, but don't hurry.*"

3. *Manage expectations.* When trouble strikes, people want it to be over very quickly so things can return to normal as soon as possible. It falls to the leader to address the size and scope of the situation. People should not be alarmed, but at the same time the leader cannot be afraid to speak to the magnitude of the situation and what may be required to manage the issues.

4. *Demonstrate control.* When things are happening quickly, no one may have full control of the event, but a leader must try to assume control. Leaders may not be able to control events, but a good leader can control the response. An effective leader jumps into the action and brings the people and resources to bear. The leader of the organization has to show that he is leading everyone through the situation.

5. *Stay calm and illustrate calm.* A leader can never afford to lose his composure. This has implications for the leader's ability to adapt rapidly. A situation can change quickly; therefore, the leader's

first response may not be his final response. In these situations, a leader cannot be wedded to a single strategy. He must continue to take in new information, listen carefully and consult with the staff closest to the situation.

Another important aspect of managing the unexpected and decision making during those times is the importance of trust. Trust is a recurring component of effective leadership and governing. In each challenging situation trust becomes an important part of the response. Trust between the leader and the governing board, trust between the leader and employees, and trust between the leader and the community of clients is essential. An effective leader can ill afford to take a moment to figure out what's going on if he cannot trust the information provided by his staff. He must trust that the information is timely, accurate and relevant. Otherwise, the decision making window becomes very small. Also, a leader cannot provide direction and respond in a timely manner if trust does not exist among the leader, governing board, and employees. The messages of reassurance that the situation is being managed will be met with skepticism if trust in the leader is lacking. Without trust, the leader's ability to manage expectations is minimized.

One of the most important requirements of a leader is the demonstration that he is in control, but that can be an illusion. There is a trust calculus that determines if the leader is actually in control. If the leader is not truly in control of the challenging situation it is very unlikely that he will remain calm. How a leader handles unexpected situations can forge a strong trust bond between him and employees, the governing board, and the public. A leader that does not manage well under difficult and challenging circumstances will be questioned and second-guessed each time another crisis has to be dealt with. A powerful example of this comes from the aftermath of the Boston Marathon terrorist bombing in 2013. Several of the deputy fire chiefs in the Boston Fire Department complained that the Boston Fire Chief did not respond well to the bombing. They claimed that the Fire Chief did not help coordinate the emergency response; was not available to make timely decisions; and at times could not be found. Consequently, the deputy fire chiefs stated that their leader's failure to respond to the crisis had eroded their confidence in him to lead.

It is important to understand and therefore recognize the origin of situations where trust is a factor with leadership during a crisis. Typically it is either because the leader is perceived as weak and consequently unable to make decisions or the leader is arrogant and does not have a history of listening to staff or others. Helga Drummond's *Guide to Decision Making* offers a rich discussion of decision making during such times. She states that *"calamity loves the overconfident."* Drummond found that *"Our innate tendency is to overestimate our abilities so that we often see ourselves as superior to other people. We also view ourselves more positively than others see us."* Consequently, many leaders do not consider the opinions of subordinates routinely and especially during a crisis. The danger, according to Drummond is complacency. She sites Toyota's response to a product failure. *"Toyota's CEOs inflicted huge damage upon the company by refusing to recall vehicles with potentially lethal accelerator pedals. Toyota had known about the accelerator pedal crisis for months before reports began appearing in the news in late 2009, but acted only when forced to do so by mounting public pressure."* Leaders at Pennsylvania State University knew about the child molestation crisis and chose to respond with an arrogant rebuttal of the accusations. The careers of several university leaders ended in disgrace and their decision making during the situation tainted the reputation of a fine university.

Another example of how a leader responds to bad news or a pending crisis comes from a rather unusual set of circumstances. The weather in Georgia is, for most of the year, very pleasant with mild seasons. It can get very hot in the summer, particularly in August, but spring and fall are usually beautiful and winters are seldom more than a few days of subfreezing weather. On some occasions the remnants of a Gulf of Mexico hurricane or tropical storm will charge into Georgia and create temporary havoc, and parts of north Georgia may have a snow or ice storm, but those situations are rare. Some years spring storms are temporarily brutal and can be extremely dangerous, but that is not a common event either. One week in late spring during a time when the southeast was experiencing unpredictably stormy weather, I received a report from the National Weather Service (NWS) that a very large and dangerous storm system was going to move rapidly from Florida straight into Georgia. Fortunately, I had developed a very good communication protocol with the NWS and they were very patient handling my phone calls. I called my contact at the NWS and asked about the storm. He said they were tracking it closely because it had the potential to cause serious property damage and threaten the safety of anyone in its path. The projected path of the storm would take it directly through our part of the state.

I informed our CEO of the storm and what the NWS said about the storm's potential danger. Despite his peculiarities, he understood how school districts operate on a daily basis, so he understood the potential for problems with this type of storm. I tracked the storm and talked several times with the NWS. Soon it was apparent that the storm was headed for our county. On radar the entire storm was a mass of red – that is as serious as it gets in the world of weather color radar, indicating severe weather conditions. I told our CEO that the storm would hit our county on Thursday of that week and that the severity of the storm would be a threat to life and property. It was possible that it would hit just as we would be releasing a thousand school buses to take 70,000 children home. More likely the storm would hit during the school day and rage throughout the day and night, which could create a difficult situation and decision whether to house students until the danger passed or send students home in storm. With considerable trepidation, I recommended that we be proactive and close all schools that Thursday. When I made that recommendation I was looking out the window of my office. It was a beautiful day – sunny and warm with hardly a cloud in the sky. I expected the CEO to explode, but he did not. I told him that I would like to talk to the NWS one more time that afternoon, but I thought we should let the news media and parents know as soon as possible. I called him back later that day convinced that the weather was going to be extremely dangerous the next day. He did not get upset or question my judgment. He calmly said, *"Contact our Public Information Officer [PIO] and get the word out that we are not having school on Thursday because we are fearful that the approaching storm will be extremely dangerous."* He never said anything about the consequences of this decision if the weather did not turn violent the next day. He never mentioned that at all. He was calm and I tried to be calm, but there was always a possibility with weather that something could change. I called the PIO about this situation and even though he thought I was crazy he made certain that the community received word that the schools would be closed the next day.

Immediately parents and the news media started hounding the school district about closing schools before the storm was a threat. I worried throughout the night. I could not sleep that night and I am certain that the CEO lost a lot of sleep, too. I did not, of course, want our community devastated by a storm; however, the CEO's career or at least his creditability was on the line if the storm did not hit our community and I certainly did not want to be the source for criticism heaped on him. He was already in the spotlight because of his combative behavior. I was in a tough spot, but he was in a tougher spot. The next day morning broke sunny and cloudless and with over 100,000 students and nearly 16,000 employees sitting at home. What made the situation worse was that none of the neighboring school districts were closed. The CEO called me at 10:00 that morning and I expected him to give me hell at best and fire me at worst. Instead, he said chuckling, *"Hey, man, I don't know where you're sitting but outside of my window I see beautiful weather. What's going on?"* He was not upset, but I'm sure he was troubled. I told him I was in contact with the NWS and I was looking at the radar screen from the NWS and a huge band of radar red was heading our way. He said simply, *"Let me know, so I know whether or not to look for another job."* It was amazing that the same leader who railed over seemingly insignificant things was so calm about a growing crisis situation that could cause great embarrassment to him and the organization.

I thought I had made a huge mistake by recommending that the schools close, and that our CEO had made even a bigger mistake by listening to me. But at 10:30 that morning, the NWS said the storm was increasing in intensity and was heading straight for our region. I called the CEO and gave him the NWS update, but all he saw was partly cloudy skies. Parents and governing board members kept calling his office to complain about schools being closed. Consequently, he called me at 10:45. While he was on the phone with me the NWS issued a Tornado Watch for our area and within a few minutes they issued a Tornado Warning. When the storm hit around 11:15 it had the impact of a hurricane. Our community and surrounding counties had tropical downpours, hurricane force winds, and there was substantial damage to buildings and property. Many of the schools were damaged and the damage to the area was so extensive that it was declared a federal disaster area. Over a third of the county lost power that day plus other days. The other school districts in the area were saddled with the decision whether or not to send students home early during and into the storm or keep them at school. Some were sent out into the storms and those leaders were roundly criticized, while others kept the students at school where they were stuck when the storm worsened. It was one of those situations where any and every decision is a not a good one, except the one that kept the students and employees out of harm's way in the first place. The storm was expected to last most of the day and into the evening, so some of the school districts started sending students home in the storm. There were numerous vehicle accidents; some students were stuck trying to get home early with no way to get into their homes; day care centers were not prepared to receive students before their afternoon staff came to work; many bus routes had to be changed because of downed power lines and flooding; and many students and parents were frantically trying to find each other. It was chaotic and dangerous for everyone, but especially for students. During the storm I was asked by the local Emergency Management Director to come to the County Emergency Operations Center. I saw firsthand the damage the storm was inflicting in the area. We even had to mobilize a few school buses to help evacuate citizens from an apartment complex that was in a flood plain. Our CEO trusted his staff members and he was there to make tough decisions. He was quick to give permission to use the school buses. The school district was able to assist because we had an emergency plan that included a quick mobilization of school buses. The damage and power outages were so extensive and widespread that all of the school districts in the area were closed for two more days. The CEO called me to his office a few days after everything was somewhat back to normal. He said, *"I never doubted you for a moment. Well, that's not entirely true."* He said that governing board members were very pleased that he had the courage and leadership to put the safety of children first. He was pleased that he could trust the opinion of a staff member. Undeniably, he handled this situation with decisiveness and calm. He trusted the opinions of his staff and made tough decisions during a crisis, and he delivered bad news clearly and succinctly that schools would close for the safety of children and staff.

Another example of leadership during a crisis comes from the H1N1 pandemic in 2009. In the spring of that year, the H1N1 influenza virus shocked the world, especially the United States and more specifically the Centers for Disease Control (CDC) and state health departments. Years of planning for a virus such as the more lethal H5N1 (bird flu) had taken place at the national, state, and local levels, but the main premise of the planning was flawed because the basic assumption was that a virus, such as the H5N1, would evolve in some other part of the world and the United States would not be impacted until three or more weeks later. By then, CDC and/or the World Health Organization (WHO) scientists, epidemiologists, and virologists would know the severity of the virus and could plan accordingly. In other words, the United States would know what to do depending on the mortality rate, how quickly the virus spreads, and what age groups were most vulnerable. What the public did not know is how much debate centered on whether or not to close schools if a pandemic broke out in the United States. CDC, state and local public health experts did not have a realistic view of the impact of closing schools and day care centers. To many of the public health experts it was rather simple: close schools to avoid the spread of a virus. However, as the debate matured it became more apparent that the public health impact, economic impact, psychological impact, and educational impact of closing schools were very significant. In fact, the Brookings Institute estimated that closing all public schools in the United States for three weeks would have a significant impact on the economy: *"We find that closing all schools in the U.S. for four weeks could cost between $10 and $47 billion dollars (0.1-0.3% of GDP)."*

When the H1N1 virus appeared suddenly in Mexico that spring and rapidly spread, CDC and other Health and Human Services agencies were shocked that this type of virus began so close to the United States; nevertheless, they all sprang into action. They reviewed all of the plans and scripts developed for a virus like H5N1 and soon realized that those plans would not apply to this situation. State public health agencies found the same. The issue of closing schools moved very quickly to the forefront, particularly since the virus came into the United States so quickly. At a National Institute of Health (NIH) pandemic public health conference that was hastily scheduled a few months into the H1N1 pandemic, a large number of the public health officials said that the most complicated situation and the situation that was causing them the most angst was the decision whether or not to close schools due to the virus. Up to that point, the opinion from educators about closing schools was not sought by public health officials either at the federal level or at state levels. This was a point of concern at a National Governors Association (NGA) meeting about pandemic planning two years before the H1N1 pandemic. I was there with a public health team from Georgia. Twelve other states were represented. The facilitators of the meeting asked how many educators were represented on the state teams in pandemic planning. Only two states had education represented on their pandemic planning team. The NGA was very concerned that public health had left education off of the planning teams and reported to governors across the United States that education should be included in all public health emergency planning. NGA also recommended this to the United States Department of Human Services. Some states took notice and followed the NGA recommendations and some did not. When the H1N1 virus spread to the United States, CDC and WHO were still trying to determine if the virus was dangerously lethal. They never planned to make that decision while a virus was in the United States and spreading. They had counted too much on advanced warning.

Without a grasp of the severity of the virus, CDC issued guidance to school districts across the nation to close school even if only one student became ill with H1N1- like symptoms, and close the school district if one student in more than one school became infected. The education community was put in a difficult situation. They were asking, *"What type of crisis decision-making is this?"* How could they justify closing schools when little was known about the virus; yet, how would they respond if a student or several students became gravely ill because they kept the schools open against the advice of public health officials? In those communities where the virus spread, schools were closed, which released thousands of students into the malls, stores, streets, and/or unattended in homes. That did not seem like a good example of social distancing (limiting social contact to prevent the spread of the virus) which was the purpose of school closures in the first place. Some school districts remained closed for up to a week or longer, and some schools reopened after closing for only a couple of days. It was a chaotic time. Fortunately, CDC, NIH, and WHO found that the severity of the virus was no worse than seasonal flu, so they recanted the guidance to close schools. In other words, the leaders in those organizations trusted their respective staff members, who trusted their local community staff members, and in turn trusted their leaders enough to be honest and forthright with them. The leaders were at the center of the decision making process and made timely and thoughtful, albeit tough, decisions during the pandemic. Public health officials around the country finally realized how important public schools are to the fabric of existence and daily life in the United States and, therefore, the decision to close schools should be taken more seriously. That showed leadership during a crisis.

The impact of the H1N1 virus hit state departments of education across the nation in more than one way. Each summer in Georgia, the state department of education hosts the Governor's Honors Program (GHP), which is a six week program for gifted and talented high school students from schools across the state. Over 700 students attend GHP each summer. It is a tradition of high honor in the state. During the summer of H1N1, a GHP student became ill with flu-like symptoms. GHP was being held at a state university that has one the most advanced medical and student health centers in the state. By the time the GHP student became ill, CDC determined that the H1N1 virus was no worse than the seasonal flu virus. State department of education staff members supervising the GHP called the organization's CEO, the state school superintendent, to report that a GHP student had H1N1, as confirmed by the medical and student health center at the university. The CEO convened a committee of the executive staff. I was not a member of the executive staff at that time; nevertheless, I was told to attend the meeting since I had worked with public health on issues and served on the state's pandemic planning committee. The CEO was in a high state of anxiety about the situation at GHP. She set up a conference call with GHP staff and the president of the state university that was hosting the GHP. As soon as I walked into the conference room, she said, *"What do you know about this?"* I did not even know the purpose of the meeting. She then went around the room and said to her executive leadership team, *"Do you think we should close GHP and send all of the students home?"* It was clear from the tone of her question that she had already decided to close it and she wanted confirmation. The GHP staff on the conference call phone remained quiet, but the university president said that the program should continue, based on the opinion of his medical staff. But the CEO cut him off, saying *"Well, I'm sorry but you're not the one responsible for the safety of these kids." "I'm not going to have the death of some student on my head."* Staff members around the table, having taken a clue from her, started agreeing with her that the program should be closed and students should be sent home. I offered an opinion that the virus had been determined by epidemiologists and virus experts to be no more lethal than seasonal flu and we would not send students home and close the program if a student contracted seasonal flu. She did not respond well to my suggestion and again expressed concern about the possible death of students. We were at a stalemate. In the meantime, the university president who was still on the conference call was trying to reassure her that the situation was under control. He said, *"We have everything under control. We have our medical staff checking on your students routinely, we provided hand sanitizers to all of your students, and we provided additional space for your program so the students can have social distancing. Also, keep in mind that my college students will be returning for the fall semester in three weeks and it would be devastating for my student enrollment if people were under the mistaken impression that the college is not safe because you closed the GHP."* Our CEO became very agitated and turned on me. She said, *"You're our so-called public health expert; what do you think?"* I tried to remain calm, but I wanted to remind her that I had already told her what I thought. Instead, I said, *"As I said earlier, the virus is not any worse or more deadly than seasonal flu. The program can take precautions such as social distancing, cancelling large group activities, and distributing hand sanitizers. We can contact all of the parents and let them decide if they want to bring their children home."* She looked at me; she stared at me; she glared at me. Then she said abruptly, *"Okay, that's what we will do."* The decision was made to keep the program open, but to call every parent and inform them of the circumstances. It was the best decision for a number of reasons. As it turned out, she was a hero to the GHP students and parents and the news media because the program did not close. Only two students were withdrawn from the program by their parents. All of the others completed the program and no other students became ill. She as the leader came to the right decision during a crisis. Despite all of the turmoil and emotion, she still possessed the leadership acumen to listen to staff, evaluate the situation, and trust the opinions of staff members and make a difficult decision.

There are other examples of decision making and sharing bad news. A church with over 1,000 members and 600 loyal weekly attendees was both happy and saddened when the long-time minister decided it was time to retire. They were happy for him and sad for the church. He was an organizational legend. His sermons, tributes, speeches, and writings were widely praised over a 30 year career. He was well versed in leadership and yet he frequently attended training sessions and workshops on leadership to gleam more skills to help him run the church with peak efficiency. The church membership had steady growth during a time when churches across the country were losing members, and the church was in a strong financial situation, with no mortgage, no significant debts, and a healthy capital endowment. He even planned for the transition to the next church leader. The committee that would select his successor was carefully chosen. The committee carefully reviewed all applicants and thoughtfully questioned them and made diligent efforts to check references. The selection was made and the transition to a new minister began. Only, there was one glaring omission during the screening and selection process. No one thought to ascertain how the applicants responded to crisis situations, nor did they pose any interview questions that focused on leadership behavior during unexpected situations. Even the retiring minister did not suggest this critical element, even though he had managed several minor and major crises in the church and crises in the community that affected the church. The new minister was welcomed with open arms and quickly became an integral part of the active church. For a while, membership continued to increase and it seemed that the selection committee had done a fine job. The problems started with a small situation; in fact, it was not even a crisis; it was more a problem than a crisis. The church's children and youth education was having a difficult time keeping teachers, so the quality of its programs and the quality of teaching became an issue for some parents. They were not upset; they only expressed concerns and ask questions about teacher retention. The youth minister explained to the church's Education Committee that the church needed to figure out a way to compensate the volunteer teachers, since salaries were not affordable nor expected. A few ideas were developed and implemented, but the problems continued. The new minister decided that he needed to become more engaged, so he attended an Education Committee meeting. During the meeting which heretofore were described as always positive and congenial, the minister began questioning the youth minister in an increasing assertive manner in front of others. The youth minister and members of the Education Committee assured the minister that they were working on some strategies and would continue to generate ideas to address the situation. Members of the committee later reported that the minister turned to the youth minister and shouted, *"You'd better get this under control or you are out of here."* A few weeks later, the youth minister took a job in another church. It became apparent over time that the minister had many qualities, but he could not handle any challenging situations well at all. He was quick to blame others; he did not take the time to discover what the most important issues were and he sought simple solutions (reactions) instead of considering the ramifications. When others did not agree with him he isolated himself with just a few of his most adamant followers; and his communications efforts failed completely during crisis situations and even when he received bad news that was not a crisis. The church suffered from the minister's failure to handle any type of challenging situations effectively. During his years at the church, membership declined steadily.

Michael Hyatt, head of Intentional Leadership, wrote in an article titled, *When Leadership Fails*, that leadership failures are often the result of poor planning; inexperience; stubbornness; lack of vision; and/or pride. Hyatt makes a very important point for all who work in organizations. He writes, *"Failed leadership in a crisis happens more often than we would like to admit. When we are the victims, though, we notice it all the time. We see ourselves as being stuck in our circumstances. We complain. We gossip. We throw our hands up in the air and ask, 'What if?' That is not necessarily a bad question. But instead of asking, 'What if those leading me were better,' we should ask, 'What if I had responded to poor leadership better?'"* Hyatt claims that a common response to poor leadership during unexpected situations is to give up. Instead, he suggests, encourage each person to continue to work hard on the tasks before them and learn from the mistakes that are made during the situation, because there will be other unexpected events, bad news, and crises. Poor leadership during such times is bad enough, but the failure to learn from those events is unforgiveable and poison for the organization.

Antidote

Tim Berry, a writer on leadership, wrote that a good measure of the type of leadership can be identified by asking this question: *"How quickly does the leader get bad news?"* If the leader is usually one of the first to hear bad news; subordinates don't wait to tell him; the subordinates don't tell each other first; and they don't try to hide bad news from the leader, then the leader is someone who knows how to handle bad news and a crisis. In this chapter, some of the leaders refused to hide the bad news and refused to deny that a crisis was present or pending. In fact, they made it clear to their leadership teams and governing boards that no one was going to hide the facts. The leaders and the their teams calmly and thoroughly identified the essential components of the situation; developed a list of responses and resources; shared the challenge with governing board members and with clients in an appropriate and timely manner, and ultimately implemented a plan with far reaching goals and results.

In an article for CBS News *Money Watch* by Steve Tobak titled, *How to Deliver Bad News*, he offers the following advice: *"The method incorporates elements of crisis management, customer service, effective communication, and even some psychology. And, if you do it with empathy and finesse, I've found that you can actually improve your relationship with the other party in many ways."* Additionally, Tobak advises leaders to be genuine;

be empathetic; develop a plan; and deliver. *"Be honest with yourself about the role you personally played in the outcome. This is critical because, if you played a direct role, i.e. you screwed up, you need to be straight with yourself about that or you'll end up feeling guilty and weird and that will come across negatively. In other words, you need to diffuse your appraisal and come to terms with your own emotional state and the impact of it all on the organization."*

Leaders should think about how they would feel from the perspective of their clients. Leaders must try to understand what clients stand to lose or how they will feel as a result of the bad news. Leaders must make sure they are clear that responsibility and accountability rests with them. Clients appreciate leaders taking responsibility, so do employees and governing boards. When leaders communicate bad news, it can be done in such a way that the leader's empathy and concern for the client is apparent. One of the worst things a leader can do is to play the "poor me" role, at the expense of the ones most impacted by a crisis.

Leaders should consider all the ways they can make the situation better, understandable, or right. This may require creative, innovative ways of thinking beyond anything the leader has attempted before. During times of crisis, in particular, leaders may need to toss out existing plans and start over, or they may need to find the most effective parts of an existing plan and focus more resources on that aspect of the plan. In any case, leaders need to have a clear picture of the options at their disposal and under exactly what conditions the leader and the organization are willing to bring them to bear on the situation.

If a leader is genuine, displays empathy, and develops an appropriate plan, he is ready to deliver. The leader's emotional state will be clear. That means he will be empathetic but not emotionally distraught. And depending on the reaction, leaders may have an arsenal of possibilities to offer to help make things right. Tobak offered a good example of the time that a company could not deliver a key component on time, resulting in a shutdown of one of his customer's production lines.

During the 'bad news delivery' face-to-face meeting with the customer, we held a conference call with my company's head of operations who, seemingly on the fly and under pressure from the customer, committed to an accelerated schedule that would minimize my customer's pain. That was a preplanned contingency to use if necessary. The result was a customer who felt that I would do anything to go to bat for him; my company would pull out all the stops to meet his needs, and he helped to make all that happen by the way he handled the meeting. We all won and our relationship was stronger as a result.

One of the most serious mistakes leaders make in delivering bad news is the emotional build up and the rush to get it over with. They typically do not take the time to diffuse their own emotional state; put themselves in the other person's shoes, and do enough contingency planning to know what can be done to make things right. Bad news and a leader's response can turn into a self-inflected poisoning.

Erika James in her article *Leadership as (Un)usual: How to Display Competence in Times of Crisis,* suggests that there are two types of situations: (1) *Sudden Crisis* and (2) *Smoldering Crisis.* Sudden crises occur without any warning and are beyond the organization's control; consequently, leaders are judged completely on how they respond to the situation within what was even possible, given the circumstances. Smoldering crises are different from sudden because they begin as bad news and escalate into a significant event. James recommends that all leaders create a situational preparation mentality and modality by starting with a signal detection strategy or plan. This can be accomplished at least in part by encouraging staff members to inform leadership when something happens or is happening that may smolder and become worse. In other words, do not hide bad news. Many unexpected and challenging situations can be prevented, but leaders must grow situational skills that include the ability to sift through a lot of information and determine what is important, what can be delayed and what needs to be addressed rapidly. It cannot be said often enough that leaders must develop trust with employees and the governing board members before challenging situations occur. Trust is essential during difficult times. In fact, the lack of trust is perhaps the most compelling obstacle during a crisis. A "bunker mentality" response is not uncommon when the leader, staff and governing board do not trust each other, and no good decisions can come from that climate. Leadership expert, Robert Freeman, once said, *"Character is not made in a crisis it is only exhibited."*

A few weeks after the Katrina storm flooded New Orleans, an editorial cartoon appeared in *Time Magazine* that showed a man standing in waist-deep water holding a sign that pleaded, *"Leadership Please."* In his book, *Crisis Leadership*, Gene Klann wrote:

Nothing tests a leader like a crisis. The highly charged, dramatic events surrounding a crisis profoundly affect the people in an organization and can even threaten the organization's survival. But there are actions a leader can take before, during, and after a crisis to effectively reduce the duration and impact of these extremely difficult situations. At its center, effective crisis leadership is comprised of three things - communication, clarity of vision and values, and caring relationships. Leaders who develop, pay attention to, and practice these qualities go a long way toward handling the human dimension of a crisis. In the end, it's all about the people and the plan.

Ken Sweeny's book, *Crisis Decision Theory,* focuses on three steps of crisis decision making theory: (a) assessing the severity of the negative event; (b) determining response options [instead of repeating what may have worked or not worked in the past]; and (c) evaluating response options. Sweeny wrote, "*Some crises have more consequences than others, but crisis decisions theory recognizes that even relatively inconsequential negative events may require considerable attention at the time they occur.*" There are no precise and exact decision making protocols that will be appropriate for every type of unexpected event. However, at the very least, every organization could build a basic protocol based on questions that should be asked and answered at the onset of an unexpected situation.

1. How serious is the situation?
2. Is the situation unexpected or has it happened before?
3. What components of the organization are most affected by the situation?
4. What are the response options?
5. What are the pros and cons of each response option?

Organizations can then combine those questions and answers with the concept of Strengths, Weaknesses, Opportunities, and Threats analysis, sometimes referred to as SWOT. For example, identify the strengths of each response option; identify the weaknesses of each response option; does a response option have opportunities for making the situation a valuable learning experience for the organization and can the decision response possibly strengthen the organization's standing by illustrating its ability to respond effectively to an unexpected situation? Rahm Emanuel, the former chief of staff for President Obama, once said, "*You never let a serious crisis go to waste. And what I mean by that it's an opportunity to do things you think you could not do before.*"

CHAPTER 3

BROADENING BOARDS

The trouble with the world is that the stupid are cocksure and the intelligent are full of doubt.

—Bertrand Russell

Poison: Governing board members that interfere with the daily operations of the organization have a detrimental effect on the entire organization, from top to bottom and all directions inside and outside the organization. Governing board members that are self-focused, narrowed-minded, self-serving and that sacrifice the best overall interests of the organization can contaminate an organization. It can be deadly to an organization's efficiency. An organization's leader that capitulates to this type of governing board has sacrificed his effectiveness and loses the confidence and trust of employees and others. This double dose of poison jeopardizes the future of the organization by leading to decisions that may cost the organization in untold ways for many years. The leader must have the courage to say no to the governing board, and they in turn, must trust his judgment and respect the purpose and operations of the organization. The lack of trust and courage poisons many aspects of the organization, regardless of the type of organization, because the primary goal of the organization is compromised by leadership chaos.

It is a simple but unfortunate truth that most citizens, employees and investors are not aware of the decisions made by governing boards. They are almost completely and totally disengaged, especially with community governing boards, such as county commissions and school boards. This is disturbing when one considers that the majority of these governing boards in the United States are elected. Citizens could have more of a voice in public education, for example, if they participated in the governing board election process. Sadly, most citizens cannot name their own governing board representatives, whether it is their school board members, local county commissioners, or city council members.

According to the *Civic Index for Quality Public Education* (*Civic Index*), a non-profit entity,

In more than 90 percent of the nation's public school districts, elected governing boards serve as governing bodies and provide leadership in support of education. District governing boards are often the smallest and most localized elected bodies of our country's governing structures. Unfortunately, the general public often overlooks its local governing board activities and elections while paying more attention to state and national elected officials. Governing board meetings are often under-attended or seem to be controlled by a few vocal individuals or interest groups. Governing board members themselves are often doubtful of the public's desire to become involved and informed about issues. In the high pressure situations common to governing boards, it is often easier to make a decision than to reach out to the public and obtain their views before voting. Moreover, in our fast-paced society, members of the public often fail to make the effort to get involved in governing board issues.

According to Fredrick Hess, *School Boards at the Dawn of the 21st Century*, most governing boards are composed of five to eight elected members. Many governing board members are professionals, but only a few have a professional education background. Individual board members work an average 25 hours per month on board tasks.

In a survey by the Iowa Governing Boards Association (ISBA), the results indicated that only 10 percent of registered voters participated in governing board election races – only 10 percent. This is an incredibly low percentage and in large part explains why so many governing boards have problems and consequently why so many leaders have issues with their governing boards. In 2007, according to the ISBA, the percentage of registered voters going to the polls dropped to six percent in some communities. It is incredible that only six percent of citizens participate in elections that have the most direct impact on their lives. The 2008 *Civic Index* found that 48 percent of citizens could not name one member of their local governing board. Also, employees of non-profit agencies and businesses could not name any members of their respective governing boards. Governing board members themselves complain that governing board meetings are generally unproductive since the few people who attend usually advocate for narrow, self-interest topics rather than improvements for the entire community.

According to the 2008 *Civic Index*,

While these individuals control education, community services, and

other essential functions, research and policy analysis on the way schools are run tells us that the public is uninvolved in keeping boards responsible for their decisions and actions. In fact, public participation has been described as disorganized and occasional.

Hess found that when governing boards focus on improving performance and adopt the strategies of working together, action planning, and evaluation, the results are positive. Too often, however, governing boards do not function that way.

A school district in Georgia lost its accreditation because of the behavior of governing board members, not because of student academic performance, teacher or administrator performance, or due to financial issues. The school district lost accreditation because of the behavior and actions of the governing board. The record shows that the governing board members tried to force the CEO to make personnel decisions that favored friends and relatives; they were frequently disrespectful to each other and to the CEO in open session; and they went into schools and intimidated principals and teachers.

The Southern Association of Colleges and Schools (SACS), an accrediting agency approved by the United States Department of Education, had previously warned this school district's governing board members about their unprofessional behavior. In fact, the school district had been put on probation several years before losing accreditation for the same type of governing board misbehavior. The school district then came off probation, new governing board members were elected (with a 10 percent voter turnout), and within just a few years the same problems were cited again by SACS. The behavior of the governing board did not change; in fact, the governing board became even more dysfunctional over several years, even after SACS warnings and intervention. At the same time, SACS officials probably began to question how seriously the local citizens and community leaders wanted the local governing board to improve.

When SACS finally pulled the school district's accreditation due to the behavior of the governing board members, the community was understandably disturbed. The loss of accreditation would have a profoundly negative impact on students graduating from a non-accredited school district, which could impair the students' chances for college acceptance and college scholarships. Also, the loss of accreditation would negatively impact local businesses and property values. Despite the outrage, over 90 percent of the community could not name one governing board member.

The Center for Public Education described the importance of boards of education in a way that is applicable to all governing boards:

The decisions made by the governing board affect virtually every important aspect of local schools, from boundaries to bus schedules, curriculum to clubs, funding to field trips. The governing board hires the superintendent, the "chief education officer" responsible for managing district staff and operations. The governing board sets the priorities and adopts the budget that determines how millions in federal, state, and local tax dollars are spent. The governing board sets goals for student achievement and evaluates progress toward those goals. The governing board decides how school boundaries are drawn and whether schools are constructed or closed. The governing board sets the policies that determine which courses and programs are offered and what texts, tools, and technology are purchased.

In an excellent article entitled *Governing Boards: Duties, Responsibilities, Decision-Making, and Legal Basis for Local Governing Board Powers,* Kent Weeks wrote:

A regular criticism of local boards is the tendency of board members to confuse monitoring of key outcomes and executive performance with prescribing how to manage the components of the system. A study conducted in West Virginia found that governing boards spent 3 percent of their time on policy development and as much as 54 percent of their time on administrative matters. A study of fifty-five randomly selected governing boards indicated that financial and personnel issues were among the most frequent areas of decision-making, displacing deliberations on policy by a significant margin. The local governing board has a vital role in providing leadership, serving as a forum for citizen input relevant to public interests, and inculcating the beliefs, behaviors, and symbolic representations that define the organizational culture of the organization. In this role, the board's responsibilities include adopting a unifying vision and mission, soliciting and balancing the participation and input of members of the community, and advocating on behalf of the needs at the local, state, and national levels. Consistent with this leadership responsibility, the local governing board should emphasize the standard of continuous improvement for its own operations as well as that of the community as a whole and undertake to evaluate its performance and improve upon that performance.

The national report *Facing the Challenge: the Report of the Twentieth Century Task Force on School Governance* recommended that governing boards focus on their rule as policy boards instead of management committees:

Clear delineation of roles and responsibilities between the board and the superintendent, clearly stated expectations, continuous sharing of information, and open, honest communication among all parties nurture a positive relationship between board members and their respective superintendents.

Governing boards select superintendents, just like a governing board of a non-profit selects CEOs and a business selects CEOs to manage the organization. The governing board must trust the CEO to make the administrative decisions that are best for the organization without interference from them as a whole or from individual members. Governing boards often select CEOs for short-term reasons and not with the future in mind, and many of the governing board members do not understand how the organization operates on a daily basis; therefore, they do not understand that running an organization is a complex task that can be negatively impacted by governing board behavior and interference. Some governing board members previously worked in the organization at some level; therefore, they think they know how the organization operates or should operate. But anyone in that position who is willing to be honest understands that once he is removed from the daily operations of an organization it all changes very quickly, so while previous experience in the organization or in a similar organization can be beneficial, it does not equate to the governing board member possessing more knowledge of management than the organization's CEO, and it certainly is no reason or excuse for interfering with the daily operations of the organization.

In a highly publicized case reported in the *St. Louis Business Journal*, a member of a bank governing board resigned, complaining that the chairman of the bank's governing board constantly and consistently interfered with the CEO and managers of the bank. In fact, the resigning governing board members wrote: *"The present management staff does not have the ability to run the bank under the conditions set forth by the chairman of the board. The board will not allow the management to run the bank."* Apparently, the chairman of the governing board had previous banking experience and thought he knew more about operating a bank than the bank's CEO, as evidenced by his constant interference in the daily operations of the bank.

It is not uncommon for a governing board member to come from a background as a community activist or a one-issue activist that provided name recognition to garner influence or votes to be selected or elected to a governing board. Then that new governing board member does not understand that his role has changed from one of activism to one of stewardship of the organization's best interests. There is a very significant difference between the two; a difference that is often ignored by the governing board member and many times ignored in training sessions. Activist governing board members often view management and other governing board members as the "enemy" - the "establishment." There is very little trust. The activist governing board member does not see what is best for the entire organization and does not trust the motives of management or even other governing board members, but is only interested in how anything and everything does or does not benefit his or her own section or special interest within the organization or fellow activists outside of the organization closest to his own base of support. This type of governing board member will jeopardize what is best for an organization as he looks for and manipulates circumstances that are favorable for only a few. This governing board member's behavior during board meetings can be an embarrassment to the organization and community. The behavior of governing board members is so bad in some communities that people watch the televised governing board meetings not for information but to be entertained by the drama and unprofessional behavior of the governing board members.

A specific example is a situation in a school district where one governing board member held the school district "hostage" because of his activist mentality and approach to governance. Consequently, millions of dollars were earmarked to renovate the high school in his section of the district even though all projections showed a decline in student population. Not only was the school renovated, it was enlarged, and a state-of-the-art performing arts center was added to the school even though the school did not have an active performing arts program. The new performing arts center was seldom used and enrollment continued to decline in the high school, but they had the nicest empty classrooms in the school district. The same governing board member was notorious for his habit of eating during board meetings. It was not uncommon for him to bring a plate of food into the board room and talk with his mouth full during governing board meetings. His outrageous, crude, and unprofessional behavior never changed and he continued to be re-elected every four years by the handful of voters that bothered to vote. It should be noted also that the remodeled high school with declining enrollment was 12 teachers over allotment one year, based on student population and declining enrollment, but this same governing board member screamed when the CEO told him the teachers were being transferred to other schools where they were needed to fill vacancies. To quell the governing board member's stormy and outrageous behavior the CEO gave in and the teachers remained at the school. The average teacher annual salary plus benefits at that time was around $60,000, so that decision costs the school district $720,000 that year and each year they kept the extra teachers at the school.

The other governing board members and the superintendent should not have allowed that to happen, of course, but they did, and the community should have been outraged, but it was not. The same community saw governing board members coerce the local school district into building an elementary school in the wrong place and a high school in the wrong place. Had those two schools been built in the right place, school consolidation could have taken place to alleviate crowded conditions. Another public school high school in that same school district badly needed renovations to make the school safer, cleaner, and efficient. However, there were so many change orders (changing the original architectural design and costs) due to the demands of one governing board member that the completion of the renovations was delayed for almost two years, leaving the students and staff in dust and confusion. Another time a new elementary school was needed to relieve overcrowding conditions, but it was built in the wrong location, also. Students assigned to the new school had to ride a school bus past an elementary school that was not overcrowded in order to get to the new elementary school. The new school was built in the wrong location to satisfy the desire of one governing board member who wanted the school in her area of the community. The governing board members were exchanging votes to appease each other's selfish interests.

This same unfortunate school district followed the demands of governing board members that resulted in more wasted tax dollars. Instead of building one new middle school and merge student attendance zones, the school district built two new middle schools even though the student projections in both locations showed declining student enrollment. Both schools never exceeded 60-70 percent occupancy. In fact, only a few years after it was built, one of the middle schools was closed. Each school cost approximately $30 million to build. What was the source of this folly? Why were two schools built instead of one? Two governing board members wanted a new school in their respective voting areas, whether they were needed or not. That $60 million decision was brought to the public's attention through the local news media and yet both governing board members were re-elected and the CEO was reappointed.

There was a time when that school district was building new schools in one side of the school district while ignoring deteriorating conditions of old schools in other parts of the school district, because of activist governing board members who did not have any interest in doing what was best for the entire school district, and because of the lack of public outrage and voter input. The waste in public dollars for building improvements and new buildings in the school district ran into the millions of dollars and failed to address the district-wide needs of all students.

In the private school world, a local activist governing board member insisted on major renovations and even a six classroom addition to the elementary section of the private school even though the school was experiencing declining enrollment. The school director and other members of the governing board gave in to the governing board member's demands, so dollars went toward the unnecessary renovations of the school. This decision cost hundreds of thousands of dollars, damaged morale, and reduced community and employee confidence in leadership. The other governing board members and the school director should have stopped it. More to the point, the parents and other stakeholders should have shown enough interest to keep decisions like this from being made by selecting more responsible governing board members.

Another example of the poison from governing board members with the wrong priorities and misunderstanding their role comes from the business world - a privately operated bus transportation company. On nothing more than the whim of one governing board member the company purchased a large tract of land that included an abandoned strip shopping mall for millions of dollars with the idea that the company would relocate to the facility after it was remodeled and the large parking lot would be used as a place to park all buses in one place for logistic, security and maintenance purposes. The CEO of the company was against the purchase of that piece of property, because the building was in such bad repair it would cost over $400,000 to renovate it. Also, upon closer inspection it was determined that the entire huge parking area would have to be repaved to handle the weight of the commercial busses. Today the building sits unused and deteriorating and the surrounding property has gone to seed. That decision cost almost $2 million, all because a governing board member insisted that it be purchased, the CEO capitulated and no other governing board member objected.

A non-profit agency that provided essential services to its community was considering expanding its outreach program. To do so, it needed a larger facility. The organization's CEO received permission from the governing board to develop the expansion concept further. The CEO and his management staff spent considerable time researching all possible pros and cons of the expansion and received many hours of pro bono work from attorneys, real estate agents, architects, accountants and other professionals. An expansion plan was developed that included the site of a larger facility, a service map of the projected expanded service area, the reallocation of existing staff, and a cost-benefit analysis. Everything seemed to be going well during the presentation to the governing board. Then one governing board member asked if the CEO considered vacant buildings in a particular neighborhood. The CEO said the management staff with the assistance of several volunteer professionals had considered several buildings and the one being recommended was the best choice. This governing board member objected. He insisted on knowing in more detail why the buildings in his neighborhood were rejected. During a governing board meeting, he said, *"I deserve the building in my area."* Showing weak leadership and little skill at negotiation or mediation, the CEO and the remaining members of the governing board invested $15,000 more in another feasibility study, even though the previous study showed that no buildings in that area of the community would fit the needs and intentions of the non-profit. The follow-up feasibility study results were the same. So, because of one poisonous governing board member and the capitulation of the CEO and other governing board members the non-profit wasted thousands of precious dollars.

In a large school district with ever-shifting student populations, three elementary schools were closed and the buildings were sold for almost nothing (for example, one was sold to a community arts center for one dollar). Over time, as populations shifted, it was determined that more classrooms were needed in that same area due to growing enrollment. The cost of a new elementary school was close to $20 million, but only two miles away another elementary school had declining enrollment and plenty of classroom space. One obvious solution was to change attendance zones and use existing classrooms, instead building a new school. However, two governing board members insisted on building a new school. The other governing board members capitulated because they had successfully pressed the school district to build unnecessary middle schools in their area of the district. Adding to this folly was the decision to tear down an existing successful technical and vocational center in order to build the unneeded elementary school. The technical and vocational center was an award-winning facility that would have been even more valuable as the school district later begin developing career pathway courses. A few years later, this same school district needed a building for a career academy, just like the one that was earlier demolished for the purpose of building an elementary school that was unnecessary.

John Jantsch, author of *The Commitment Engine*, referred to this type of dysfunctional leadership as *"Disconnected Influence,"* where the influence is focused more on what leadership wants instead of what the organization needs. A governing board member suffering from Disconnected Influence views almost everyone, including fellow board members, as either adversaries or allies and uses what Jantsch refers to as *"Conditional Compliance"*, only complying when the outcomes are in his favor. This type of governing board member takes adversarial positions personally and only focuses on the short term so his biggest influence is on the issue at hand, regardless of what the long-term impact may be. Contrast this to the healthier and more productive "*Connected Influence.*"

The Connected Influencer tries to influence in a positive manner for overall better results. Jantsch says that the Connected Influencer is a governing board member who views other people as collaborators, regardless of whether they disagree with him or not. If there is disagreement, he will make an effort to better understand why someone disagrees with him. This governing board member also "*strives to gain sustained commitment and communications.*" The power of a Connected Influencer governing board member is that he "*persuades without pushing.*" Therefore, his influence is more profound because it is meaningful but not at the expense of other governing board members or the organizational leadership.

Leadership and governance must co-exist and there is no time to waste. As Jantsch points out, those governing board members who insist on "pushing" their point of view without listening to or considering other points of view have a flawed and failed strategy that may work in the short-term but not in the long term and certainly not to the benefit of the organization. Jantsch says this approach is deeply flawed: "*Pressing your case too much instead of striving to understand your counterpart's point of view*" is not good for the organization. Take, for instance, an example that resulted in a disastrous decision by an organization that costs a lot of money. In an effort to save money for the entire school district an elementary school was closed, but a local governing board member forced the school district to use the same building to house students for a magnet school (a school that draws students from different attendance zones to attend high achievement classes). The elementary school that was "closed" to children in the community because the student enrollment of 240 students was so small that it was considered a drain on the school district's operations cost was replaced with a program that had only 100 students from outside of the community. The CEO allowed it to happen, as did the full governing board.

The behavior of governing boards and the failure of an organization's CEO to make tough decisions and stand by them is not an exercise in petty politics that impacts only a few people. It is a serious poison. One year an internationally known commercial development company was trying to buy large parcels of land in order to build a shopping area that would be surrounded by apartments, condominiums, houses, office buildings, and a park. It was slated to be a "Live, Work, Play" community. The only remaining parcel of land the company needed was owned by the local school district, and that parcel of land was in a strategically important section of the proposed development. The project could not proceed without that parcel of land. An old high school building that housed a non-traditional high school, a small performing arts school, and a teacher training center were on the section of property the development company needed to begin the project. Also, there was a 40 year-old high school football stadium in bad repair behind the school buildings. Two governing board members who lived in that area were worried about traffic problems, even though the developer's plans would have actually relieved traffic in the area, so they spoke out against selling the property. They never said anything about what was best for the entire school district and what the long-term plan was for the property, or even what was best for students and the neighborhood. However, those local governing board members pressed hard to refuse the developer's offer on the land. The offer was $64 million. The only portion of the $64 million that would be obligated was for replacement of the stadium, which was altogether about $10 million (purchase of land and the cost of building a stadium). The balance of the money would not have to be obligated because a new facility for the non-traditional high school and the other program occupants of the building was already approved and funding was available through a special purpose local option sales tax (SPLOST), which was used to avoid bond debts.

Because the school district owned the last essential piece of property to complete the site plan, the school district could have received, in all probability, several million more dollars for the sale of the land. With resistance from only two governing board members, who refused to see the value to the school district overall, and who had small agendas for a large organization, the possibility of funding a new regional stadium to replace the dilapidated one and the availability of money that could have been used for other essential projects to help students was forever lost, so was an opportunity for the community to benefit from the revitalization. A few years later the same school district struggled with its budget because of the declining economy, reduced local revenues, and education cuts at the state level. Instead of $54 million in the bank, assuming $10 million would have been spent on a new stadium, for the first time in the school district's 80 year history, employees were being laid off and the operating reserve was down to just a few million dollars, enough to operate the school district for one day in a financial emergency.

In an article written by Lisa Iannucci, she describes the behavior of a governing board member of a community association through the voice of a governing board member who was demoralized by what he witnessed.

There are the WIIFMs (What's In It For Me) and the Idiots. The WIIFMs get on the governing boards because they have an axe to grind or a pet issue they want to promote. The Idiots either get roped into it by some well-meaning family member or neighbor, or they think they know everything and actually know nothing. To be good governing board members they have to be able to set aside their personal biases and ambitions, be willing to learn and listen, and think about the good of the whole community and organization. Many folks find that very difficult.

Iannucci strongly suggests that the other governing board members *"...have a talk with the difficult board member, explaining to him what he is doing wrong. If there is a bad board member and it affects your situation it may be worth trying to win him over."*

To further illustrate this point, a school district had a parent run for a governing board seat only because he did not like the way his son was disciplined at school. He accused the school's police officer of pushing his son around. He made serious accusations because he took his son's word over that of a police officer. He insisted that the school district fire the officer. The principal looked into the situation and found that the police officer did nothing wrong. The parent then complained to the police supervisor, who found that the police officer acted appropriately. The parent then insisted on a meeting with the CEO. The CEO asked his senior staff to attend the meeting. The school principal called the CEO's office a couple of hours before the meeting and said he had a lot of parents who were upset with the complaining parent. They were afraid that the popular and respected police officer would be fired or transferred because of this one parent. To show their support for the police officer, over 50 parents showed up at the CEO's office at the same time the complaining parent showed up.

The police officer was not fired or transferred; consequently, the complaining parent made public accusations and decided that he would run for a seat on the governing board to get even. He had no political experience, very little education, had never attended a governing board meeting, and he did not know anything about the school district. He ran on a so-called platform of, *"They are picking on your children."*

Much to everyone's shock he won with less than 10 percent of eligible voters caring enough to vote. He was immediately a disruptive factor on the governing board. He created problems from his first day on the governing board. He frequently interfered with school principals. Referring to Jantsch's description, he *"turned every discussion into a fight."* He also attended a lot of school functions for the sole purpose of grandstanding. Anytime he appeared at a school event, invited or not, he insisted on being allowed to speak. Reports are that he did not represent his governing board well or the organization. One time he attended the opening of a parent center at a school where 95 percent of the students were Spanish-speaking. He was not on the agenda to speak but that did not stop him from insisting that he be allowed to participate. He stood before a large audience of Spanish-speaking parents and guests and instead of saying "Hola," (Spanish for "hello") he said "Aloha." Some parents were amused, but most of them were offended, and the school administration was extremely embarrassed.

Another time he attended a meeting that was for only staff members to discuss prevention and intervention strategies and activities. After the meeting he told a staff member, *"Several times today I was about to say something but before I could say it you said what I was about to say. You must have ESPN."* It is a fair assumption that he meant ESP (Extra-Sensory Perception).

Many governing board members and others firmly believe that every type of organization should be run like a business. All the ills of every organization would be or could be remedied if the business model was adopted. Non-profits, schools, colleges, and government organizations hear the same lament; that they should run their organizations like a business. It is a popular notion. But should school districts or non-profits or for that matter any organization really operate like a business? Should all businesses operate the same? Do all businesses operate the same? Should a background or experience in the business world be a qualifying requirement of prospective governing board members? Many governing board members with a background in business readily agree that the organization should be run like business. It certainly is an opinion that can be shared with governing board members and leaders of any organization, but those that advocate so ferociously for the business model should be cautious about forcing it on organizations and fellow governing board members.

According to the United States Bureau of Labor Statistics, there are on average 15,000 business failures per year in the United States. Which business model does governing boards want organizations to adopt: Enron, Eastern Airlines, AIG?

I had first-hand experience in this debate. I was asked to make a speech to a local Rotary Club, as I was often asked to do. During the course of my speech on that particular night the forks and knives stopped in mid air and mouths dropped open because of what I said about business failures. I was asked by a member of a business board of directors why school districts and colleges could not be run more like a business. The room became quiet, the air was still, and heads were shaking from side to side. I was speaking heresy. Then a peculiar thing happened. Someone from the audience spoke up, *"He's right. If we want other organizations to improve, businesses have to be more actively involved in school and community programs and if we want them to run like businesses we have to be more specific about what that really means. In this room today we have several different types of businesses, and I bet we all run our businesses differently."*

As fate would have it this same Rotary Club meeting got me into trouble. During the meeting I was asked if I would endorse a particular governing board member candidate for office. I explained that employees cannot participate in elections or comment on governing board member candidates. I was then asked to profile what makes a good governing board member. I responded with what I could remember from the National School Boards Association's (NSBA) publication about effective governing board members. Apparently, a member of the Rotary Club audience made notes of my comments and consequently on his own concluded that the governing board member representing his area did not meet the NSBA's standards. He then proceeded to call that governing board member to let him know of his shortcomings as a governing board member.

Because governing boards have a lot of power and influence, there has to be more accountability. Many of the examples given in this chapter focus on large or relatively large organizations, but much smaller organizations have the same issues with leadership and governing boards.

In a small community with a long tradition of art appreciation, a governing board managed the policies of an arts council and helped raise money. Over the course of many years, the reputation of the community's appreciation of the arts grew statewide. For decades, the arts council thrived and the community benefitted greatly from the business, industry, and education that developed from this central pride in the arts. A member of the governing board became disenfranchised with the director of the arts council because he did not include one of the board member's relatives in an arts exhibit. The director assured the governing board member that the art work was judged to be good by the advisory committee that selected art for the arts exhibit, but many other art pieces were superior to that particular piece of art work. For decades, the process of selecting art for the annual art exhibit was sacrosanct. The likelihood that a governing board member would interfere with the selection process was absurd. This overbearing governing board member was selected by his peers primarily because of his financial standing in the community, not because of a reputation of supporting the arts. In fact, he had shown very little previous interest in the community's arts endeavors and exhibits.

It became painfully obvious soon after he joined the governing board that his only attribute was his financial wealth, for he added no value to the purpose of the arts council. The director and the governing board had sacrificed their purpose and commitment to the arts for the power status and possible financial contributions of the new governing board member. After the director explained the process of selecting art for the exhibit and the critical role of the advisory committee, the new board member was unmoved. He insisted that his relative's art work be included in the exhibit. The director informally and formally addressed the issue with the other governing board members. Rather than maintaining its integrity and focus on the tradition of art work selection; instead of standing strong against one governing board member's inappropriate demands; instead of appreciating and respecting the authority and responsibility of the director's position and important role in the council and community, the governing board told the director to include the substandard art work in the exhibit. The governing board members were obviously thinking that no harm would come from their decision; after all, it was just one piece of art in a large exhibit. However, shortly thereafter other governing board members begin to question the selections of the advisory committee, and each one began to name their own art piece favorites. Over a short period of time, the selection process broke down; the quality of the arts exhibit declined; the trust of the director diminished; and the once broad support of the community started to erode. Soon after the selection process for the art exhibit deteriorated, the director was removed and a successor was selected that was unqualified for the position but who clearly followed the dictates of the governing board.

The issues facing organizations, particularly when there is a stressful relationship between the governing board and leadership, or even when there is conflict between and among governing board members, often affects the succession of leadership and thus sustainability. Even in the best of times and under positive circumstances, according to an article by Dayton Ogden and John Wood, *Succession Planning: A Board Imperative,* governing boards understand the need for succession planning, but too often they just do not do it very well. Many governing boards do not give themselves strong marks for planning for a leadership change. Only about half of public and private corporate boards have leadership succession plans in place, according to a recent survey by the Center for Board Leadership. A report from the National Association of Corporate Directors found that only 16 percent of governing boards had an effective leadership succession plan. The succession planning process must be thoughtful and deliberate and not sabotaged or hijacked by governing board members with personal agendas and a power ego. According to the Society for Human Resource Management, in an article titled *Succession Planning with Your Board,* the editors wrote:

Succession planning is a means for an organization to ensure its continued effective performance through leadership continuity. For an organization to plan for the replacement of key leaders, potential leaders must first be identified and prepared to take on those roles. It is not enough to select people in the organization who seem right for the job. Not only should the experience and duties be considered, but also the personality, the leadership skills, and the readiness for taking on a key leadership role.

In other words, succession planning and selection is a very difficult process, and it is a very important governing board function. Everyone seems to agree that succession planning is essential for any organization, but if it is not done very effectively during smooth times, it is very unlikely that a successful succession will occur during difficult times. It is another insidious outcome of ineffective board governance behavior. But there is more. The failure of successful succession planning is in many situations centered on the attitude of the governing board about its role in the operations of the organization. Governing boards that are involved in the operations of an organization far beyond their proper role, seldom make good CEO selections.

When we return to the story of the small arts council with board governance interference problems, we find years later that the once proud and prestigious arts council is now a shell of its former existence, and its decline started with one governing board member who put himself over the best interests of the organization and was supported by a governing board that failed to carry out its duties and responsibilities. Once the trust was eroded and the focus of the organization shifted from its mission to individual self-interests, the core of the organization was poisoned from the inside out. The purpose of leadership was lost. But more importantly, sustainability of the effectiveness of the organization suffered. There are many examples, almost too many to note, where sustainability was lost and the organization faltered because of the conflict between a governing board and leadership of the organization. In every story told in this chapter, the goals and the effectiveness of each organization were compromised and the organization's ability to sustain good, effective programs was weakened substantially.

Antidote

In his book, *The Speed of Trust*, Stephen Covey states that an effective leader must have the trust of everyone in the organization in order to reach maximum efficiency. He conveys that micromanaging comes from a lack of trust and over self-indulgence from the leader. Covey asks the questions: *Do people trust their boss and does their boss trust them?* If that trust of leadership is diminished it reverberates across the organization. Of course, trust works both ways and any discussion about trust or the lack therein must be an honest appraisal of the behavior of employees and leadership. Leadership based on trust means that employees can trust that leaders are dependable and honest, while leaders can trust that employees are doing their jobs and are not falsifying records or stealing from the organization, for example, and that governing board members are fulfilling their role instead of trying to manage the operations of the organization. Covey's emphasis on trust focuses on leaders that do not trust any employee to do anything without intrusive supervision, even when there is no indication that employees are doing anything wrong. This applies to the behavior of governing boards that do not trust the CEO. This approach to leadership minimizes production and leads to employee turnover. In organizations with a history of employee misbehavior, the CEO and governing board cannot be naïve about the leader-employee relationship. Trust is earned and is not an entitlement. In the book *The Twelve Absolutes of Leadership*, Gary Burnison suggests that the lack of trust and the forfeiture of leadership develop when an organization loses its purpose which can be the result of governing board interference.

In this chapter, there are examples of governing board members replacing the purpose of the organization with their own purposes and agendas. When the CEO abdicates his role in order to please governing board members the purpose of the organization is sacrificed. The antidote to this type of poison is an absolute, unbreakable devotion to purpose and commitment to purpose. Burnison writes: *"To be a leader is to be passionate about purpose – authentically and genuinely. Leaders make purpose their North Star and continually lead the organization toward it. Embody purpose – people will watch you and follow your lead; personally shape and continually deliver the message about purpose; walk the talk of purpose in everything you do – if you don't, purpose is just the slogan du jour; be grounded in purpose over time."*

Governing board members, CEOs, and communities must maintain the purpose of the organization and protect it, because the insidious effects of even the smallest amount of self-purpose can ruin it. They must understand their role as leader and governing board members. Carlo Corsi, Guilherme Dale, Julie Hembrock Daum and Willi Schoppen list essential things governing board members should be thinking about.

The effective functioning of a board depends on a number of factors, including the mix of knowledge and experience among them, the quality of information they receive and their ability to operate as a team. The [governing board] chairman's role...is pivotal in managing the group dynamic, playing to the board's strengths and maintaining regular contact with organizational directors between meetings. High-functioning boards rotate meetings around...locations.... Boards not only evaluate the performance of the CEO, but take the formal assessment of their own work seriously and use the findings to develop — and hold themselves to — objectives for improvement. Transparency and trust prevail.

An effective governing board should take the time for self-evaluation, using the role of the governing board and the mission of the organization as cornerstone indicators of effectiveness. The effective governing board member stays focused on the purpose of the organization and each governing board member's role in protecting and encouraging the purpose of the organization.

Effective boards put their companies [organizations] at a distinct advantage; nowhere is this more evident than in the way they address strategy, from formation through to execution. The conventional delineation of responsibility is that the executive team develops the strategy and the governing board fine tunes it and then oversees its execution by management, measuring the CEO's performance against a set of agreed-upon objectives. (Corsi, et al.)

The distinction is clear – an organization's leader and her executive team create the strategy and execute the strategy. The governing board offers support and holds the leadership accountable, but governing board members should not be involved in the daily operations of the organization. It cannot be stated too often how disruptive governing board inference is to the operations of an organization. The long-term impact can compromise the quality of work and jeopardize staff morale. Also, there are other ramifications of role confusion.

Ultimately, it is sustainability that is the measure of success. There are many organizations and businesses that found short-term success at one time but do not even exist now. Take for example, the Fortune 500 list. In the 1980s it took five years for one-third of the Fortune 500 to be replaced; in the 1970s it took a decade to replace the Fortune 500, and prior to the 1970s it took two decades. Jim Collins, author of *Built to Last*, notes that only 71 companies on the original 1955 Fortune 500 list are there today. Sustainability should be a major concern to governing board members, which means for example that constant changes in an organization's leadership because of the failure of the governing board to understand its proper role jeopardizes sustainability of the organization. It can be a challenge to get governing boards and CEOs of organizations to understand and accept this. An organization's governing board or a CEO that focuses on self-interest and role confusion has no real goal or plan for sustainability and therefore focuses only on the short-term. Chip Heath wrote in *Made to Stick*, "*Many armies fail because they put all their emphasis into creating a plan that becomes useless ten minutes into the battle.*" Some organizations have recognized that sustainability is too important to depend solely on whatever quirks of board governance might jeopardize them, so they are developing sustainability managers. These managers work with the organization's CEO and the governing board to point out how decisions and the behavior of governing board members may impact the future of the organization in positive or negative ways.

CHAPTER 4

PUT LEAD BACK IN LEADERSHIP

The first responsibility of a leader is to define reality and the last is to say thank you. In between the leader is a servant.

—Max Dupree

Poison: The selection of a leader based on personal agendas of the governing board or on perceived short-term needs of the organization can poison critical components of the organization. This is toxic when the leader aims to maintain the status quo and when the leader relinquishes leadership functions and lets the organization drift on its own. Equally destructive is totalitarian leadership because an overbearing, bullying leader does not work well in problem-solving situations and typically creates morale issues within the organization. No organization can survive or thrive with those types of leaders. The laissez-faire leader is often controlled by the governing board, thus, decisions such as personnel decisions are driven more by the leader's desire to please the governing board than by the needs of the organization. The totalitarian leader tries to control everything and ends up controlling very little. Without the right type of leader, one who has effective communication skills, understands the value of trust and good support staff, and seeks independence from the governing board, a once successful organization can decline rapidly and irreversibly.

There are, of course, several different types of leadership in the literature on management, from Robert Greenleaf's "*Servant Leadership*" style to George Patton's "*Military Leadership*" style, but there are three leadership styles, with some crossover, that seem to be central to the circular pattern of leadership selection used by governing boards and even some businesses: benevolent, laissez-faire, and totalitarian. The cycle may start, for example, when a benevolent leader is replaced with a laissez-faire leader who is later replaced by a totalitarian leader before cycling back to the benevolent and so on, but it may start with any of the three and circle back through. This seems to occur most often when the governing board falls into the trap of selecting a leader based not on qualifications for the long haul, but instead on perceived short-term needs of the organization and their own biases. Jack Welch, in the article *5 Types of Directors Who Don't Deliver*, labeled this type of governing board member as "The Meddler" — *"...meddlers get all mucked up in operational details. They seem oblivious to the fact that board members are there for their wisdom, sound counsel, and judgment, not the day-to-day running of the business."*

There is a fourth leadership style that I do not include with the others because it is unclear how common it is and under what circumstances it emerges; plus, it is a leadership type that is not included in most articles or other literature on leadership. I cannot name it with certainty but I can describe it from experience. It is the *"Lemon"* leadership style, which is slick, shiny and colorful on the outside and bitter and seedy on the inside.

Even though the circular pattern of leadership can start with any of the three, these leadership styles are listed in this order for a reason – it is surprising how often the different leadership styles follow one another, and the order has as much to do with the purpose for their selection by the governing board at the time of the selection as anything else. In other words, circumstances on the governing board and the condition of the organization often determine what type of leader is selected by the governing board instead of the qualities of the individual and the match with the organization's needs. Many governing board members have preferences about what type of personality a leader needs to possess to be successful. This makes sense if: (1) the personality type is a good match for the mission and purpose of the organization; (2) if it is grounded in a positive attitude toward subordinates coupled with superb communication skills; and (3) not a personality that is perceived as the perfect match because it either mirrors the personality of governing board members who expect the leader to act as they do or is the personality type that can be easily dominated by the governing board.

If a leader is viewed by the governing board as dictatorial, much like a bully, who intimidates the governing board, staff members, clients and service providers the governing board will soon grow tired of this behavior. They will become weary of the complaints from others who find the behavior of the bully wearisome and disrespectful. However, it is very likely that the bully was selected by that same governing board fully aware of the leader's personality and management style because they wanted the new leader "to shake things up; to move the organization beyond the status quo."

At the time a domineering leader is selected the governing board typically wants a mover and shaker - someone who is not afraid to make changes. A short time later, when the governing board sends the bully packing, it seldom selects someone of the same leadership style as a successor. Instead, the governing board will often select a benevolent, servant type leader to replace an irascible leader. The servant leader is hired to make peace, to solve problems with a wise and steady hand, to restore morale and good relations, to calm things down so the organization can focus again on its mission and purpose. The governing board expects the servant leader to be all things to all people. He will have a wholesome vision and mission for the organization and will communicate with and support employees, clients and the governing board. This type of leader will have a good sense of humanity and humility so he will know how to interact with people.

The servant leader is just as comfortable meeting with other CEOs, politicians, and benefactors as she is meeting with employees, customers, service providers, citizens and others that communicate at a different level. The servant leader understands and embraces the value of social capital – community support and interaction. Yet, she is smart enough to know that hard decisions have to be made and someone has to be the bearer of tough news sometimes. However, the servant leader is agile enough to understand that during such times, she must rely on other staff members. For example, she may select a skilled financial officer, an experienced human resources officer, and a no-nonsense chief of staff to handle the toughest duties. This is not avoidance behavior; instead, it is a wise delegation of responsibilities.

The legendary expert on leadership, Robert Greenleaf, wrote in *The Servant as Leader*, that *"It begins with the natural feeling that one wants to serve, to serve first. Then conscious choice brings one to aspire to lead. The difference manifests itself in the care taken by the servant--first to make sure that other people's highest priority needs are being served."*

The servant leader knows how to blend the organization's vision with the realities of day-to-day leadership and the challenges of leading the operations of an organization. In this regard the servant leader, much to the surprise of others, can be shrewd. This type of leader tends to last longer than leaders with more abrasive or lackadaisical styles of leadership, because their leadership style serves the organization well and because he is generally well liked. Consequently, the servant leader is given more time to accomplish goals and address issues. It does not mean necessarily that this type of leader is always successful, of course, but he has better odds for success than most other types. Servant leaders are typically successful because the nature of their leadership style is a good match with the needs and challenges of many organizations. He leads by example of a positive approach to leadership by encouragement, by motivation, by focusing on the needs of clients that the organization serves.

The servant leader also has the ability to build a strong team. He recognizes the needs of the organization at many levels and consequently selects team members that will meet those needs. It does not mean that he will not ever make an appointment that is political. Politics is part of any organization, but he will not select a team member based solely on that reason and certainly will not sacrifice the good of the organization with a politically-based selection. The servant leader is not intimidated by intelligent staff members and is not threatened by team members that do not always agree with him. In Marcus Buckingham's book, *The One Thing You Need to Know*, he writes:

Some managers claim that they don't have the time to select the right person for the team. I have openings now, they say, and these openings must be filled. Good managers know the folly of this approach. They know that, when it comes to building the right team, time is nonnegotiable. You will spend the time. The only question is where you will spend it: on the front end, carefully selecting the right person, or on the back end, desperately trying to transform the person into who you wished he was in the first place.

Many organization leaders have a thankless job. It is a job that many members of the public do not understand and do not care much about until something happens that draws media attention or impacts them or someone they know. According to Cooper, Fuserilli, and Carella, the public perception of organizational leadership positions is that of a job so daunting that only a few individuals desire to pursue the challenge.

An example is the dilemma in public education leadership. The most comprehensive study about school superintendent characteristics is from the American Association of School Administrators (AASA). An AASA survey sampled 2,262 superintendents and found that the average tenure of superintendents was between 5 and 6 years, slightly lower than the previous surveys. The Council of Great City Schools (GCS) survey conducted with member districts that showed average tenure for urban superintendents was only 2.75 years, while the mean tenure for the immediate past GCS superintendents averaged over 4 years. The Council of Urban Boards of Education reported the tenure of urban superintendents to be between 4 and 5 years.

The brief tenure of leaders is not limited to public education leadership. The average tenure of a leader in non-profit settings and businesses is not much longer. According to *Forbes Magazine*, in an article by Steve Denning, *Seven Lessons Every CFO Must Learn,* CFOs last about six years, and based on research by The Center for Association Leadership the average tenure of non-profit executive directors is less than four years.

In some cases, the length of time a leader is able to maintain his job is related to his ability or inability to work with and satisfy governing board members. Too often if a leader stands up to a governing board member who is out of line with their role on issues that are essential to the organization, the leader is considered uncooperative. A cooperative relationship between the leader and the governing board is the number one quality governing board members look for in hiring and retaining an organization's leader; at least that is what most governing board members claim. If, however, a leader gives in to governing board member's whims, the same governing board may be quick to label him as weak. It is a delicate balancing act for leaders. Many business leaders and their boards have the same issues. One of the crisis of leadership is this situation, where the leader must work with a governing board without drawing battle lines all of the time; yet, some governing board members view compromise as weakness and lose respect for the leader, but if the leader takes a stand, the same governing board members may label him as uncooperative. On the other hand, leaders that do not communicate with governing board or that mislead them or provide incorrect information to them are not acting in the best interests of the organization. A leader will not be successful if he views the governing board in an adversarial way. There are few things more distracting to an organization at all levels than the leader and the governing board locked in one battle after another. The causalities of these battles are the employees, clients, volunteers, and others who matter the most.

While research cited by the *Civic Index* shows that most of the time governing board members vote to approve items brought to the board by leaders of public organizations and non-profits, that does not include personnel issues or budget issues, which are critical to the operation of the organization. The research also does not include the pressure some governing board members exert on the leader about operational matters – the day-to-day operations of the organization. This is a critical distraction because the daily operation of any organization can be very complicated – providing services or materials each day to clients; maintaining order and cleanliness in facilities; taking inventory and processing countless purchase orders; answering dozens or hundreds of phone calls, emails and letters; and much more, and all of that on a good day. If something unforeseen happens, all operations functions can be further stressed. The responsibilities are multi-faceted, so the last thing a leader and his staff needs is an interfering governing board member. Therefore, how the governing board interacts with the leader is crucial, so crucial that the relationship can and frequently does impact the vision, mission, performance, morale, and operations of the organization. This tenuous relationship depends on a lot of factors.

One of the main factors related directly to the governing board and leader relationship is communications. Many studies indicate that communications is a major obstacle to a positive relationship. In fact, a study by Young, Peterson and Short, *Complexity of Substantive Reform*, found that communication skills related directly to the quality of the leader and governing board relationship which in turn influenced decision making more than any other factor. In his book, *The Twelve Absolutes of Leadership*, Gary Burnison lists communication as one of the essential leadership functions; he states that, *"Communication is where leadership lives and breathes. In good times, people look to the leader for validation and in difficult times they look to the leader for assurance."*

Where I worked, a successful CEO who lasted over 16 years understood the power and necessity of clear communication with the governing board. Notice that I did not say "positive" communication but "clear" communication. Research distinguishes between positive and clear communications because they differ in the management of expectations. Many times, governing board members expect positive communications when instead they get clear communications. This then can be perceived by the governing board members as negative communications when the CEO sees it as clearly conveying information or an opinion. The successful CEO understood that communications with the governing board, employees and the community cannot always be positive but it can and should always be clear and timely and respectful. He understood that there is a time and place for clarity. He avoided open confrontations during public governing board meetings, but behind closed doors he could be very clear and firm with them. He was always very tactful and strategic with his communications; yet, he was no one's fool. It was not wise to mistake his kindness for weakness, for he was a very strong-willed person. The following story is just one example.

I was leaving the central office building one evening after a long local governing board meeting. It was a chilly night as I stepped out of the back door of the office complex building after the meeting. As I neared the back corner of the building near the parking lot where staff and governing board members parked, I heard the voices of the CEO and a governing board member who had been continually critical of the CEO and his staff members during public board meetings. The CEO tried diligently to resolve issues with this governing board member behind the scenes away from the public. He was not inclined to have a public debate and he did not want to drag staff members into the disagreements either. I did not want to walk up on the conversation because it was obviously not a pleasant conversation and since the door to the building locked behind me I was stuck there in the semi-darkness with no place to go to. So I just waited, and listened. I heard the CEO say to the governing board member, *"I have worked with you for weeks on this issue and we have had cordial disagreements. I've respected your opinion and thought you respected my opinion, but it seems you want to deliberately embarrass me and my staff members during the board meetings. I will not get into a running battle with you in public. I've told you that. It's not good for anyone or the governing board or the community and therefore serves no purpose. But let me tell you one thing you can count on - within six months either you'll be gone or I'll be gone."* That was clear and timely communication. It did not sound like a threat. It was just a statement made in a calm manner. I do not know the details of why, but that governing board member resigned a few weeks later.

Most of the studies, research and articles on communications focus on timing, technique, and process, but some of the recent books written by successful leaders point out the importance of humor as a communication method, because communication can be enhanced with the insertion of a well-timed bit of humor. One interesting contrast in the use of humor in communications at the leadership level comes from the same company and two distinctively different leadership communication styles. For years, the iconic CEO of IBM was Thomas Watson, Jr., the son of the legendary founder of IBM. Watson was an enormously successful CEO who made IBM into a world known power and business giant. He was unpredictable in his communication style, serious minded and by his own admission a tyrant at times with little or no sense of humor. Watson's tenure at the top was an unqualified success, but IBM declined slowly after Watson retired. Many of the CEOs that followed Watson tried to emulate his leadership style. Contrast that communication style with another IBM CEO, Edward Gerstner, who took the helm of IBM at a time when the company was struggling. In fact, when he took over the helm at IBM the giant company was bleeding money and had a bleak future. Gerstner managed to pull IBM from the brink of being dismantled into small companies and returned IBM to its former glory. In his memoir, *Elephants Can Dance,* Gerstner points out the importance of communications and he states that humor is a very important component of effective leadership. Of course, the timing and circumstances have to be right and the humor has to be relevant and in good taste, but he noted that humor can create a positive work environment.

In Watson's memoir, *Father, Son and Co.,* he frequently points out the importance of communications with the executive staff, executive board, line staff, sales staff, media, and IBM clients. But at one point in the book, Watson laments almost painfully about his failure or reluctance to show his humorous side more often at work and more importantly at home. He felt that he could have improved the work climate and his home climate if he had not taken everything so seriously all of the time. Dwight Eisenhower stated, *"A sense of humor can be a great help...a sense of humor is a part of the art of leadership, of getting along with people, of getting things done."*

Understanding the importance of communication, including humor, is one reason why the CEO I worked with for several years was successful and lasted almost two decades in the leadership role. He understood that used tactfully and appropriately, the right touch of humor can diffuse a tense environment. In staff meetings, he often used humorous stories and examples to make a point without embarrassing anyone. Abraham Lincoln was famous for the use of humorous stories to make a point or to reduce tension, but never at the expense of someone.

A good example of our CEO's use of humor to make a point or diffuse a situation was how he once handled a section of the governing board agenda that had spiraled out of control during several board meetings. The section of the governing board agenda that everyone dreaded was the "New Business" section which always came last on the agenda. Any governing board member could bring forth an item for discussion during New Business without any advanced notice or warning. New Business was a euphemism for, *"This is what's on my mind and by God everyone is going to hear about it."* It was not uncommon for a governing board member to go off on a tangent about some obscure point or concern or self-promoting speech or even make some demand on the organization's leadership. This had become a very controversial part of the board meeting, because sometimes certain governing board members would make critical remarks about staff members or the CEO, criticize each other or go on a tirade about a controversial political position. Typically it was always the same few governing board members who did this, while the other board members, the CEO, staff members, and others sat quietly and stared off into space. The CEO seemed very tolerant of this practice, but privately it greatly disturbed him. In private sessions with them he had several conversations about the inappropriate comments made by some of them during the New Business section of the meeting. No matter what he said, the New Business fiasco continued and seemed to be getting worse. Something had to be done, but the governing board showed no interest in managing this increasingly embarrassing practice. Most likely, they did not know what to do with their colleagues.

One evening at the end of a very long board meeting just as the governing board chairman moved to the New Business section of the agenda the CEO signaled a staff member and through the board room sound system everyone heard the music score from the attack shark movie *Jaws*. For a moment no one understood what was going on. Everyone looked up at the ceiling where the rumbling, sinister theme music was pouring out in ominous tones. The governing board members looked at each other and then at the CEO, who sat still with a poker face. Then suddenly everyone almost simultaneously laughed; most curiously those governing board members who were the ones most likely to turn the New Business section into a gripe session laughed loudest. While this tactic might be viewed as irreverent or risky, which it was, it made a point in a humorous way and the point was well received, for after that the New Business portion of the agenda took on a whole new purpose and the attack-mentality faded.

After the CEO retired, some of the fondest memories of him according to the governing board members were his uncanny means of communications, including his use of humor. This highly effective veteran CEO was what Kowalski would view as an expert communicator. Each governing board member had his or her own unique means of communication, yet the CEO was known by each of them as a master of communications. One of his favorite quotes was from Plato: "*Wise men speak because they have something to say; fools because they have to say something.*" Unlike many CEOs who do not communicate directly with their governing board members on a regular basis this CEO talked with governing board members routinely. He spent time almost daily in direct communication with governing board members. A CEO who does not communicate with the governing board except just before and during governing board meetings can expect difficult board meetings and maybe even confrontational board meetings. Some CEOs have found that governing board members interfere less with the operations side of the organization if the CEO communicates with them on a regular basis, even the most insignificant communication effort is important to governing board members. According to General Colin Powell, former Secretary of State, it is through communications that trust is built between and among people in an organization. The successful CEO's philosophy is that the number of conflicts and the number of confrontations during governing board meetings is diminished if he communicates with the governing board members *before* the board meetings. This gives him the opportunity to gauge the opinion of the governing board members about certain agenda items before he takes those items to the board meeting.

Sometimes leaders have to mediate or breakup disagreements between and among governing board members. That is part of the communication function of a leader with a governing board, maybe an unwritten part, but an important part nevertheless, especially when they are disrespectful to each other. This makes the leader's job even more difficult. In a study by Jason Grissom, he found governing boards that utilize more professional decision practices and whose members share a common vision for their work experience conflict with each other at substantially lower rates. He also found that governing boards that monitor their own behavior were more successful in their role of supporting each other, the leader and the organization.

The interaction of governing board members can be a tenuous situation. I was in a closed governing board executive session one afternoon. I was there only for the purpose of answering questions about a personnel case. The board chair reviewed the relevant issues of the case and a governing board member asked for clarification. The board chair in a condescending manner, complete with a dramatic sigh, said *"I'll make it easy for you."* The governing board member who asked the question lost his temper. Rising from his chair as his temper flared, he said, *"I'm goddamn sick and tired of you treating me like I'm something under your fingernails. You think you're so wonderful and so smart. Well, you may be smart but you're a bitch and I'm not going to put up with it anymore."* Even though he was an elderly man he moved quickly around the large conference table and was heading for the board chair with pure rage in his eyes. I was close to the conference table so I stepped in front of the angry governing board member while the target of his anger was backing up. I did not touch him but I darted in front of his every effort to get past me and at the board chair. After his temper abated some, the CEO took the board chair and the angry governing board member out of the room together and into a small private conference room. I was not privy to the communications that took place after that incident, but by the time the next public governing board meeting was held two weeks later the board chair and the angry governing board member were on good terms. It was apparent that after the incident, the CEO talked at length to both of them and helped them work out their issues. The incident was forgotten. The bad feelings mended. The work of the governing board continued and all due to the communication skills of the CEO. In *Elizabeth I, CEO, Strategic Lessons from the CEO Who Built an Empire* Alan Axelrod wrote, *"Effective Leadership is still largely a matter of communications."*

Another important factor in the relationship between an organization's leader and the governing board is how they react to tough decisions, which includes, of course, effective internal and external communications. In an article about the CEO of the Gloucester City Public Schools, who was retiring after nine years in the job, she said her otherwise good relationship with the governing board was challenged when difficult and unpopular decisions had to be made, but in the past with a different governing board they always worked it out. Now it is different. She said, *"Now, as soon as you make a decision a board doesn't like, you're out."* She added, *"A lot of people come onto boards with personal agendas. Sometimes you have to make decisions that aren't popular. A lot of it is politicking. No matter what you do, it is wrong, and a lot is driven by politics. My blood pressure medicine has quadrupled."*

The governing board of Hewlett-Packard seems to fire CEOs that bring bad news to them or that disagree with them, or perhaps they are just not very good at selecting leaders. Hewlett-Packard is currently on its fifth CEO in seven years. In a different type of organization, the same issues are prevalent. A non-profit organization with national offices has gone through five CEOs in less than five years. It seems as if each time a leader is shown the door, the governing board has a press release that sights the lack of communications between the governing board and the leader. This implies that the leader had to make some tough decisions for the organization that governing board members did not like.

An article in *Forbes Magazine* by Glenn Llopis, *The Most Successful Leaders Do 15 Things*, lists five critical components of making tough decisions by leaders that impact how decisions are made. These five components can also shape how governing boards receive or accept decisions.

1. Make no decision before its time. *"Clay Mathile, former owner of the Iams Company and now founder of Aileron believes that this is the key for any leader. If you don't make those decisions that you don't have to make, invariably, there's new information that comes, there's more information, better information, better data."* Making a decision at a later date, unless there is a crisis, may lead to a more informed one and thus is more likely to be accepted and trusted by a governing board and employees. This is sometimes difficult for governing board members to accept, particularly the ones who are high pressure and intense and who consequently want all questions answered immediately.
2. Accept that there are few easy decisions and there are seldom "exact right" answers. *"Stop searching and doubting and exercising repeated second-guessing. There is only a "current" right decision based on the information that is available now."* It is important to convey this to the governing board, also.
3. Deciding with heart or head? *"The leader has to admit if he or his staff members are making decisions based on emotion or the facts. While it is not necessarily bad to make a decision on emotion, this*

needs to be clear and the rational sensible and relevant." When leaders make a decision out of anger with a governing board member, it seldom stands the test of reason and good sense, especially if the decision serves no purpose or is contrary to what is best for the organization.

4. Make the decision after careful consideration, but then do not waver. *"Commit to one path and take action. Wavering will almost guarantee that the desired outcome is not accomplished."* Governing boards want and demand decisiveness from the leader, but they may encourage the leader to reconsider his decision if it goes contrary to governing board's wishes. The leader must examine his decision and if it is the right decision based on circumstances, he must be committed to that decision and stand by it. Governing boards, employees, and the public develop doubts about leaders that waver and constantly change decisions.

5. When definitive action is taken, learn from the results and then plan the next move. *"Success is typically a series of patient interim steps, not giant wild leaps. Often governing boards expect a new leader to take giant wild leaps because the board wants everything to change immediately; they want all of the problems to be addressed at the same time and with positive outcomes."* Organizational change and decision-making does not work that way. Systematic change comes from a series of connected, related, mindful, and thoughtful decisions with the long-term in mind. Short-term solutions that are reactionary, poorly planned, and based on emotion or pressure from the governing board often create even more serious long-term problems.

The reaction to leadership decisions often centers on the perception and belief of role responsibilities. Ted Glass found that 30 percent of organizational leaders, for example, thought some of their governing board members were unqualified. Though there may be some truth regarding the qualifications of some governing board members, it is a dangerous and counterproductive view by a leader, because it may adversely shape his decisions and communications on important issues with the governing board. Also, if the leader holds a negative view of governing board members he is likely to frame communications in a condescending manner. Whether the leader believes that the governing board is qualified or not, he has to work with them, communicate with them and align on tough decisions.

The first CEO I worked for was the quintessential bureaucrat. His leadership style was clearly "by the book." He was very bright, but very temperamental and irascible. He invited confrontation when it was not necessary. He even managed to get into a public fight with the governing board over what should have been a win-win situation – a large budget reserve.

At a governing board meeting one of the board members asked the CEO what he planned to do with the substantial amount of money in the reserve. Instead of explaining the importance and necessity of a budget reserve during economically tough times - to help the organization face any type of financial shortfall or react to unforeseen circumstances, the CEO made the statement, *"You're not going to tell me to use up the reserve and you're certainly are not going to tell me how to use that money."* He should have and could have told the governing board that the amount of money seemed large for a budget reserve, but the fact of the matter was that the budget reserve amount equaled the organization's operating costs for only one month. It was very prudent of the CEO to manage the organization's budget so frugally and thoughtfully. Had he explained the budget reserve that way, instead of being arrogant and condescending, the issue would have ended then and there. In reaction to his unprofessional demeanor and challenging comment, the governing board turned against him very quickly even though he was a very competent CEO. The governing board had each heard complaints about the CEO's derogatory demeanor toward just about everyone and they were growing very tired of it. Even though he was a good steward of the budget and a very intelligent person, he did not delegate authority, did not have any interest in building a team, had poor communication skills and had no interest in anything associated with *servant leadership*. Additionally, he had no respect for the governing board and avoided communicating with them at all costs. The CEO's tenure was very early in my career so I had only a few opportunities to interact directly with him, but one such occasion illustrates his lack of social skills necessary to build a team and build trust with the governing board.

I was summoned to his office without a reason given. This was very unusual for two reasons: (1) I had only been in my job for a couple of years and (2) I had absolutely no authority over anyone. I was a low level, inexperienced employee – a member of the working class. When my immediate boss, who we called the Dragon Lady because of her temperament, heard that I was going to see the CEO, she demanded to know what I had done or said. She was upset because the CEO did not go through her and did not ask her to accompany me. That was typical of his disinterested communication skills, which created problems at the operations level and at the staff morale level. My boss slinked up behind me while I was in my little cubicle one day and before I sensed her presence she shouted at me loud enough for everyone in the room to hear, *"What the hell did you do this time?"* I stammered, *"I don't know."* That really made her mad. She said, *"Bullshit, you know what it's about. You'd better watch your mouth because I'll find out exactly what you said to him and you don't want to deal with me."* That was the type of leadership behavior the CEO was modeling and reinforcing throughout the organization. She was following the CEO's example of bullying and intimidation and lack of effective communications.

When I was escorted into the CEO's office he never said a word and he kept busy with a task on his ostentatious desk. I did not know whether to stand, sit, clear my throat, or slowly and quietly back out of his office. Suddenly, he looked up and blurted out, *"Why should I pay low level employees like you above the minimum wage?"* *"What do you do?"* There was a hard edge to his voice and his expression was a pained one, complete with furrowed brow and clinched eyes – it was like Ebenezer Scrooge talking to Bob Cratchit. Other than the shock of his demeanor and the subject of his concern what struck me was his use of the pronoun "I," as if it was his money, his personal money. I half expected him to ask me for a refund then and there. He peppered me with question after question. The questions were more statements of opinion than questions. He never said hello or introduced himself or stated why I was summoned or even asked my name. He never gave me the chance to answer any of the questions, not one. After he peppered me with a litany of questions and statements that I had no time to respond to, he went back to his work and seemed shocked a few minutes later when he looked up and found that I was still standing there. Temporarily befuddled by my failure to see that I had been silently dismissed earlier at the conclusion of his tirade, he barked, *"That's all; that's it; you answered my questions."* I opened my mouth to point out that I had not answered any of his demeaning questions, but I could not find the words. From that experience and others I can see why a governing board would grow weary of a CEO with that temperament and disrespect for people. However, that same governing board hired him because of his financial acumen and his no-nonsense leadership style, which were the qualities they thought the organization needed immediately. There was no consideration given to his long-term abilities and how his abrasive personality would impact the organization.

I have witnessed governing boards and the leaders get into many battles over a variety of topics, but this confrontation between the CEO and the governing board became increasingly more intense and ultimately centered on the budget reserve. The governing board wanted him to use some of the budget reserve so that services could be expanded. However, the CEO said he would not be told how to spend the reserve and to spend the money for the sole purpose of temporarily expanding services could cripple the organization during difficult economic times. Instead of focusing on that point he fought the governing board over its efforts to tell him what to do. The issue became a struggle for power, not a debate about fiscal management. It became one of many power struggles. The CEO seemed to think that he took a brave stand on the battlefield of the budget reserve and his career in that organization died on that hill. However, that was not the issue. He failed to understand that the issue shifted to his behavior and lack of leadership skills, even though the financial points he raised were legitimate. How he communicated was not effective. About this topic, Sydney Harris wrote: *"The two words information and communication are often used interchangeably, but they signify quite different things. Information is giving out; communication is getting through."* The CEO's message was not getting through to the governing board members because of his arrogant, condescending communication style. A few years later when the local economy took a downward shift and revenues declined significantly, the governing board realized that even though the then-former CEO was arrogant, uncooperative and argumentative, he was right about the budget reserve and expanding services.

In a study cited by T.L. Alsbury, researchers interviewed school district superintendents from several states and found that role incongruity was a key concern: *"In one example, governing board members, principals, and teachers seemed to gravitate toward 'turf protection' of their own agenda, building, or classroom and failed to understand or practice what was best for all students."* This is not unique to school settings. If role incongruity, communications, and consternation over decisions divide governing boards and leaders, how are leaders selected in the first place? What leadership style and leadership expectations do governing board members have in mind when they select a leader?

Let's look at the typical selection process of a school district CEO, for example. It starts with describing the characteristics the governing board is looking for in candidates. Some school districts contract with executive search firms to conduct the search and make recommendations for three to five finalists. Then they leave the final selection to the wishes of the governing board. These search firms can be for-profit companies or state governing board associations or even contracted individual consultants. A typical qualification checklist for a school district CEO candidate includes the following, which is used by several school boards associations: (1) possession of the doctorate level degree is important, though not mandatory; (2) master level administrative or higher level certification is mandatory; (3) Successful experience as a superintendent is important, but not mandatory; successful experience as a teacher and as a principal are mandatory; (4) has a record of proven public relations abilities, participation in community organizations, and other community affairs; (5) possess the interpersonal skills to effectively deal with all people in a respectful manner and a willingness to become a fully functioning member of the local community; (6) has outstanding experience, understanding, and abilities relating to the areas of curriculum, and personnel; (7) has a proven record of sound fiscal management, experienced and knowledgeable in budgeting and educational finance; (8) capable of delegating authority; (9) has a goal-oriented management style; (10) has a record of a team-building approach to educational leadership and is committed to fostering cooperative relationships among the school district, the board of education, and community CEOs and organizations.

Is this any different in other organizations with governing boards? Not really. They are looking for the same or similar traits in the next leader of the organization. On the *Opportunity Knocks* job website, which lists non-profit sector jobs, almost every executive level job description includes most of the same traits as listed above. If governing boards are seeking essentially the same qualifications and qualities in their next leader, why is the longevity of the selected leader so short-lived? Certainly, the candidates for the leadership positions are not all misrepresenting themselves. That may occur, but infrequently. The capricious nature of leader selections has more to do with governing board member's *perception of the situation* within the organization.

New leaders are very susceptible to pressure from governing board members and; of course, they want to keep their new job, so an awkward dance takes place between the governing board members and the new leaders. For example, organizational leaders, especially leaders new to the organization, who succumb to pressure from governing boards to hire family members, friends, or relatives seldom last very long and much of that is because of the loss of respect but also the amount of time spent, as Buckingham says in his book, *One Thing You Need to Know*, desperately trying to transform that employee who is ill-equipped to help the organization. Then the cost of training someone to eventually replace that person or the cost of engaging another employee to "carry" the incompetent but politically connected employee is significant. When that type of employee clearly becomes a liability for the organization, it is virtually impossible to terminate him or even transfer him to another job or location, because of his ties to a governing board member. This jeopardizes the leader's reputation within the organization and ultimately with the governing board.

The arrogant autocratic CEO who fought with the governing board about the budget reserve was followed by a servant CEO. The governing board wanted someone to calm the turmoil and work with them and the staff and community in a more collaborative manner. The person they selected was such a masterful CEO that he was CEO for several years and could have continued ad infinitum if retirement had not looked so much more attractive to him than the problems of a large organization.

The transition from the arrogant CEO to a more servant type CEO was an interesting study in leadership and governing dynamics. As do many dominating and controlling CEOs, the previous CEO consolidated power so that virtually every decision came from his office. He never delegated any decision-making authority. He controlled or tried to control every aspect of the decision-making process and woe be to anyone who tried to make a decision or express an opposite opinion. No one told him what to do and no one survived any effort to exert influence on his decisions. He showed virtually no respect for the governing board or his own staff members. His style and talent combined to produce an efficiently run organization for a time when he was its CEO, but he had difficulty adjusting to change and challenges to his authority and for that reason the efficiencies weakened over time. Leadership effectiveness is often measured by inspiration and seldom by domination.

When the new CEO took over he wanted to decentralize the decision-making process by delegating authority and placing decision-making closer to the daily operations of the organization. He was surprised and baffled to see so much activity around his office and the constant flow of office staff members coming in his office with questions. It took him a while to understand that many of his executive staff members could not or would not make decisions on their own. He later talked about the blank stare reaction when he asked a veteran executive staff member, *"Well, what do you recommend we do?"* The staff member did not know what to do or what to recommend, because all he had done under the previous CEO was to carry out orders. He was not expected to think, analyze and offer solutions or an opinion.

The new CEO spent a great deal of time studying the organization, including the role of the governing board. He visited sites and talked to hundreds of people inside and outside of the organization. He met with each governing board member and he held meetings with the central office staff to discuss the issues facing the organization. During this time he made no significant changes at the central office level. He was very respectful of people and thoughtful about the opinions of others. In the book *Influencer - The Power to Change Anything*, the authors discuss the importance of enlisting social support, if a CEO is going to be a significant "influencer."

When it comes to creating change, you no longer have to worry about influencing everyone at once. If you preside over a company with 10,000 employees, your job is to find the 500 or so opinion leaders who are the key

to everyone else. Spend disproportionate time with them. Listen to their
concerns. Build trust with them. Be open to their ideas. Rely on them to
share your ideas, and you'll gain a source of influence unlike any other.

The new CEO realized that the central office would have to undergo
some significant changes, and in what became his trademark, he talked
individually with the governing board members to explain what he was
going to do and why. He showed them courtesy and respect by sharing
his thoughts and plans but he was not asking them for permission to make
operational and personnel changes. He made that clear to a few of them
who initially misinterpreted his intent. After working with an arrogant
and disrespectful CEO, the governing board was enamored with this new
CEO who actually communicated with them and the staff on a regular
basis in a meaningful way.

He met with the central office staff he inherited from his predecessor's
regime. He told them that his leadership style dictated a change in everyone's
approach to their jobs. He took the time to explain his expectations. He
also explained the difference between approaching a problem in a task-
driven manner instead of taking a purpose-driven problem-solving track.
In a task-driven approach, there is interest in addressing the presenting
or current problem by seeking a remedy that temporarily resolves the
issue so all involved can move on to other work. Thus, there is seldom
any follow-up or thoughtful consideration of the causes of the problem, so
the problem is more likely to reappear. With a purpose-driven strategy to
problem-solving, there is a deliberate effort to determine the basic problem
beyond the current circumstances. There is a commitment to seeking a
solution instead of settling for a short-term remedy.

He did not "clean house" and start replacing staff and he did not threaten
to replace them, which is exactly what some CEOs do. In Clemens and
Mayer's extraordinary book on leadership, *The Classic Touch*, they focus on
this issue through the ideas of the famous Edmund Burke, the 18th- century
British statesman, parliamentary orator, and theorist of leadership. During
change, Burke warned against expelling all traditions of an organization.
He believed that some of the traditions in an organization have great value,
"They are the storehouse of the organization's collective wisdom." He said
that a new leader who does not recognize this can easily destroy the good
aspects of the organization's traditions, and once destroyed may not be able
to rebuild them. He wrote, *"Any effort to change the organization, therefore,*
should be implemented slowly, a little at a time; and always carefully, so
that the changes are in agreement with its history and its tradition." This
approach is the long-term strategy of sustainability. A quick, dramatic,
traumatic change seldom works and rarely lasts, according to Burke.

The new CEO listened and observed and he told his staff that he trusted them to make decisions and to make good decisions. That is the only way he could determine the value of their contribution to the organization and if their efforts were important to the long-term mission of the organization. He also expected them to keep him abreast of issues, and he encouraged them to be proactive – to look for and anticipate what may become a problem. He wanted them to think. He wanted them to be creative. He wanted them to be leaders. Additionally, he addressed the role of the governing board and what he considered appropriate interaction with them.

This transfer of decision-making from the CEO to staff members for purposes of efficiency was met with skepticism by the governing board and across the organization. Some of the central office staff could not handle making decisions. They did not know how to be responsible for making decisions. They were adept at gathering information that would guide the decision-making process, but they became catatonic when asked what they thought. Consequently, some staff members retired, some moved to other jobs, a few made the conversion and a small number of staff members complained to the governing board.

This is certainly not unique to any particular type of organization. Louis Gerstner took over IBM at a time when many experts did not think it would survive. He found a workplace culture that discouraged individual thought and initiative. Thoughtfulness, creativity and initiative were the very things that had made IBM successful in the past. Gerstner wrote: *"Many used hierarchy as a crutch and were reluctant to take personal responsibility for outcomes. Instead of grabbing available resources and authority, they waited for the boss to tell them what to do; they delegated up. In the end, my deepest culture-change goal was to induce IBMers to believe in themselves again – to believe that they had the ability."* Peter Drucker once said, *"Culture eats strategy for breakfast."*

The new CEO in our organization was smart and intuitive enough to know which central office staff members could work efficiently during his administration. He did not force anyone out, but under his steady and thoughtful ways central office staffing and operations changed and became more effect, which prevented bureaucratic stalemates that hampered the organization. He also knew that even the most inept central office staff members had their own supporters on the governing board, so it was important not to embarrass anyone and create enemies who could be the genesis of destructive rumors. He found that the management style of his predecessor had negatively impacted the flow of decision-making and problem-solving with staff and the governing board. What appeared at times to be efficiency was actually more control processes in place than actual efficiency.

The transfer of leadership and the shift in leadership style regardless of whether the CEO is a servant leader or not is never easy in any organization or business. One incident illustrates how the leadership and management style transition can cause confusion and even resentment.

Our new CEO was advocating the integration of schools by encouraging students who were in a majority school (a White student in a predominantly White school or a Black student in a predominantly Black school) to attend a school where the student would be in the minority. The student transfer program was an important strategy for the school district. Transportation was provided to any student interested in making this transition. At the time the school district was still under the supervision of a federal judge who provided oversight for the desegregation lawsuit. The federal judge approved the transfer program as a legitimate and innovative way to achieve integration.

The implementation of the student transfer program was never easy. It was a difficult decision for families because of social issues but primarily because of the necessary long school bus ride to another part of the school district. In fact, some of the bus rides were an hour or longer. The point is that the transfer program was a daily operations challenge even though it was a good program that worked effectively.

One of the central office administrators left over from the previous regime simply could not make a decision. He had relied on his standing with some governing board members; plus, the previous dictatorial CEO told him what to do regarding all issues. One important area of his responsibilities was transportation for the student transfer program. The transportation complications of moving so many students across the district to other schools were daunting. During a staff meeting with the CEO and executive cabinet, he expressed concern about the ongoing transportation complications of the transfer program, including logistics and additional buses, and he said, *"What are we going to do?"* over and over again. The CEO asked this administrator, *"What do you recommend?"* After getting no reply except more whining about the problem he asked the question in a different way. He said, *"What are you going to do?"* Again, the administrator restated the problem and how difficult the whole situation had become. Finally growing weary of the constant complaining and whining, the CEO said, *"Enough is enough - just stop it, will you."* The befuddled administrator was so use to being told what to do that he apparently took the CEO literally. He completely misunderstood the CEO's comment; in fact, he thought he was being told to discontinue the program. Everyone else in the room knew exactly what the CEO meant, and it certainly was not to stop the program. It was abundantly clear that the CEO wanted the transportation administrator to stop whining and stop asking *"What are we going to do?"*

A storm broke over this because the administrator told others that the CEO instructed him to stop transportation for the student transfer program! This was an incredible gaffe. Parents, local governing board members, and the integration oversight federal judge were outraged at the CEO, as word spread quickly. When he heard what had happened, the CEO confronted the ever-befuddled administrator who replied, *"That's what you told me to do so that's what I told others. You told me to stop it."* When the CEO said that he had misconstrued the meaning, the administrator repeated, *"That's what you told me to do."* The poor soul was not insubordinate, willful, or disrespectful. He had forgotten how to be a leader and how to make decisions. The philosopher Jean-Paul Sartre wrote: *"It is only in our decisions that we are important."* A leader who cannot make decisions is of no use to an organization.

There is no doubt that any other CEO would have taken steps to fire him, but not this CEO. After many embarrassing moments and awkward meetings with stakeholders, the situation was cleared up. The CEO had every reason to put that administrator's head on a platter and everyone, including the governing board, expected him to do just that after the truth was revealed. That is what most CEOs would have done. Instead, he never said another word about the incident to anyone and he let the confused and humiliated administrator leave several months later on his own and with dignity. Of course, during the time before he retired, his duties were gradually shifted to another administrator.

The organization was very lucky or the governing board was very astute in the selection of this new CEO who was communicative, patient, intuitive, and smart, because the turbulent social times could not have been handled by a tyrant or laissez-faire type leader. Those days were charged with emotion and litigation. Those times called for change, collaboration, innovation and thoughtful decisions, and he rose to the challenge time after time. Not only was he an excellent communicator, he was a trusted communicator; he recognized the importance of trust, and he conveyed the necessity of trust to the governing board. Stephen Covey would later refer to the concept of *Speed of Trust* – when trust improves production increases, but this CEO recognized a simple but important fact long before Covey wrote about trust – effective communications depends on trust.

It came as a shock when after several years on the job, the CEO announced his retirement, but he knew it was time for a change. He told the governing board that he did not want to hang on like an aging King Lear, unwilling to let go. The governing board started the search for a replacement with the idea in mind to maintain and sustain the CEO's vision, mission and goals. The retiring CEO discouraged that idea. In fact, they wanted the retiring CEO to be on call as the new CEO moved into the position, but he said that was not a good idea and declined the offer. He believed that such an arrangement would be unfair to the new leader.

The governing board was pleased with the work and the progress of the organization, and like many governing boards in a similar situation sought a clone of the retiring CEO. That can be and usually is a very difficult task. Picking a successor to a successful leader is not an easy task for any governing board, organization, or business. Clemons and Mayer wrote:

Picking a successor is rarely easy, and there are no general rules for how this task is to be accomplished. At Exxon, for example, the personnel department uses a forced distribution scoring system to rank potential candidates. Those who make the grade are placed in a waiting line for the next executive vacancy. Even selecting a successor in a family-owned organization is difficult. Freedom Newspapers, Inc. was involved in a battle that rivaled the feud between Cain and Abel.

The governing board could not easily find another CEO like the one leaving, so the prevailing thought was "*don't rock the boat.*" Consequently, an administrator from inside the organization was selected as the next CEO. This is not uncommon in the business world or the world of non-profit organizations or in any other organization. Selecting a successor to a successful leader is one of the most difficult challenges facing governing boards, and governing boards are especially concerned when they have to replace a successful leader because the new leader's performance is clearly seen as a measure of the governing board's judgment. Consequently, an internal successor-as-status-quo-supporter is frequently selected in those circumstances.

Laissez-faire leadership style is described by experts as the "hands-off" style. The leader gives employees as much freedom as possible and considerable authority and power is given to employees. Laissez-faire leadership style was first described in 1938 by Lewin, Lippitt, and White. According to leadership experts, this style of leadership is acceptable and even productive when employees are skilled, experienced, placed in positions that match their talents and motivation and are resourceful. This is a very critical point to remember.

The leadership style of the successful CEO I worked with was clearly formulated over the course of many years as a leader in different settings while his predecessor's dictatorial leadership style was merely a reflection of his personality. The laissez-faire CEO who followed the successful CEO had the necessary skills and he inherited a talented central office staff, but he tried to follow too closely the whims and wants of the governing board. Also, some of his personnel decisions compromised his good intentions. Eventually, he was caught between two worlds with shifting leadership expectations and operational needs. He was expected to follow the success of his predecessor and ensure continued success, but at the same time he was not confident enough in his own leadership skills, unlike his predecessor, to stand up to the demands of the governing board and the ever changing challenges and needs of the organization. He experienced what Goethe once said, *"He who moves not forward, goes backwards."* That's the reality that a laissez-faire leader faces. It is impossible to maintain status quo in organizations because change inevitably impacts operations. He was under the impression that his predecessor made decisions based on the governing board's whims and that by maintaining their support he could protect the status quo, but that clearly was not the case.

Laissez-faire leadership may work over a long period of time in an organization that has strong leadership at the operational level where the work is accomplished and when an organization has strong and talented managers throughout the organization. But even that is compromised over time, because every organization in some way is active, ever changing, with diverse needs growing out of changes. Laissez-faire leadership does not typically handle change well at all.

Dissatisfaction develops when the leader's style is not what was expected by the governing board or the governing board changes its philosophy or political view of the organization's needs. Louis Gerstner talks about this situation in his book, *Who Says Elephants Can't Dance?* When he was selected to bring IBM out of the malaise of financial problems, morale problems, and operational problems, he learned that the internal leadership training program for young executives encouraged and even embraced the status quo; they were training them to be laissez-faire leaders. Through the years, this philosophy was supported by the board of directors, so a string of laissez-faire CEOs led the company into a destructive malaise that depended more on past successes than addressing current issues and preparing for future needs and challenges.

It is not unusual for a laissez faire leader to recruit staff members that are in good standing with governing board members. The skill set of the central administration staff members supporting the leader is too often less important than who they know on the governing board. After all, a laissez faire leaders reasons, if the organization is coasting along and there appears to be no need for major changes, what harm would come from strategically placing staff members who can have something positive to say to governing board members about the leader? However, this runs contrary to the type of workplace environment where a laissez-faire leadership style can be effective, for at least a short period of time, when the supporting staff is very competent. A laissez faire leader compromises his standing and the success of the organization when he puts status over competence. That is when the wheels started to come off in the organization. That was the beginning of the negative change. That was when the name of the Department of Human Resources should have been changed to the "Department of Who Is Your Daddy?" Some promotions were earned, but too many were based on who one knew and who governing board members told the CEO to hire and to promote.

Many governing board members have no idea about the ripple effect of such a seemingly insignificant change in leadership style. Some of the examples of personnel changes influenced by governing board members were mentioned earlier in the book. Imagine those scenarios played out throughout an entire organization. Add to that the impact of such appointments at the operational level, where the services are provided and products are manufactured.

The following is an example of the ripple effect of poor personnel decisions at the leadership level and interference at the governing board level.

An ineffective principal was very close to two governing board members, so the CEO promoted him to a central office position where he was expected to provide leadership and oversight to several schools in his area of the school district. He was abrasive, dictatorial, argumentative and a prima donna. He made an effort to "run off" principals he did not like. Whether they were good, effective principals did not matter to him. If he did not like them they were gone. In other words, he exhibited all those behaviors of leadership that research has shown for years to be totally ineffective. In meetings with principals he tried to humiliate the ones did not like and in those schools he was constantly trying to undermine the principals. For example, all a parent had to do was to call his office to complain about a disciplinary action against their child and he would be on the phone directing the principal to put the student back in class. Ken Blanchard's *One Minute Manager* research found that, *"Not supporting, believing in, or championing direct reports was cited as a problem area that can undermine leadership effectiveness."*

Many employees experienced his caustic leadership style on more than one occasion. At the time I was the student discipline hearing officer for student discipline tribunal hearings. This is the body that heard the most severe student discipline cases – weapons, drugs, violence, etc. He tried to use his position to influence tribunal decisions – clearly an ethics violation. In one case, he found out who was scheduled to serve on the discipline tribunal for a case against one of his friend's children. The student was accused of inappropriate bodily contact. The student was arrested and charged. The school suspended the student and referred him to the student discipline tribunal for possible expulsion or transfer to an alternative school. Despite the seriousness of the case this administrator called each discipline tribunal member before the hearing to influence their decision. Each one of the five student tribunal members called me because they were offended and angered by his actions, so I told each one of them that they did not have to attend the hearing. I then selected five different tribunal members to hear the case. The administrator was furious at me. His next move was to contact his favorite governing board member in an effort to sabotage any appeal of the student tribunal's decision to the governing board. When I reported his behavior to the CEO he did nothing about it. He did not even take time to talk to the administrator about it. In fact, the CEO named this same administrator to a human resources committee that was responsible for selecting and promoting school administrators at the school level. Of course, he advocated for his friends, his relatives, friends of his relatives, and friends and relatives of governing board members. It did not matter if they were the best qualified for the position or not. I actually heard him say in one of the meetings when principals were being selected, "*I think this guy is off his rocker.*" He was referring to a very smart, popular, talented young assistant principal whose only negative feature was that he was pitted against a friend of the administrator's for promotion to a principal position. That talented young administrator was soon thereafter offered a principal's job in another school district and has had a distinguished career. Many times the final selections were not the persons best suited for the principal position or other positions. The laissez-faire CEO was aware of this; nevertheless, he did nothing about it.

Unfortunately through much of his reign as CEO this type of decision making happened more frequently each year, and over time eroded the employee talent base that is essential for a successful organization. It seemed that he became more and more fragile in his position and less inclined to say no to certain employees or governing board members. There were families where every adult and child in the family was employed by the school district. Friends and relatives of governing board members were hired frequently during his administration. Had all of them been qualified for the jobs and performed up to expectations it would be less of an issue, but many were not qualified and most underperformed.

This type of leadership crisis is not limited to public education. A church in Georgia with 500 members was lead by a minister who was selected after a careful review of applicants. After becoming close to a couple of the church's governing board members, he decided abruptly and without any warning that the long-time associate minister needed to be replaced. His dilemma centered on the fact that for whatever reason he did not like the associate minister. The associate minister was effective, so he did not have just cause to terminate him. Undaunted, the minister begin undermining almost all of the associate minister's work, strategic plans, and decisions. It was later revealed that this was a systematic effort to replace the associate minister with a relative of a governing board member. Even with inside knowledge of what was taking place in the church, the regional leader did nothing to stop this and the fortunes of the church over a short period of time made a turn for the worse, with attendance dropping significantly.

Antidote

In the book *Influencer: The Power to Change Anything* the authors note that the attraction of short-term strategies is to make short-term progress. There is something positive to be said about immediate success to build motivation and morale and to let everyone inside an organization and outside know that a new leader is in place and the governing board is taking care of business, as Louis Gerstner did when he first joined troubled IBM. However, there is a dynamic chain of events that spiral downward from the selection of a leader by a governing board based on short-term needs, and most of those events are not good for the organization. Governing boards must be very thoughtful about the selection of the organization's leader and refrain from the overwhelming temptation to select for the short-term or select based on a desire to maintain the status quo. It behooves the governing board to take the time to review its strategic plan; conduct a self-assessment; survey the employees; determine the future needs of clients and the organization, and conduct a "Gap Analysis" to determine the gap between the organization's goals and the outcomes. From that thoughtful approach, the governing board can create attributes that the next leader must possess in order to move the organization toward short-term and long-term goals. Also, the governing board should annually sign an Assurance of Governance that compels each governing board member to refrain from nepotism. The organization's leader should also sign an Assurance of Governance. This is a commitment on part of the governing board and the leader to stay true to their different roles in the organization and focus on selecting and promoting talented employees.

Contrary to many of the myths and assumptions surrounding the selection of new leaders, experts such as James Citrin and Julie Hembrock argue that the process of choosing a leader should begin with a deep understanding of the organization's needs and the kind of person who will both fit into its culture and bring the right experience and skill-set to get the job done — and only then seek the person who best matches those needs. This may seem like common sense, yet in practice this represents a different way of thinking for many organizations.

Contrary to many opinions, research by LaBelle found that the first hundred days do not comprise a sufficient indication of how the leadership transfer has succeeded. The key is communications. LaBelle wrote,

> *To keep the organization steering in the right direction requires constant and constructive communication between the leader and the governing board. Open communication links should allow the leader to bring both good news and bad news to the governing board. In turn, the governing board needs to listen appropriately and give honest feedback. Change in leadership is hard. Support from the governing board is imperative. The new leader's personal successes will serve as an encouragement; the governing board's recognition of the new leader's results will reinforce and strengthen the process and outcomes.*

Research by the Hay Group and reported by Gilmore, has found that if a new leader is following a well liked leader it is important for him to avoid falling into a popularity contest in an effort to fit in and be liked by everyone. Gilmore recommends that the new leader,

> *Simply put, you need to be yourself and follow your own vision and communicate effectively. In establishing credibility and a loyal following amongst the team it is important that they see you for yourself and not a mold of the previous leader. You have to let them all know that you are not your predecessor, but you have your own talents and motivation.*

New leaders that pressure themselves or that feel pressure by governing board members to protect the status quo are not following sound advice. The new leader needs to let the organizational staff members and the governing board know what he stands for and communicate that effectively and often, and maintaining the status quo should be quickly dismissed. New leaders must recognize and develop key relationships and build networks in the organization in order to convey the clear message that they are team-oriented and not status quo oriented. Additionally, according to Goodyear and Golden, "*It is important that a new leader convey trust in the organization from the beginning, through delegation. Focused discussion between leaders and followers about successful outcomes and accountability mechanisms can result in focused and successful implementation.*"

CHAPTER 5

ORGANIZATIONS HAVE FEELINGS, TOO

It is a terrible thing to look over your shoulder when you are trying to lead and find no one there.

—Franklin Roosevelt

Poison: The leadership requirements of any organization are very complicated, and the leader must never forget that each organization has basic needs that must be met before it can expand or excel. Too often, leaders and governing boards fail to understand that organizations have work climates that live and breathe, and must, therefore, be protected and nurtured. The complexity of the work climate requires an understanding of what motivates employees. Leaders and governing boards must strive to identify and meet the basic needs of employees. This is especially true in two vitally important areas: change and safety. Organizations have to be prepared for change and must take safety seriously. Some of the dynamics related to change also apply to safety, because both are directly related to the workplace climate. Many organizations do not have a plan to manage change nor do they have a clearly defined and fully developed safety plan until after something happens or fails. Research shows that employees and clients in every part of society are acutely aware of change and safety and there is a full expectation that every organization understands the importance of both and, consequently, have plans in place that includes all of the essential elements for managing change and safety, based on functions of the organization. The lack of change and safety planning and training of employees is poisonous to leaders, employees, governing board, clients, and ultimately to the organization.

There is a rubric from cognitive psychology that highlights, and in some ways measures, the effectiveness of change while describing the basis for the behavior and attitude of employees. The rubric is based on the status of five components: vision, skills, incentives, resources, and action plan. The rubric lists five possible outcomes of change based on the prevalence of the five components of change. While this is a change model it can also serve as an indicator of what happens in an organization over time when the focus shifts to a reactive mode rather than a planning mode, which typically occurs when change is unexpected and/or not managed well. To manage change effectively, an organization needs to have a vision; employees must be hired and trained to possess the skills necessary to do their jobs; the organization must develop incentives, such as financial incentives or flexible work schedules; the organization must provide the resources necessary to enable employees to do their work at the levels expected by the organization; and the organization must have an action plan that guides the work of the organization and by which progress or lack thereof can be assessed.

When a change indicator is missing, there can be a significant impact on employees. When vision, skills, incentive, resources and action plans are in place, there is much greater likelihood that employees are satisfied and productive. If an organization lacks a clear vision or does not share that vision with the employees and stakeholders, it creates confusion inside and outside of the organization, which eventually will threaten individual and organizational effectiveness, job satisfaction, and possibly the future of the organization. In organizations that do not recognize the skill sets of employees and match training to those needs, the employees are put in recurring situations where they are expected to produce even though they do not have the skills necessary to be successful. This causes employee anxiety – the fear of going to work each day knowing or wondering if the lack of skills and subsequent non-productivity will result in embarrassment or termination or both. Organizations, consequently, must determine what skill sets are necessary and then provide the training or retraining and match employees with the appropriate job. Too often an employee is demoted or terminated not because he could not do the job, but because the organization did not take the time to match the employee with a job that matched his skills. Additionally, if the organization ignores incentives, this oversight jeopardizes the goals set in the organization's strategic plan. The need for recognition is a basic human trait, and research has shown that neither money nor threats are as powerful a motivator as many leaders believe. When describing this fact as a significant component of an effective "influencer" leader, Patterson, et al, in their book, *Influencer*, state:

People with power over others often trump all other sources of motivation by relying on threats. Now that others have been warned, surely they will be motivated to do the right thing. Unfortunately, negative reinforcement yields at best mixed results and needs to be constantly monitored. People who develop a change strategy based on a single extrinsic motivator typically miss the importance of creating circumstances in which intrinsic rewards carry their share of the motivational load. Savvy influencers increase their likelihood of achieving success by building in multiple sources.

The factors related to motivation are essential to the success of an organization because the lack of attention to motivation breeds overt or covert, intentional or unintentional resistance between and among individuals within the organization. It is important for leaders to know that research for many decades has found that motivation typically falls within two categories: *content* and *process*. Ivancevich, Szilagyi, and Wallace, in *Organizational Behavior and Performance*, defined *content* approaches to motivation as factors that start or arouse motivated behavior. This is motivation centered on satisfying individual needs for money, status, achievement, and/or working conditions. Process approaches to motivation are concerned not only with behavior but *"also the choice of behaviors and factors that increase the likelihood that desired behavior will be repeated."* Process motivation recognizes that motivation comes from clarifying the individual's perception of work inputs and by rewarding desired behavior through several different means other than or in addition to money or status. The content approach requires the leader to answer the question, *"What specific things motivate people?"* Many researchers have found that promotion, salary, recognition, fringe benefits, friendly coworkers, flexible work hours, teleworking opportunities, compensation time, covered parking spaces, compensation for commuting to work, employee recognition programs, employee birthday recognition, occasional extension of the lunch hour, etc. can be equally effective in motivating individuals because they meet the needs or motives of employees.

In the *process* motivation approach, the leader deliberately tries to determine the expectations of individuals and the satisfaction or dissatisfaction that accompanies those expectations. That is why it is critically essential for an individual to be matched with the job and not hired just because they know someone with influence or because they are well educated but in a field that does not match the requirements of the job. Using rewards that are content based, plus matching outcomes with individual expectations will most likely result in a motivated working environment. A study of Vroom's *Expectancy and Valence Theory* conducted by Sheridan, Slocum and Richards gives an example. In a study of nursing school graduates, it was found that nurses choose hospitals that let them satisfy a variety of work-related outcomes (flexible work hours, pay, leisure, work in specialized fields of interest, and challenging work assignments). Hospitals that gave nurses opportunities to satisfy these outcomes were chosen by the nurses to a greater extent than hospitals that did not give the nurses the opportunity to achieve these outcomes.

Related to motivation but important separately, too, are resources. Resources are often tied to the expectations of individuals within the organization. The lack of resources necessary for an employee to adequately perform her duties is commonly viewed as an example of a leader's disregard for the individuals within the organization and therefore indicative that the leader does not care about the work climate. Nothing is more frustrating to a motivated employee than not being able, for example, to have his computer problems fixed in order to complete a project. The pressure of completing a project can be motivating – to get the job done on time and with quality is jeopardized by the lack of resources which causes high levels of frustration and employee dissatisfaction. Frustration is a morale killer, especially with a motivated employee. An effective leader will take a resources inventory periodically to inquire if individuals within the organization have the resources they need to be effective and productive and satisfied. A resource inventory can often reveal some surprising and useful results for leaders. In one organization all staplers were removed because a floor manager wanted to cut the cost of staples. He told employees they could use the copying machine's built-in stapler. This meant that each time a report needed stapling, employees had to leave their work space and stand in line at the copy machine. The CEO discovered this during the course of a resource inventory review and quickly changed the practice.

Even if a leader has focused on vision, skills, incentives and resources, the absence of an action plan that ties everything together can jeopardize the effectiveness of the organizational outcomes. In Peter and Waterman's book, *In Search of Excellence*, they found that all successful organizations have one thing in common – "*a bias for action*". This bias for action starts with an action plan that consolidates and validates every person's value to the outcomes enumerated in the action plan, so that not only will individuals see the value of their work, they will also see the relevancy of their work as it relates to the success of the organization. This becomes a self-fulfilling motivation for employees because they have worth and value.

Without these essential components, vision, skills, resources, incentives, and an action plan an organization will never reach its potential and probably not its goals. This model is turned on its head, as are any successful models, if people are assigned to positions based on who they know rather than their skill set or potential for learning. Even with everything else in place, the lack of skills creates significant anxiety because work is not completed at the level of quality as before. Serious employee issues then start to arise when people who are qualified to receive promotions or recognition see others who are not performing receive rewards, promotions or other perks. This creates resentment and resistance to leadership and work flow and jeopardizes the work climate.

A laissez-faire leader is more prone to create this latter type of work climate than any other leadership style, because it is rudderless and lacks a clear action plan. This puts most everyone in the organization in a state of ambiguity. In practical terms this means that employees dread coming to work. As a result, the organization's outcomes or services suffer.

What follows is an example of a negative work climate stemming from poor leadership. An employee was asked to join the central office of a large school district where student achievement test scores, student attendance and graduation rates had declined. Parent and community complaints about schools and administrators were increasing. At the onset of his administration a laissez-faire CEO decided to add three top level administrators. In previous years, the school district never had more than one top-level direct report to the CEO. The three new top-level assistants did not get along with each other and at times worked against each other. The work climate became negative. They were each in their own way constantly testing the loyalty of staff members. They were picking sides instead of working to improve the working climate of the organization. Eventually two of them made peace with each other so that they could combine resources to neutralize the third top administrator. This drama, pettiness, and absurdness bled over into the CEO's Cabinet meetings where one's loyalty and competence were measured by seat selection rather than performance. The rectangular arrangement of tables for the meetings had the CEO at the head of the table with two top administrators on one side of him and the other one on the other side. Staff members were expected to sit on the "appropriate" side of the rectangle. If a staff member knowingly or unknowingly departed from this arrangement, he or she could expect an informal meeting with one of the top administrators or a phone call to "correct" the employee's behavior.

Ignoring the basic infrastructure of an organization and the accompanying work climate is one of the most telling elements that generate the decline in the performance, reputation and trust of an organization. Many executives new to companies or other organizations are surprised to learn that the basic needs of work climate have been ignored, dismissed as unessential, or set aside as a future project. According to *Forbes Magazine's* review of takeovers, the majority of leaders that were hired to turn a company around found that infrastructure problems had been ignored in the struggling companies, which means that that work climate and the needs of the employees were ignored.

A leader's style and priorities can impact work climate, including safety. It is rare when a governing board asks prospective leaders about their work climate and work safety history or attitudes toward both. Yet, one of the basic and most important infrastructure essentials is a safe working environment. Safety in the workplace in any organization has to be the top priority, but often that aspect of infrastructure is minimized until a tragedy takes place. It so often happens that the follow-up story to a tragedy was a disregard for work safety, work climate, managing change, slack security essentials, poor safety planning, insufficient staff safety training and awareness, and/or reduction in safety related services and staff. Due to leadership indifference about work climate, some organizations have a crisis management plan that is so outdated and so seldom referenced that it has become worthless. Typically, these organizations do not manage change well either. Even worse, some organizations do not have a crisis management plan, so that a thoughtful, deliberate response that might otherwise mitigate a disaster only acerbates the situation. This leaves an organization in a very vulnerable position when change or a crisis occurs.

In his book, *Winning*, Jack Welch lists five assumptions to keep in mind when a crisis appears:

1. The problem is worse than it appears. *"The vast majority [of crises] are bigger in scope than you could ever imagine with that first phone call and they will last longer and get uglier."*

2. There are no secrets in the world and everyone will eventually find out everything. *"Information you try to shut down will eventually get out and as it travels it will certainly morph, twist, and darken."*

3. You and your organization's handling of the crisis will be portrayed in the worst possible light. *"The media's professional calling is to question authority in its every form and topple empires and emperors."*

4. There will be changes in processes and people. Almost no crisis ends without personnel or changes in processes. *"Most crises end when with a settlement of some kind or when a crisis is handled effectively enough for the daily routine to return."*

5. The organization will survive ultimately and could be stronger for what happened. *"There is not a crisis you cannot learn from, even though you hate every one of them and even though you may not have managed it well."* Welch warned that the common response after a crisis subsides is to *"put it away in a drawer."* That is asking for more trouble; consequently, a chance to improve the work

climate is missed.

In surveys of employees regarding work climates, in both for-profit and non-profit organizations, workplace safety is always in the top three lists of priorities. For example, a *Campus Safety Magazine* Survey found:

35 percent either disagree somewhat or strongly with the statement: 'If an active shooter or bomber came onto my campus, my department and my organization would be able to respond effectively.'

A significant percentage of college and university respondents indicate they are receiving good support from campus administration; 80 percent say their top administrators take safety and security on campus seriously, but only 65 percent say they have enough authority to carry out their responsibilities appropriately.

Lack of resources is another challenge, which, in light of the current economic recession, it's not surprising. Two in five say their organizations don't dedicate enough money, resources and personnel to safety and security efforts and technology.

Hazmat incident preparedness is the one significant weakness. Nearly a third of respondents (29 percent) either disagree somewhat or strongly with the statement: 'My organization is adequately prepared for a hazmat incident.' One in five survey takers are not satisfied with their organization's emergency/crisis plans (20 percent) or weather emergency/natural disaster preparedness (21 percent).

Probably the most troubling statistic of the survey involves hospitals and their inability to respond to active shooters and bombers. A whopping 40 percent of hospital respondents disagree somewhat (21 percent) or strongly (19 percent) with the statement: 'If an active shooter or bomber came onto my campus, my department and my organization would be able to respond effectively.'

Staffing data also correlate with the active shooter/bomber and weapons statistics. More than two in five hospital respondents (41 percent) disagree somewhat or strongly with the statement: 'My department has enough staff to respond appropriately to incidents.'

Almost four in five (79 percent) of hospital survey takers say that their top administrators take safety and security seriously, but only 74 percent of hospital respondents say they have enough authority to do their jobs well.

In some instances, the lack of leadership in managing work climate can have tragic results, especially if work climate is not a top priority or if leadership has not been given the authority to do what is necessary to secure the work climate. No one will imply that any organization is fully safe, because it is impossible to plan for and prevent every type of tragedy or crisis that can occur, but leadership at all levels, especially at the top, in every organization must understand how seemingly unrelated series of events and decisions may and can be connected to create an unsafe situation.

In a large school district, a teacher at an alternative school for discipline problem students was shot and killed by a student during class. The student who shot the teacher was later diagnosed by several psychiatrists (psychiatrists for the defense and different psychiatrists for the prosecution) as paranoid schizophrenic. The student was receiving special education services until his father removed him from the program against the recommendation of the school district. The district attorney and police investigators found out that the student's father left his .38 caliber handgun on the kitchen table the morning of the shooting. That morning the student put his father's handgun in a bookbag. He carried the gun to school and the student went to his first-period class as usual. No one noticed anything unusual about the student's demeanor that morning.

Ironically, the teacher was one of the student's favorite teachers, according to comments made by the student and his father. The teacher was one of the most popular teachers in the school, also. He loved teaching and had asked to be assigned to the alternative school because he wanted to work with students who had the most serious needs. The teacher was well known for his teaching skills and kindness to others. On that day, as he did each day, the teacher greeted each student as he or she came into the classroom. The student did not say anything or acknowledge the teacher's greeting. He walked up to the teacher as if to ask him a question or tell him something and suddenly pulled the gun out of his book-bag and shot the teacher in the chest. It happened that quickly. After he shot the teacher, the student just stood there. One student described him as *"staring off in space."* The school resource officers (school police) ran to the classroom and administered first aid until the ambulance arrived, but nothing could be done to save the teacher.

The site of the shooting was an alternative school that was very well run with a good balance of strict discipline and academic support. In fact, some considered it a model non-traditional school for students with discipline problems. The school district was applauded for the enlightened attitude that suspended and expelled students deserved another chance. Only the best teachers were assigned to the alternative school. But let's take a closer look at the tragedy. One of the strong features of discipline in the alternative school was what the school called the demerit and merit system. It was a demerit system with built-in rewards and punishments. This system created a positive school/work climate. If a student misbehaved he would receive a demerit. If a student received 10 demerits, he was expelled from the alternative school. Keep in mind that the students were at the alternative school in the first place because of misbehavior. The most important part of the demerit system was the opportunity for the students to remove the demerits for good behavior. This was a unique feature of the plan and the key to its success with most students. A demerit could be removed if the student went five school days without receiving another demerit. It became a matter of pride to the students to remove all demerits before the end of the semester. Students that accomplished this were recognized and encouraged by the staff and students. The concept was based in large part on William Glasser's concept of "positive addiction", with the belief that a negative behavior is more likely to be neutralized by replacing it with a positive behavior than by trying to eliminate the negative behavior through punishment. The importance of a healthy, supportive climate was reinforced. The demerit and merit system worked because of the recognition for good behavior and the possibility to remove a demerit. Many of the students had not experienced recognition for good behavior before, so this was a new positive experience for them. It also gave teachers and administrators the chance to have a positive relationship with students. Of course, some did not care enough about school or self-control to adjust to the school and the demerit system, so they left voluntarily or were removed from the school, but that was a small number. Several students had to learn self-control, so it was not unusual for a student to get eight or even nine demerits before changing his behavior and attitude and working the demerits off. All of that changed, however, because a very vocal and belligerent parent complained about the demerit system one semester to a central office administrator.

The central office staff member told the principal of the alternative school that he would have to discontinue the demerit system – the demerit system that worked and that had been in place at the school for many years, and was the centerpiece for a positive school/work climate. The students and teachers were very upset about the elimination of the demerit system. Many people talked to this arrogant central office administrator about the benefits of the demerit system. It was a major underpinning of the school's success in changing the behavior of students, and it was at the core of the school's positive climate. But he would hear none of it. He did not think students should be disciplined, he had no understanding of school/work climate, and he was always looking for an excuse to control others. This was a situation where the safety of the environment was compromised by an organization that made two critical decisions – one was a personnel decision and the other was a decision about workplace safety.

So why did the CEO in the school district assign this central office administrator to oversee the alternative school? Actually, that decision was made by one of the top level administrators because they were friends and the CEO was convinced to go along with assignment.

The demerit system had worked well for several years. In fact, several schools around the state adopted the same demerit and reinforcement system for their alternative or non-traditional schools. Even the students said it was very effective in positively changing behavior. Worst of all when it was removed it was not replaced with another school-wide discipline strategy. Consequently, some of the best teachers wanted to leave because the work climate deteriorated. No one can say of course for certain, but is it possible that the student who shot the teacher would not have been in school or may have changed his behavior if the demerit system had remained in place?

Workplace violence is impossible to completely prevent, but leaders and governing boards must take an honest and realistic view and measure of safety. Sometimes change that is unmanaged is the culprit. No decisions that undermine safety should be tolerated, especially personnel decisions, operational decisions, facility decisions and budget decisions. There are several examples of workplace violence where the safety of the facility, training of the employees, and/or leadership response was called into question, because the work climate was non-productive and negative or there were no effective strategies to manage change. Workplace violence is not limited to certain organizations. In August 20, 1986, a part-time letter carrier named Patrick H. Sherrill, facing possible dismissal after a troubled work history, walked into the Edmond, Oklahoma, post office, where he worked and shot 14 people to death before killing himself.

The genesis of violence in the workplace has become a source of concern and study. It is becoming more obvious that behavior such as bullying is a contributor to workplace violence, or at the very least is a symptom of a climate of harassment. Bullying is a major issue in public and private schools, but bullying also takes place in other work environments.

In a 2010 *Zogby International* survey about bullying in the workplace, some of the key findings included: (1) half of all workers have either witnessed or been bullied in the workplace; (2) 35 percent of workers have experienced bullying firsthand; (3) 62 percent of bullies are men; (4) 58 percent of targets are women; (5) women bullies target women in 80 percent of cases; (6) bullying is four times more prevalent than illegal harassment; and (7) the majority (68 percent) of bullying is same-gender harassment.

Why is bullying so often ignored? Much of the issue is related to a generally held perception that bullying is a way of life and it is a rite of passage and that it is so pervasive that nothing can be done about it. Too often the burden is put on the victim to "fight back" or "be tougher."

In addition to the emotional toll and the added risk in the workplace, it is a fact that bullying in the workplace is expensive. The *Orlando Business Journal* cited an estimated cost of $180 million in lost time and productivity to American businesses each year due to bullying in the workplace. *The Workplace Bullying Institute* (WBI), as reported by *No Work Place Bullies*, estimates between turnover and lost productivity that bully in the workplace could cost a Fortune 500 company an *"astounding $24 million in lost productivity and another $1.4 million in litigation and settlement costs."* Here is one way an organization can calculate the expense of bullying in the workplace, according to WBI:

1. *The bully's direct manager counseling the bully = 80 hours*
2. *The bullying victim's direct manager counseling the victim = 150 hours*
3. *Witnesses of the bullying counseled =100 hours*
4. *Human Resources staff members talking with managers, bully and victim = 10 hours*
5. *Human Resources staff members talking with executives about the bullying problems = 5 hours*
6. *Human Resources recruiting and training replacement of victim employee and bully =160 hours.*
7. *Based on average salary scales, the total cost could be from $50,000 to $80,000.*

I have conducted bullying prevention and intervention workshops for several years for schools, school districts, non-profit organizations, businesses and professional associations. A few years ago while I was working with school bus drivers at one of my presentations about bullying, an incident occurred that was so powerful it surpassed anything I could say about the negative impact of bullying. Toward the end of that particular presentation a school bus driver raised her hand, as if to ask a question. As I scanned the room during the presentation to see if I was communicating well enough to keep people from falling asleep I noticed that this bus driver had kept her head down during most of my presentation. I did not know if she was asleep, bored, upset or a combination of all three. Consequently, I was somewhat taken aback when I saw her hand rise in slow motion to ask a question. I stopped and nodded toward her, encouraging her to ask her question or make her point. Beneath the papers on her table she pulled out a photograph of a baby and held it up for everyone to see. She did not say a word; she just slowly showed the picture from one side of the room to the other as if to make certain that everyone there, all 100 school bus drivers, saw the picture of the baby. She then said,

"I want everyone to know that this is a photograph of my new grandchild. She is a beautiful baby and she is such a sweet little baby; however, she was born with only one arm. Do you know what I thought of first when I learned that she had one arm? I worried then and there that she would be picked on in school. The fact that she was born with only one arm does not break my heart; she will adapt and so will we. The thing I worry the most about is her being bullied in school because of her appearance. That bothers me and her parents more than anything. That's what I want the other bus drivers here to know; we have to stop bullying. We cannot let kids be mean to others and pick on them and make fun of them. It's got to stop."

There is no excuse for anyone to adopt a cavalier attitude about a tragedy that could have been prevented by focusing on a positive and safe workplace climate. The tragedies that stem from negative workplace climates are at the feet of those that ignore it in any organization, because issues such as bullying can be addressed, reduced, and even prevented. Providing a positive workplace climate is a leadership function and basic responsibility.

It should be noted that social isolation has the same impact as confrontational and physical bullying, and is a symptom of a negative work climate. This is how social isolation works. The students or colleagues ignore the victim by not speaking or walking away. Then they start whispers of rumors about the victim or will not let him or her participate in any activity or discussion or meeting. I was at a training session for executives being held at a Fortune 500 training center. The training center participants were allowed to gather for lunch at the company's employee cafeteria. As I waited in line to be served, I noticed an employee wandering around the crowded cafeteria trying to find a place to sit. It was clear to anyone who took the time to observe that social isolation was taking place in front of hundreds of people. The social isolation was tragic enough in itself, but to be publicly humiliated added to the sad situation.

Another example of what this type of behavior can do the climate of a school or workplace and its impact at the personal level comes from my experience working in a school system. I received a phone call from a very upset parent. A student discipline tribunal hearing had been scheduled for her son because he supposedly made a "hit list" of students that he was going to harm. This was shortly after the Columbine High School tragedy, where 12 students were murdered, so people were on edge about school violence. All of the students on the so-called hit list were females. The mother of the accused said that her middle school-aged son had been setup by precocious female students and was a victim of bullying through social intimidation, which was pervasive at the school. The accused middle school student was described as quiet, shy, and studious. The girls made fun of him for being a "nerd", like they probably did other students. One of the girls stopped the boy in the hallway one day and said she was going to help him be more popular with the girls, but she first had to know which girls he liked and didn't like. She convinced him to write down the names of girls he liked and the ones who had been mean to him. I found out later when I investigated that the girl showed the list to her friends and then they took his list and wrote "Hit List" at the top of the sheet of paper and passed it around the school, making certain that every girl whose name was on the list saw it.

It spiraled out of control from there. The girls on the hit list told their parents who then rushed to the school or called the school and demanded action be taken against this "terrorist." Some even called the police. The school administrative staff reacted more to the parents' pressure and hysteria than they did the facts and there was a rush to judgment; consequently, the student was charged with making a terroristic threat and was suspended 10 days and referred to the student discipline tribunal for possible expulsion. The student denied the accusations. I met with the parents because of the extraordinary story and conducted an investigation. I spoke to the student, who was the quintessential nerd, and I went to the school and spoke to several of the female students that had convinced the boy to write the list of students. The girls were very precocious and arrogant to be only 13 years old. It was clear that the boy was no match for them socially and the difference in level of maturity was significant. The parents of the girls were there during the interview. Some of them, but not all of them, were appalled at the behavior and cavalier attitude their own daughters had about the incident and the harm done to the young boy. One of the quieter, more reserved girls finally admitted fully what they had done. I knew then what had happened; consequently, we put the student back in school and the school administration sent a letter home to all parents explaining what happened. It is interesting to note that four years later that same student, the so-called terrorist, graduated in the top five percent of his high school class.

The impact of school climate, like workplace climate in businesses, cannot be overstated. While there is evidence that workplace climate can positively or negatively impact production, there is equally compelling research on the impact of school climate on student outcomes. In a study conducted by the Georgia Department of Education, researchers found that a 1.0 percent increase in school climate (based on a school climate rating using attendance, discipline and surveys) decreased discipline actions per pupil by 1.35 percent and decreased suspension days, while improving student attendance. In a soon to be released study by CDC, it was found that improving school climate has significantly positive outcomes for students with disabilities.

Stories like this are not limited to schools. A story covered by *ABC News* in 2010 revealed a disturbing set of circumstances in the workplace related to bullying.

In the days before Kevin Morrissey committed suicide near the University of Virginia campus, at least two co-workers said they warned university officials about his growing despair over alleged workplace bullying at the award-winning Virginia Quarterly Review. 'I told them, I'm very concerned about Kevin; I'm afraid he might try to harm himself,' said a colleague and friend of Morrissey, who asked not to be identified. 'They asked me to clarify what I meant and I repeated that I was afraid he might harm himself. If someone had just done something....' On July 30, Morrissey, the Review's 52-year-old managing editor, walked to the old coal tower near campus and shot himself in the head. Morrissey's death underscored the turmoil at the high-profile journal, according to co-workers. Maria Morrissey said her brother's phone records showed that he placed at least 18 calls to university officials in the final two weeks of his life. The phone records, obtained by ABCNews.com, showed calls to the human resources department, the ombudsman, the faculty and employee assistance center, and the university president. 'Kevin was asking for help,' said Maria Morrissey, who had been estranged from her brother in recent years, but has started looking into the circumstances of his death. Kevin Morrissey, former managing editor of Virginia Quarterly Review Morrissey's sister and co-workers acknowledged that he long suffered from depression. But they insisted that he took his life only after the university failed to respond to repeated complaints about alleged bullying by his boss, Ted Genoways. Other employees, they said, also complained about being bullied by the journal's top editor. 'Bullying seems to make it like some sort of schoolyard thing,' said the colleague who asked not to be named. 'It's really a much more subtle kind of erasure. I'm not going to talk to you. I'm going to come in the side office and shut the door. I will pretend you don't exist.' The university has these [human resources] people, but they don't do anything. After one of your colleagues has killed himself, it's beyond the point of mediation. They didn't protect us. We went again and again and again and they didn't protect us.'

Workplace climate, including safety, can be enhanced by the strategic use of law enforcement trained officers and staff members. The United States Office of Personnel Management's *Workplace Security* workbook advocates the use of security officers in the planning phase with the following recommendations of how they can help leaders secure the workplace and plan for emergencies:

1. *Identify types of situations they can address and when and how they should be notified of an incident;*

2. *Indicate whether their officers have arrest authority;*

3. *Identify their jurisdictional restrictions and alternative law enforcement agencies that may be able to provide assistance;*

4. *Identify threat assessment professionals who can assist the agency in its efforts to protect threatened employees;*

5. *Advise on what evidence is necessary and how it can be collected or recorded, so that law enforcement can assess the information and decide what action to take, if appropriate;*

6. *Explain anti-stalking laws applicable in the agency's jurisdiction and how and when to obtain restraining orders;*

7. *Suggest security measures to be taken for specific situations, such as in cases where Employee Assistance Program counselors or other mental health professionals warn the agency that an individual has made a threat against an agency employee; and*

8. *Arrange for supervisor/employee briefings or training on specific workplace violence issues such as:*

    a. *Personal safety and security measures*

    b. *Types of incidents to report to law enforcement/security*

    c. *Types of measures law enforcement/security may take to protect employees during a violent incident, e.g., explanations of what it means to "secure the area," "secure the perimeter," and "preserve evidence"*

    d. *Suggestions on how to react to an armed attacker*

    e. *Suggestions for dealing with angry customers or clients*

  f. *Suspicious packages*

  g. *Bomb threats;*

  h. *Hostage situations; and*

  i. *Telephone harassment and threats.*

9. *When potentially violent situations arise, law enforcement/security officers can work with the incident response team to:*

10. *Provide an assessment of the information available to determine whether law enforcement intervention is immediately necessary; for example, whether a criminal investigation is appropriate and whether a threat assessment professional should be consulted;*

11. *Identify what plan of action they deem appropriate; and*

12. *Determine who will gather what types of evidence.*

According to experts on workplace safety, it is imperative to take measures to ensure that everyone understands the importance of safety. If any organization has to make budget cuts, the employees and clients should remind the governing board and leadership that safety measures, safety staff members, and safety strategies are essential and cannot be compromised. One of the basic needs in Abraham Maslow's *Hierarchy of Needs* is safety and security. Employees in any organization cannot be expected to dismiss safety issues and forget safety concerns. Countless numbers of employees miss work because of workplace safety issues. It negatively impacts productivity, retention of employees, creativity, and client services.

Antidote

An effective leader must understand the dynamics that can negatively impact workplace climate and an organization's ability to effectively handle change. Leaders must also understand the relationship between leadership, change, conditions for change, and how all of these link to workplace climate. A safe work climate is a basic and essential requirement of every organization, but many organizations are finding it more difficult to provide safety because of continued budget cuts and because safety is not a top priority to some governing boards and CEOs. No one's health or safety should be at risk because of budget issues or a lack of safety planning and preparation. Also, most courses and books on leadership or governing, whether it is directed to schools, colleges, non-profit organizations or business environments do not address the need for a safety plan nor do they establish the link between the organization's climate, managing change, leadership and productivity. This is a major oversight. Every organization, regardless of mission and size, must take the time to develop a positive workplace climate and safety management plan. Studies have found that organizations that understand the dynamic nature of workplace climate find that respect for the climate through actions such as safety awareness and planning create conditions for success, transitions, and change in the workplace. Leaders and governing boards can seek assistance on the development of a safety plan from the local emergency management agency and from the Federal Emergency Management Agency (FEMA). A crisis can occur at any time, change is inevitable, and it is unlikely that any organization will escape the necessity of responding to a crisis or deal with change. A comprehensive approach to workplace climate places a strong emphasis on prevention, using strategies which range from building design to policies and programs which improve the organization's climate. One example of this is the Atlanta branch of Ernst and Young, an international accounting firm. The workplace design was changed to eliminate the dreaded work cubicles. They were dehumanizing, created social isolation, discouraged creative interaction, and created a mob scene during evacuation drills. The redesign opened up the floor space to allow interaction between and among employees, and the redesign offered a more open design for safety and emergency evacuations. In a short period of time, the workplace improved substantially, as measured by improved employee productivity and attendance.

Crisis management is that part of an organization's approach to safety and change which anticipates potential problems and establishes a coordinated response to minimize stress and disruptions in the organization; thus, it is both prevention and management. It is not possible, however, to anticipate all events. Crisis management functions as a time-limited, problem-focused intervention designed to identify, confront and resolve the crisis, restore equilibrium, and support adaptive responses. Developing safety-related policies provides both a foundation and a framework for action and a climate of support and care for employees and clients.

Leadership is necessary to ensure effective implementation of plans and maintenance of preparedness and a positive workplace climate. The essential and basic components of a plan can be used for any type of crisis, as well as for significant changes in the workplace.

There are four major components of planning that are essential to a workplace that is safe, positive, and prepared: *Crisis Response Team*; *Critical Management Plan*; *Critical Incident Management Plan* and *Training for Preparedness.*

Crisis Response Team - A Crisis Response Team can be a highly effective organizational unit for dealing with a variety of crises. Well-functioning teams provide a network that can support action whenever crises arise. *Crisis Management Plan* – An organization that is prepared before a crisis occurs will be much more likely to deal with it effectively during and after a crisis. The plan should be designed to result in a differentiated, coordinated response to crises. *Critical Incident Management Plan*- A critical incident management plan focuses more narrowly on situations that involve imminent danger to life and limb and require a coordinated response involving public safety resources and public health resources. *Training for Preparedness* – Preparation for and response to crises rely on people understanding policies and procedures and knowing what they are to do during a crisis. These are achieved through training. Maintaining preparedness is an ongoing process which involves debriefing following crises, periodic review, updating, table-top (practice) exercises, and ongoing training. When a crisis occurs, effective communication is essential within the organization, with the governing board, with all stakeholders and clients, and with the media. Effective communication can speed the restoration of equilibrium; poor communication (i.e., lack of communication, incorrect information, etc.) can make a bad situation much worse.

All organizations must focus on workplace climate and develop plans based on strategic needs and aims. The failure to do so jeopardizes the organization's effectiveness and ultimately its purpose. A comprehensive workplace plan should lay the foundation for a positive work climate, effective response to change, safety, and crisis management. All of this is directly related to the organization's leadership.

CHAPTER 6

T-REX AND OTHER EXTINCT LEADERS

The man who smiles when things go wrong has thought of someone to blame it on.

—Robert Bloch

Poison: There are many leadership traits and styles that are poison to an organization. Leadership that does not match the needs of an organization, regardless of good intentions makes for an unsuccessful present and future. The organization can lose precious momentum and ineffective selection of support staff can actually jeopardize the future of the organization. This situation, however, is quickly exacerbated by a governing board's decision to hire a leader who is either already arrogant or who becomes arrogant with the bestowed and perceived power of the position. This arrogance of power and position becomes a poison that spreads throughout an organization.

A non-profit organization hired a new leader to replace a very effective long-term CEO who had brought prominence and distinction to the organization. Upon his retirement, the governing board sought a new CEO who would continue the work of the retiring CEO, thinking that maintaining the status quo was desirable and possible. The laissez-faire CEO did very little to help the organization respond to internal and external changes. He tried to hold on to his predecessor's programs and strategies and never made an effort to update anything in the strategies, goals or actions. A general malaise settled over the organization. The laissez-faire CEO remained in place for few years but was basically a figurehead during the last two years of his administration. By then any effectiveness and influence he had had been marginalized by his leadership style, the infighting of his staff, the growing control and influence of the governing board on the operations of the organization, questionable hiring and promotions, and looming budget issues. With its growing power and influence in the vacuum of leadership created by the laissez-faire CEO, the governing board decided it was time to bring in a firebrand to spark the organization back to life. A CEO was hired who had a reputation for making drastic changes in organizations in a short period of time. As Louis Gerstner, Jr. wrote in his book about taking over IBM, "hired guns" do not always shoot straight and they seldom last very long. Within three months, the new CEO of the non-profit that was once known for its dynamic community presence and positive workplace environment had alienated employees, clients, contributors and grantors, service providers, vendors, and even the employee parking lot attendant. He once handed a towel to the parking lot attendant and instructed him to *"wipe the dust off my car, and if you do a good job, you won't have to wash it."* He told a female senior vice president to *"fetch me a cup of coffee, and fix it like I like it."* At a local Rotary Club dinner where he was invited to give remarks, he talked a full 30 minutes about himself without one time mentioning his organization or the Rotary Club.

An outside accounting firm completed its annual financial audit and the auditors had questions about the CEO's travel claims. There was nothing out of the ordinary; the auditors simply ask the CEO for more documentation for some of the travel claims. The CEO was rude, insulting and accused the auditors of conspiring to embarrass him. He had a negative attitude toward the governing board, too. He showed little respect for the governing board members, and often blamed them for his failures, which he also did with staff members. At one governing board meeting, a confrontation ensued between the CEO and the chairman of the governing board. During the confrontation he reminded the governing board that they hired him because of his leadership style, and he added that they were being disingenuous by now claiming that his confrontational style of management was unacceptable. He finally said, *"You knew exactly the type of leadership I would bring to this stale and dying organization. Now that I've made most of the uncomfortable decisions, you want me out. All of a sudden you want a saint who will capitulate to your efforts and intentions to run the operations of the organization. None of you individually and certainly not collectively have the skills and knowledge and experience to run a complex organization like this."* A few days later, the CEO was fired.

Another example comes from a public school district. The governing board thought it was time to "shake things up," so the search for a new leader focused on finding a "tough" one – someone who would reduce the number of central office staff, motivate the school administrators and teachers, and who would break the mold of the outgoing CEO. After searching for over a year, the governing board hired a leader who from day one of his administration to the end of his administration two years later was a totalitarian manager. He was abrasive, dictatorial and brilliant. This new leader, nicknamed T-Rex by central office staff members (behind his back, of course), was intelligent and well-read. He had a vision for public education that came from his sincere belief that public education could and should provide quality education for all students. He was a tireless worker who was in his office or at a school early in the morning and well into the night. It was not unusual to get a phone call from T-Rex after midnight or be asked to come to a meeting in his office at 7:00 in the morning or 7:00 at night. He took the school district and the community by storm. My first encounter with T-Rex was the afternoon of the press conference that would introduce him to the public and the school district. The press conference was to be held in the central office board room. As with most board meetings, the school district arranged for low level and discreet security. One of my duties was to make sure security was in place. That afternoon T-Rex burst into the board room early to make sure the room was set up to his liking. The tall, physically intimidating leader cut a path no matter where he entered or what he was attending. If he did not like something, he barked orders to change it. I approached him and introduced myself. I told him that in case of an emergency all he had to do was to follow me and I would direct him to the "safe room" (an office that could be quickly secured) until the emergency passed. He said, "*That's bullshit!*" and then he stormed off. That attitude and demeanor did not serve him well, as confirmed by his short tenure.

T-Rex's personality and abrasive management style offended almost everyone he came in contact with, but he felt like he was on a mission and that change was essential to return to the days when the school district provided a quality education. In fact, the governing board hired him for that purpose. He felt that he did not have time to be a "Mr. Nice Guy". Using the Hersey-Blanchard Leadership Model terminology, T-Rex's mission was "*high task and low relationship*" because of the urgency of his mission. His leadership style was not to be confused with Fielder's Contingency Theory where the effective manager assesses a situation and the needs of the organization and determines if it is a low task, high relationship situation or a high task, low relationship situation. T-Rex was full bore low relationship, high task all the time. Besides, he had the full support of the governing board who instructed him to make changes and to make changes quickly. He was empowered to be an overbearing, dictatorial CEO. Had T-Rex tempered that approach, as suggested in the Hersey-Blanchard Situational Model, he could have been very successful for a long period of time. In the Hersey-Blanchard Situational Model, the leader takes time to determine the amount of direction (task behavior) and amount of socio-emotional support a leader must provide given the situation and the level of maturity and ability of the staff. The task behavior is how much the leader engages in explaining the duties and responsibilities to employees – telling them what to do, how to do it, when to do it, and where to do it. This requires no or little dialogue. The communications is one way and the expected outcome is compliance. Leadership behavior that is focuses on socio-emotional dynamics is more two-way communications, where the leader listens, facilitates, directs when necessary, clarifies goals and supports employees. The key difference and what determines the appropriate leadership style in a given situation is decided in large part by the maturity and skill levels of the employees.

Immediately upon his arrival in his new job, T-Rex thought he could send a power message if he eliminated the three top jobs in the organization and within a few weeks they were either reassigned or retired. He did not respect their maturity or skills and did not trust them. One retired soon after T-Rex took office and the others lingered for a while until their jobs were so marginalized that they too left. The other members of T-Rex's central office staff were intimidated, chastised, criticized, and at times humiliated. He also approached mid-level staff members the same way. At monthly school administrators' meetings he gave mixed messages – browbeating them one minute and telling them about team work the next. At one meeting he brought a football to the podium. He tossed the football in the air as he talked about teamwork and the importance of each administrator. He talked about the value of each "player" in the schools. Then he tossed the football to an administrator and said, "*Now, what if he drops the ball? See, the game stops.*" As administrators listened and watched, they got caught up in his speech and illustration; he had their attention. He was making good points and he was focusing on important points about individuals on a team. He was talking about the importance of teamwork. Then abruptly he said: "*And if you drop the ball, I'll be all over your ass with no mercy.*" His real message always drifted back toward intimidation. He just could not find the balance.

With research to the contrary, it is puzzling why so many leaders think the intimidation style of management will be productive in any type of setting. That leadership style is contrary to all research on effective management. Research by Jim Collins on effective companies reported in his books *Good to Great, Built to Last,* and *Great by Choice* does not support dictatorial leadership. Research conducted by Daniel Goleman and reported in *Leadership That Gets Results,* on the different types of leadership notes that the "*Coercive Style*" is the least effective in almost all situations and in all types of settings.

The style of leadership is important at all levels, and in all types of organizations. Employees report that a good, effective, caring, organized and efficient leader is just as important as salary. Mid-level administrators say the same thing about their supervisors. This leadership style issue starts at the top and filters down eventually to all levels of an organization. If a leader's leadership style is intimidation that is passed along by example to top management, middle management and line management.

T-Rex brought his own "hired guns" with him. He named one of them as his top aide. She was very bright and was an expert in many areas, but she was given the impossible task of filtering virtually every decision so it did not take long for the decision-making process to bottleneck and therefore adversely affect operations. This decision-making bottleneck caused confusion and delayed many important decisions. In addition to that burden, T-Rex made her life miserable. One evening I was monitoring the weather because a line of extremely heavy thunderstorms was moving into our area. I constantly watched for anything that might pose a danger to our students and staff, even after hours, because we always had activities going on in schools well into the evening and because anything could happen during the night that might hinder schools the next morning, especially weather. On this particular night I sent an electronic notice to principals about the storm system to make certain that students were not outside. I knew the new CEO's top aide was working late, so I called her and warned her about the dangerous storm system. She was very appreciative and said she would leave the office and head home. I found out later that T-Rex called her about 10:00 that evening and when he found out she was at home instead of at her office he became furious at her. She explained to him that she went home because of the dangerous storm. He said he did not care about the "*damn storm*" and she had better get her "*ass*" back to work. The next day he talked to her and praised her for the good work she was doing. They had a very strange workplace relationship, but she was very loyal to him despite his ill and bipolar treatment of her. The way he treated his top staff member sent a message out repeatedly to all employees – the new CEO is not trustworthy; he does not care about people; he is unrealistic in his expectations of staff members; he is unpredictable; he does not trust staff members or the governing board, and he is an ineffective communicator.

It was reported in a study by the Center for Creative Leadership that 40 percent of new CEOs fail within their first 18 months. Of those that failed, 47 percent did not communicate effectively and 21 percent tried too hard to "*show who's in charge.*"

One of the staff members T-Rex brought with him was supposed to develop a district-wide reading enhancement program. There was a lot of fanfare about this initiative, including training sessions for central office staff, plans to train staff district-wide, and a press release. This was supposed to be something more than a fad. T-Rex made the opening comments on the day of the training for central office staff, which included this statement, *"...listen and learn and by God if you don't you will have to deal with me."* I am not sure he understood the research on positive motivation. Not only did the reading program initiative falter, it never took one breath. In fact, the highly paid staff member was seldom seen again. He was making in excess of $100,000 per year, and yet no one ever saw him do any work. He never attended cabinet meetings or any other meetings, and amazingly the governing board never asked about him or the reading initiative, but his salary continued to be paid. During the two years of T-Rex's tenure, the reading initiative director was seen a grand total of three times – each time in a hallway heading out the door early in the afternoon. The message was clear – T-Rex was holding everyone accountable for immediate action except the few that he favored.

In an article by Rick Piraino on leadership titled *Leadership and Favoritism,* he states that *"Favoritism is a leadership and morale killer. It's natural for leaders to have people they enjoy working with more than others, but this can never be justification for special privileges or breakdowns in the consistent application of accountability."* Every leader in any organization has favorite employees and trusted confidantes, and those individuals may be judged by a different standard; that's only natural and is generally recognized and accepted by others in the organization, but there is a line that cannot be crossed – where the favorite employee's work is so lacking or behavior is so egregious that it is known to all within the organization. Enabling that behavior by ignoring it seriously jeopardizes the effectiveness of the leader. Typically there will not be an overt protest of favoritism by employees, but the diminishing influence of the leader is insidious and persistent. In the long run, he will suffer.

T-Rex also brought his own public relations person with him. He was unquestionably the most arrogant one of the group, and he was the spy, or was suppose to be the mole, and he also thought of himself as the enforcer. I do not think T-Rex expected or even wanted him to be the enforcer; he took that upon himself, but he clearly wanted the public relations guy to be his spy. In reality, he lacked the skills and insight to be any of those. Appropriately enough, many people called him the Mole, among other names. T-Rex did not trust employees; therefore, he thought the Mole was a necessary part of his administration. However, the growing rumors of favoritism and spying further diminished his influence with staff members and the governing board. Spying on employees is not unusual in the business world or in the non-profit sector; however, spying on employees taints trust and thus production is negatively impacted.

My first encounter with the Mole was not a positive one. He called me to set up an appointment to talk about my job duties and responsibilities. Fair enough, I thought, – it is a new administration and T- Rex needs to know who is doing what and for what purpose. He insisted that the meeting take place in my office at 1:00 that afternoon. He called twice to say he was running late. When he did show up at 4:00, he was arrogant, rude, and very condescending. I had prepared a packet for him that included my job description and other information about the work I was doing. Without any greeting or introductions, he said in a commanding tone, "*We want five things from you, starting with your job description. We want to know what you do, how you do it, why is it important, how could it be done differently, and who you talk to.*" I was listening very closely. After he listed the third of the five things, he demanded, "*Well, why aren't you writing this down? We want this before the end of the day.*" I told him I could remember what he wanted and it would be no problem to get that information to him. In fact, I told him, most if not all of that information was in the packet I had prepared for him. I was somewhat confused and disappointed when he refused to accept the package, but then I quickly decided what this encounter was all about. After all, how would it look to T-Rex if the public relations guy returned to him carrying all the information he demanded? For some reason, he wanted me to look or act intimidated or worried. He lost his composure and made some comments that he regretted. He did not regret his abrasive, rude, disrespectful response to me. He regretted that he had revealed more to me than he intended to. He said, "*Just what we thought. You've created your own little kingdom here and we're going to cut you down to size.*" I'm certain that T-Rex did not want him to say that, even if he did feel that way.

Here was another $100,000 per year employee brought in by the new CEO offering nothing that would help the organization and who presented himself in the same manner as the new CEO. In the book *The Classic Touch*, the authors speak to a basic failing of many leaders – the failure to encourage their managers to show good manners and courtesy to all employees. The new CEO and the managers he brought with him were not kind or courteous to anyone, which seriously diminished the influence of the CEO.

I put together the information he wanted and sent it to him by email, as instructed, by 6:00 that same afternoon. He never acknowledged that he received it and I never heard another word from him about my job. However, I was summoned to T-Rex's office a couple of weeks later. I was not told the purpose of the meeting, but I guessed it had something to do with the Mole. T-Rex had me wait in his lobby for almost two hours before he called me into his office. That was his common practice, to keep people waiting in his lobby for at least an hour, usually longer. It did not matter who had an appointment with him; he made them wait. This is a very Machiavellian strategy, based on the belief by some leaders that it is better to be feared than loved because there is more security in fear than in love. Some powerful and influential community leaders did not appreciate that strategy – to the point that some refused to meet with him again. Having people wait for long periods of time was by design. It was a power strategy to him. To have an employee wait is one thing, but to make people wait who are essential to community and business collaboration was not wise and was counterproductive.

When I entered his office that late afternoon I stood before his desk and he immediately started in on me. He was in a rage, but I could not figure out why or about what. I did catch a few phrases during his tirade, such as, *"You don't know who you're messing with…," "You're a smartass…," "I own you…,"* and other similar unprofessional and disrespectful phrases. He was jerking and twisting around in his chair with his arms waving in the air. He never looked at me. When he finally looked at me he seemed startled. He said, *"Why are you just looking at me?" Why don't you say something?* I said, *"I was waiting for you to finish your comments."* T-Rex went berserk. He shouted, *"You smart-ass…. That sounds like some smartass thing you would say."* I said I was just being respectful. He stood up abruptly, pushing his desk chair back so hard it smashed into the credenza behind him. He then stormed around his desk toward me. As I mentioned, I am a calm person, but I do have my limits. As he stormed around his desk in a very angry, aggressive manner, I put both of my hands up with my palms open toward him and I said sternly, *"You had better stop right there, and you're better stop right now!"* I added, *"I've only been afraid of one man my entire life and that was my father; he's dead and I ain't afraid of you, so you'd better stop right there and not take another step toward me."* He stopped abruptly and stood there looking at me. We stared at each other for a long time. He then broke out into a broad smile and said, *"I bet you would beat my ass. Now, get out of here and we'll talk later."* The meeting ended that abruptly; it ended that strangely.

As I drove home, I could not figure out what just happened, but I did wonder what kind of leader we had on our hands. The sad truth is that he really had some great ideas and he was determined to make the school district better for students and staff, but his approach was flawed; his leadership style compromised all of his ideas and strategies. Apparently, his leadership behavior and philosophy mirrored that of Machiavelli: *"It would be best to be both loved and feared. But since the two rarely come together, anyone compelled to choose will find greater security in being feared than in being loved. For this can be said about the nature of men: that they are ungrateful, fickle, dissembling, anxious to flee danger, and covetous of gain...when the need arises, they will turn against you."*

When governing boards are looking for leaders, they should take the time to learn about a candidate's management style and management belief system. Too often governing board members seem influenced more by ideas and proposed strategic initiatives rather than what a candidate offers as a complex person with fundamental beliefs about leadership and organizational management. Too often governing boards make selections of leaders without contemplating how the candidate will implement strategies successfully with staff members' full participation. A bold strategic plan for any type of organization is not that difficult to develop. The difficult part is implementation and sustainability with an effective leader showing the way.

Because of his leadership style, T-Rex eventually became embattled with the governing board over ideas that were good and farsighted, but were presented and pursued in a very impatient and clumsy manner. He thought the school district was not challenging students - that the bigotry of low expectations was leading students and the school district down a path of mediocrity. So he wanted the governing board to increase graduation requirements. He knew that students who learn math are more likely to graduate from high school and he learned that most of the school district's seniors goofed off during their senior year and were therefore ill prepared for any post-secondary challenges, so he wanted to make students take four years of math. He also saw how ill-prepared many of the middle school students were for high school math, so he wanted to make Algebra mandatory for eighth graders. He saw students coming to school dressed in the most inappropriate ways possible and he thought that was a distraction from school work and it caused discipline problems, so he wanted to make students wear uniforms. Almost all of his other observations, opinions, and ideas were right on target. He increased graduation requirements. He added more math requirements. He made seniors take more challenging classes in order to graduate. He added Algebra to the eighth grade requirements. He even had brief success when he added school uniforms at the elementary level in some schools. But also many of his efforts were so ill-conceived that they either failed miserably or led to confrontations with the governing board, staff members, and even with the community.

A leader who is implementing change must be thoughtful in how the strategy should be implemented. Scott Edinger, the author of *Three Cs of Implementing Strategy*, states that implementing a strategy is among the highest priorities of any organization, and he offers three areas that cause the most problems for leaders implementing change: (1) Clarify the strategy. *"Unfortunately, if people don't understand the strategy, they are unable to connect with it. So the first step is to clarify the strategy in a way that people in the organization can rally to support its implementation."* (2) Communicate the strategy. *"Powerfully communicating the essence of the strategy at every level of the organization using multiple mediums is the key here."* (3) Cascade the strategy. *"If you want the strategy implemented well, you need to cascade it throughout the organization and get to the practical and tactical components of people's jobs every day."*

A leader must be cognizant of those things that may distract from the strategy and waste good intentions and cause morale issues. The leader must be effective at communicating the strategy to those that implement the strategy. Some leaders just do not seem to know how to do this effectively.

T-Rex decided that he could motivate the entire school district and share his vision for the entire organization by bringing all employees together in the school district's largest football stadium. In other words, he wanted to put 16,000 employees on hundreds of school buses on a hot August day and transport them without air conditioning to a stadium that was miles away so they could sit in the blazing sun on concrete bleachers and listen to him. That was his idea of a motivational event. This event was not part of any strategic thinking and it was hastily conceived. The first I learned of his idea was when he asked me if I could get a police helicopter to bring him to the football field at the stadium. He had this narcissistic vision of a helicopter landing at mid-field to let him jump out to wave to the standing and cheering masses. I was stunned and I mumbled something about that being against FAA regulations. I did not dare say what I was thinking. When I nixed the idea of a helicopter he then contemplated having a hot air balloon land him in dramatic fashion in the stadium. I told him the balloon would probably get tangled up in the nearby power lines. He settled on a school bus as his chariot.

T.S. Eliot wrote, *"Humility is the most difficult of all virtues to achieve; nothing dies harder than the desire to think well of oneself."* On a hot August day the school district spent thousands of dollars to transport thousands of employees on hundreds of school buses to a football stadium for a motivational event so T-Rex could validate his leadership. T-Rex instructed his central office staff members to meet at the main office to ride a school bus with him to the stadium. We all had to wear baseball-type shirts with "Excellence" written across the front. Many of us did not want to go; it was humiliating. I lingered at the back of the line boarding the bus. I was going to slip away and later claim that I missed the bus or was kidnapped. But he made sure everyone was present for the bus ride. We boarded the bus and within minutes everyone was sweating, both from the heat and the thought of the event. He even had some governing board members on the bus. He timed it so that the stadium was already full before the bus pulled onto the track that surrounded the field, which meant that the teachers, principals, secretaries, counselors, etc. had been sitting in the hot sun for at least 30 minutes before the bus arrived. We had no idea what was going to happen in the stadium. T-Rex never told anyone what he was going to do and say or what if anything he wanted his staff members to do or say. When the bus stopped to unload us near the center of the football field I was almost physically sick from embarrassment. I had determined that I was not going to get off the school bus. I thought I could hide underneath one of the seats, but a good friend and colleague told me that T-Rex would fire me if I did not participate. Reluctantly, I lined up and made the most humiliating walk of my professional life across the field to the makeshift stage.

We could hear a few boos and hisses as we gathered on the stage. I took a seat in the back. T-Rex approached the stage podium as if he expected a swelling and thunderous applause. He got silence instead. Just as I was thinking that this could not get worse; it did get worse. In one of the most stunning moments in the once proud history of that school district, its new CEO started singing the children's song *If You're Happy and You Know It*. This was his plan for motivating 16,000 staff members – singing a children's song? It was another example of a spur of the moment decision without staff input that focused entirely on himself. He tried to communicate his vision and motivate employees at the same time, but his method was more focused on himself rather than on the most effective way to communicate with and respect the employees. He forced a bad idea on everyone and I am certain that employees still talk about that awful and somewhat humorous day when an intelligent CEO expected to inspire thousands of employees with a children's song. Machiavelli turned over in this grave.

Human Resources Brain Bank, an executive study and research entity describes that type of approach to motivation as a *"morale killer."* In article about morale killers titled, *The Role of Company Leaders in Change Communication*, Daisy McCarty found that, *"Workers agree that their jobs are easier and less stressful if their supervisor or manager treats them well. If leadership is dysfunctional, motivation and productivity levels plummet."* McCarty adds that leadership-caused morale killers are perfectionism (no allowance for mistakes); lack of focus; aloofness; moodiness; cruelty; and greed (money, power, or influence).

Leaders, of course, have varying ideas about motivation. T-Rex thought motivation by intimidation was the most effective way, while most laissez-faire leaders think motivation is not their responsibility. A servant leader motivates by example and a positive attitude. Motivation was not T-Rex's strength. Every time he tried to create a motivational moment, it fell apart or fell short.

Eventually, as is the case with most leaders that rely on intimidation, he began losing support from the governing board and eventually from the principals, teachers, parents and community leaders. They often acknowledged his brilliance, his good ideas and good intentions, but he did not know how to or did not attempt to seek the support of others when he wanted to try something different or sustain something proven to be successful.

In the book *Influencing Up* by Allan Cohen and David Bradford, they cite the example of similar leadership by the CEO of a Fortune 500 company, Jeff Kindler. He was thought to be highly qualified for the job and was brilliant, but his leadership style was permeated with outrageous behavior toward employees. He was dictatorial, did not want input, was bullying and intimidating and eventually valued employees left or were demoralized into non-productive behavior. Some of Kindler's good ideas were never developed simply because of his negative leadership behavior and his disrespect toward and lack of trust for employees. Cohen and Bradford offer advice to leaders: *"Some experts will advise you to become totally Machiavellian and seek power for its own sake. From these people you will hear advice such as don't be afraid to bully, intimidate or use fear if you want to keep your power; you get an advantage from appearing to be tough. Forget being honest and self-disclosing because they will turn that against you."* That advice, according to Cohen and Bradford, is not uncommon and there are many leaders who still feel that being a dictatorial and intimidating leader is the best insulation from insubordination and efforts to take power away from them. Cohen and Bradford add that research and reviews of effective companies and organizations do not support the use of that type of leadership.

There were news media reporters and some governing board members who thought the decline of T-Rex as CEO started with the controversy over school uniforms, when he tried to force school uniforms on all students at the same time without a phase-in plan. Even now any time a school district in Georgia suggests school uniforms there is a reference to T-Rex's combative experience with the issue and a subtle reminder that T-Rex was the CEO for only two years. However, his idea of school uniforms was not the only controversy created by T-Rex. There was a strong negative reaction to his efforts to move all of the high schools toward "Block Scheduling" in one year. Block scheduling is a type of academic scheduling where each student has fewer classes per day but each class is longer. Rather than the traditional 50 to 55 minute class periods, block scheduling allows for classes of 90 minutes or longer. There is a body of research indicating that students benefit by having fewer classes, fewer class changes, and more time in class to learn the material. However, there also is a body of research that basically says block scheduling sounds good, but all it means as a practical manner is that some students have more time in class with poor teachers, so instead of spending 50 minutes of boredom they have 90 minutes of boredom in each class. It is good for students with excellent teachers in front of them for 90 minutes. Some students, parents, and teachers were very skeptical about block scheduling. They were not totally against block scheduling; they wanted to learn more about it. Teachers were concerned because block scheduling requires a lot more class preparation time. Students were concerned about the boredom factor and sitting for longer periods of time, and some parents thought it was another education fad that would cause turmoil for a while and then fade away.

Welch stated in his chapter on change, *"A leader should attach every change initiative to a clear purpose or goal. Change for change's sake is stupid and enervating."* On the other hand several students, teachers, and parents who supported block scheduling saw nothing but positives: reduce conflict in the hallways because of fewer class changes; more substantial lesson plans and time to learn material; fewer classes to keep up with; fewer lesson plans; fewer teachers to contact, etc. As with many of T-Rex's ideas, block scheduling was divisive and controversial and he was not deliberate and patient with implementation. Further, he did not communicate effectively why he thought this would be a good change for the schools. The message he gave was that this was his idea and therefore no one should ask questions about it, not even the governing board. Years after his departure, many schools still use block scheduling. The idea was good, but the implementation was clumsy and centered on the CEO and not on the purpose, as Welch advised against.

Louis Gerstner, Jr., the architect of IBM's reemergence in the 1990s said that one of the primary keys to his success was team building, but he added that team building does not work if the CEO does not listen. A CEO can create the idea of team building, but it is only a false concept if the CEO is not willing to listen to members of his team. T-Rex never understood that important point. Many leaders in organizations do not take the time to listen, because they are too busy barking out orders and expecting staff and the governing board to accept every dictate as gospel, sometimes because they simply don't know and have not tried another way to do it. However, T-Rex knew better. He knew that his leadership style would be perceived negatively, but he had an excuse; at least he felt justified, because T-Rex thought that the organization was failing. He was convinced that all of his ideas were going to change that, so he did not need to hear feedback or opinions of any type from anyone inside or outside of the organization. He did not care what the research showed. He had already made up his mind. Besides, he did not think he had time to waste. Just like a new leader of a business or other organization who has power, who sees things that need to improve, and yet who has no clear strategy for implementing significant change, T-Rex ignored the time it takes to develop a sustainable strategy and instead opted for forced tactics. Henry Mintzberg suggests in *The Nature of Managerial Work* that activities of most leaders are *"characterized by brevity, variety, and fragmentation."* These types of leaders are always on the move and seldom take the time to study, listen and plan effectively. Mintzberg says that this type of leader's only interaction with his staff is when he demands to know why certain initiatives have not been implemented.

For implementing change, there are valuable lessons from Albert Bandura's research for leaders of any type of organization (see Bandura's *Social Foundations of Thought and Action*). Bandura is considered the father of social learning theory and the preeminent authority on influence. At a time when leaders and many psychologists thought that the most influential way to change the behavior of people was through direct rewards and punishments, Bandura's research found that observing the behavior of others is a power shaper of behavior. Through decades of social learning theory research in hundreds of different settings, Bandura and associates found that people will attempt to change, and will accept change such as new ideas about work, new strategies, and new expectations if: (1) they believe it will be worth it and (2) they can do what is required. With these two requirements in place, most individuals will at least try to enact change. With T-Rex, he did not try to convince staff members, parents, governing board members or others that his ideas were worth the effort and turmoil and he gave no recognition that staff members had to have different information, knowledge and skills to implement the changes he demanded. Bandura would have predicted T-Rex's failure as a CEO.

Many people believe that the negative effect of his clumsy method of handling change was the reason T-Rex was released from his contract before it expired. Even though leaders are fired for such types of controversy, to say T-Rex was released from his contract because of his awkward and rambling way of handling change is not an accurate perception of T-Rex's demise in the organization, just like it would not be accurate to say that Jeff Kindler's demise at Pfizer was due solely to his inability to move the company into new markets. T-Rex's decline was much more complicated. He did not trust people and sometimes he was not very good at selecting the few that he did trust. Also, T-Rex was very impatient and a poor communicator. Above all else, however, he was a sore loser. It is important to recognize that he was a sore loser. Most leaders have a competitive nature, which can be an asset. It can be a good trait. On the negative side, very competitive leaders who aim to dominant staff and governing boards do not know how to lose, or more importantly how to learn from losses. With T-Rex, he simply hated to lose. Not only did he hate to lose; he was an incredibly sore loser. He was extremely competitive and he took everything personally. That sore loser mentality seems to be a common denominator with leaders who rely on bullying and intimidation, regardless of the nature or type of organization. They are always keeping score.

Rosabeth Moss Kanter, author of *Confidence: How Winning Streaks and Losing Streaks Begin and End*, talks about the sore loser: *"Being a sore loser is usually blamed on the person. But when people are sore losers, it is often because they have been wounded; they are sore in the sense of being in pain, covered with aches and bruises.... An ailing system inflicts wounds."* And this, she added, can start or escalate a losing streak.

The organization that T-Rex came into was ailing, but that same organization when T-Rex left was still ailing. He felt the bitterness of wounds, even though many were self-inflicted because of his coarse personality, and because he kept losing and did not learn from those loses. He trusted only a few and then he found out that a couple of them were working behind his back so they could be in good standing with some governing board members. He took that personally, and he characterized that betrayal as another loss. He knew he had good ideas to improve the organization, but he took all rebuttals personally. A more effective CEO would have encouraged feedback without personalizing the feedback. But T-Rex was constantly keeping score. He wanted what was best for the organization - no doubt his motivation was sincere, but he also wanted all of the credit and no criticism. He wanted total control. All of the elements necessary to start a losing streak were in place and T-Rex's decline was in motion.

His decline followed Kanter's nine "pathologies" that started the chain reaction leading to T-Rex's removal from the job: communication decreases; criticism and blame increases; respect decreases; isolation increases; focus turns inward; rifts widen and inequities grow; initiatives decrease; aspirations diminish; and negativity spreads. Kanter could not have described T-Rex's decline in more exact terms. First of all, T-Rex became less communicative, almost to the point of paranoia. His communication with Cabinet members became more guarded and his speeches in the community were less frequent and more defensive. His communication with the governing board almost stopped. He began to constantly criticize people, and when something happened that was even remotely negative he found someone to blame to blame it on, in addition to overreacting. One painful example involves his reaction to criticism of him in a local high school student newspaper.

A high school student wrote an article for the school newspaper criticizing T-Rex for things such as the school uniform decision. It was in a school newspaper, not a city, county, metro-area, statewide newspaper. The article was concise and reasonably well written and very far removed from public attention. After all, how many people actually read a high school student newspaper? Other than a few students in the high school one else knew anything about the article, but when it came to T-Rex's attention he reacted like a real loser. He castigated the school's principal and demanded that the school staff members gather up all of the copies of the newspaper and destroy them. He demanded that they immediately stop distribution of the newspaper. It did not take long for news of his overreaction to reach the community, and the local news media soon picked up the story as an example of abusive "censorship." There was a front page article in the local newspaper and then other news media sources picked up the story. The story even hit the national news briefly. The entire incident made T-Rex look like a petty tyrant, and he started acting more and more like a petty tyrant thereafter, because he "lost" and he was convinced he was set up to lose – everyone was against him.

T-Rex came into an organization and community that was ready for change. Almost everyone wanted him to succeed, but over time the respect toward him diminished and instead he became an object of ridicule. During his first year in the organization, people thought there was three of him, because he was all over the place seemingly at the same time. He visited schools, religious gatherings, Rotary Clubs, community meetings, etc. every day and night of every week, but toward the end of his tenure he started spending more and more time in his office and in the central office complex and less time in essential places. He and others knew he was shifting from the innovative winner's mode to the loser's survival mode. His once widespread cadre of supporters became a small band of single-minded activist who he encouraged to speak out against his "enemies." He was growing desperate and paranoid. When a leader shifts to a small group of activists to speak out for him, the end is near. There are countless examples in many different settings of this, where the leader circles the wagons when his influence is diminishing, because he has miscalculated his decisions, has overextended his change strategies, and has failed as a leader. Such examples can be found in warfare, politics, businesses, universities, schools, religious organizations, and others.

In an article by Sara Weaver and George Yancey, *The Impact of Dark Leadership on Organizational Commitment*, the authors describe the behavior of the *"paranoid leader"* as the loss of touch with the purpose of the organization and his role in the health of the organization. The paranoid leader's focus shifts from what is best for the organization to what is best for him and what he can do to find supporters and fight off the challengers. There is never a good ending when a leader becomes paranoid.

T-Rex's relationship with the governing board deteriorated. The same governing board that selected him because of his energy level, his intellect, his no-nonsense demeanor, his willingness to take risks, his innovative ideas, and his toughness was now turning on him because of some of those very same traits. Instead of working through the differences, he became defensive, which compromises almost all efficiencies and effective organizational changes. Instead of working with T-Rex in a constructive manner, the governing board listened to those that were complaining about T-Rex. The negativity spread. The confrontations with the governing board became more frequent, intense and combative. T-Rex began losing more and more battles with the governing board.

Jim Collins' book, *From Good to Great* confirmed that dysfunctional communications between the leader and the governing board is destructive. Collins found that most successful businesses were not headed by a flamboyant, outspoken CEO. They were led by thoughtful, intelligent, team-building CEOs that had a clear vision of strategy and implementation and that unquestionably understood the value of servant leadership and communications. Businesses led by tyrannical leaders were not successful.

The governing board meetings, which were frequently the epitome of local petty politics, became an open battlefield between T-Rex and some members of the governing board. They battled over almost everything on the agenda. And they were a divided board – some liked the work T-Rex was doing, a couple of them tolerated him and the others were ready to fire him immediately. This type of disharmony between a leader and the governing board jeopardizes the operations of an organization. Often decisions are delayed by the conflict. These delays and accompanying confusion can have a devastating impact on the operations of an organization. At one time, T-Rex seemed to have given up and accepted the fact that he was going to be released from him contract, but then his competitive nature kicked back in and he was hell-on-wheels, determined to fight back. He openly fought and connived against the governing board, and it became very ugly. His final miscalculation involved the accrediting agency for schools and colleges.

Rosabeth Kanter states that the competitor that thinks he is losing will try almost anything to salvage his standing. T-Rex knew that the accrediting agency was concerned about the behavior of the governing board, so he tried to take advantage of that negative situation and turn it to his advantage. He could smell victory. The accrediting agency officials were concerned about possible governing board member interference with the daily operations of the organization and threatened sanctions if they did not cease such interfering involvement, such as trying to influence personnel decisions. As is often the case when an embattled and arrogant leader misreads a situation, T-Rex tried to play this to his advantage. He wrote a letter to the accrediting agency about the governing board that led to a deeper investigation. The accrediting agency team came to the school district to interview staff members, governing board members, and T-Rex. More than a few people opined that T-Rex was trying to minimize the conflict at the last minute in an effort to reconcile with the governing board. If that was true, he badly misunderstood the circumstances.

The accrediting agency report said that the rift between the governing board and the CEO was a strain on the school district's operations, morale, and ability to improve education. The accrediting agency was contemplating sending the school district a scathing report and was preparing to put the school district on probation. Probation is a warning that the school district is in danger of losing its accreditation. When a school district loses accreditation, graduating students may not be able to get into college and it could interrupt their ability to receive financial aid or scholarships. It is front-page news when a school district is put on probation.

The accrediting agency was ready to issue the findings and the probationary status, but governing board members were unofficially asking what could be done to avoid probationary status. The accrediting agency officials were brutally blunt with the board members. They said basically, *"Quit trying to run the organization; that's not your responsibility."* T-Rex was going to use the probationary status as "proof" that he was not allowed to run the organization effectively due to interference by the governing board. T-Rex thought that would force the governing board members to back off and let him run things as he pleased. However, the governing board members told the accrediting agency that the governing board had to step in because T-Rex was making bad decisions, was alienating and intimidating staff members, was making insane personnel decisions, and was unresponsive to them. When T-Rex heard this, he shifted tactics and tried to reconcile with the governing board, but it was too late. The accrediting agency understood the role of the CEO and the role of the governing board, so it wisely determined that the truth was somewhere in the middle. This meant that T-Rex had to go and the governing board had to change its ways. The accrediting agency was not drawn into the fight between T-Rex and the governing board; it did not take one side over the other.

The governing board did not have a contractual performance reason to terminate T-Rex, but they told him he should resign. He refused, at least until they offered to buy him out. They paid him a substantial amount of money to leave the organization. They paid him to leave and had to pay the same amount at the same time to the person that replaced him. The governing board lacked the will and they opined that they lacked the "evidence" to properly terminate him so he would not be eligible for any compensation. This "compromise" kept both sides silent, so the public would not have an inside view of what was actually transpiring. Therefore, after a short and stormy tenure in the organization, T-Rex resigned (was bought out). And interestingly enough, the accrediting agency did not put the school district on probation. It indicated that it wanted to give T-Rex's successor an opportunity to work without the burden of probation. Actually, that decision took pressure off the governing board and in their mind relieved them of any responsibility for T-Rex's failures.

Antidote

Arrogance, the need to "win" at the expense of the organization, according to Grady Bogue in his book, *The Enemies of Leadership*, is an enemy of leadership in the extreme, primarily because the collateral damage to the organization can be significant. The authors of *In Search of Excellence*, Thomas Peters and Robert Waterman, noted the importance of treating people right: "*Treat people as adults; treat them as partners; threat them with dignity; threat them with respect.*" All leaders and all governing boards are selected by someone who has the authority to make such selections or by a public that has the power of the vote. Those in position to make these decisions, no matter the type of organization, must give more attention to the future of the organization and base selections of leaders on their ability to hold the future in mind while developing short and long-term strategies. That is not possible in the minds and actions of arrogant leaders. Therefore, arrogance must be avoided at all levels, from the CEO to the lowest level manager; an arrogant leader cannot lead and should not be selected for any leadership position. According to the Society for Industrial and Organizational Psychology, the angst of arrogance is clearly illustrated by one former CEO at American International Group (AIG), Joe Cassano.

Cassano was the president of AIG's financial products unit and is credited by some as single-handedly bringing about the downfall of AIG. Many accounts describe Cassano as a quintessential arrogant CEO. Former coworkers report that in stark contrast to his predecessors, Cassano had penchants for yelling, cursing, bad-mouthing others, and belittling colleagues, as well as little tolerance for opposing viewpoints. In the absence of Cassano's persistent arrogant behavior (and unwillingness to tolerate dissent regarding his management practices), it is possible that AIG's crisis would have been considerably less severe or altogether avoided. However, despite the fact that it was the practices he sanctioned that led AIG to be regarded as one of the most notable examples of excess associated with Wall Street, Cassano remains unapologetic about his role and blames others for the crisis.

Can an arrogant leader change? Robert Greenleaf opines in his book *Servant Leadership* that leaders can be taught how to lead effectively. If that is true, then staff development in every organization should include training on treating employees, clients and each other with respect.

In an article for *Inc. Magazine*, the magazine's staff compiled leadership pointers from experts that were categorized into several components:

1. Focus on employee happiness rather than employee motivation. *Inc.'s* researcher, Max Chafkin, interviewed successful business CEOs and found that many of them focused on the happiness factor of employees and customers. He found that working environments that include humor were strong on camaraderie and production. Customers that felt pleased with the employees' treatment reinforced the positive behavior with positive feedback.

2. Set a good example. *"A leader's attitude is contagious. Communication is a key to making members of the organization's team feel included in major decisions. Employees are more motivated when they feel needed, appreciated, and valued."*

3. It is important to make sure employees share in the organization's success. *"Employee performance, productivity, and motivation can all be tied to how invested a worker feels in his or her company (or organization)."*

4. It is also important to create a culture of support and collaboration. In his book *Drive: The Surprising Truth About What Motivates Us*, author Daniel H. Pink writes that the crash of Wall Street is a striking example of the peril of motivating employees strictly with cash. He advises that instead, companies and organizations should create conditions for employees to find the joy in work itself. That can mean giving workers the autonomy to choose what they do and with whom, which can help foster a desire for mastery of tasks and skill sets and simply doing more, better.

5. Leaders should encourage workers to voice complaints. *"When Dell amassed an online 'anti-fan club,' excoriating the PC maker across the blogosphere, it not only acknowledged criticism, but also actually fixed things,"* according to Jeff Jarvis in his book, *What Would Google Do.*

There are scores of reasons why employees are reluctant to offer critiques of management or their company's culture. However, it is important to remember, as *Inc.*'s Leigh Buchanan writes, "*When the heat's not lowered, steam escapes.*" One motivational strategy that works well in some organizations is to take on volunteer assignments. A significant way to improve morale and motivation is to encourage and then provide ways for employees to do volunteer work in the community where they live or in the community near the workplace. This becomes even more powerful when the leader of the organization also participates in volunteer events. This may be supported by compensatory work time, by public recognition of the volunteers' work during an organization's meeting, and/or by articles in the organization's eLetter, newsletter, etc. The volunteer work itself can be so rewarding that the benefit is a happier and more productive employee. These types of projects not only help charities, but also help employees create some of their most inspired work.

Another motivational consideration is to appeal to the creative spark in employees – there is a distinct energy in start-up companies that can be captured in any organization or business. Some businesses and organizations operationalize this practice by periodically gathering employees in small clusters at the office and for about 15-30 minutes in a very informal way, with laughter and banter, collaborate by brainstorming ideas. Some call this "controlled chaos," but it can energize an organization.

There is poison for all when an organization's leader pays scant attention to the needs of the employees and organization. People will attempt to change and will accept change such as new ideas about work, new strategies, and new expectations if they believe it will be worth it and they can do what is required. This response to change is consistent with those essential components specified in the *Three Cs of Implementing Strategy* that Scott Edinger insists are necessary for strategies to be implemented successfully: Clarify the strategy to all employees; communicate the strategy to all employees and stakeholders; and cascade the strategy so that employees and others know how the strategies are related to their daily jobs/work. With these in place, and with the motivation and good will of its leader, most individuals will at least try to enact the change.

CHAPTER 7

ASSESSING THE ASSESSORS

There are risks and costs to a program of action. But they are far less than the long range risks and costs of comfortable inaction.

—*John F. Kennedy*

Poison: **The assessment of leadership is critical to the success of an organization. In many circumstances, the assessment comes from an outside source, such as the Better Business Bureau, non-profit rating institutions, bond rating organizations, accrediting associations, popular news magazines, and others. Are these organizations held accountable for how they assess organizations? Does a "good score" or "negative score" actually mean that an organization and thus its leadership are truly good or bad? If there is a poison, it comes insidiously from assessments that go easy on organizational leadership which in reality is not effective. An organization can be poisonous and no one knows until problems erupt that could have been dealt with much earlier and much more effectively had it been revealed honestly. Organizations that aim for success or that desire to continue successfully, must contemplate how to best assess its operations and not depend solely on organization whose existence is dependent on its evaluation of other entities. An organization and its leadership can die from the poison of false or misleading assessments.**

Leaders, governing boards and the public should learn more about those organizations that rank businesses, financial organizations, public education school districts, private schools and governing boards. Sometimes their methodology is mysterious.

U.S. News and World Report's annual rating of colleges, both public and private, is the magazine's best selling issue each year. It is a highly anticipated report that ranks the quality of colleges and universities. Many parents and students read the magazine's annual issue and make decisions about colleges based the rankings. The annual ranking of colleges has been an annual event for over two decades, but during that time very little if any attention was given to exactly how the magazine determined the rankings. Did anyone assess the assessors? Apparently no one did.

In a 2012 news story that spread quickly across the nation it was revealed that *U.S. News and World Report's* rankings of colleges was based on information that was self-reported by colleges and universities with no one at the magazine checking to see if the information was correct and up-to-date. This was revealed when it was discovered that a prestigious private university, Emory University near Atlanta, was exaggerating data and submitting those reports to *U.S. News and World Report* for the annual rankings. Emory was exaggerating its numbers in order to get a more favorable ranking by the magazine, and it worked. The self reported misinformation was not revealed by the assessor, *U.S. News and World Report*; instead, it was discovered and revealed by a different news media source. Everyone just blithely accepted this very important annual report without any questions about the assessors, and leadership at the universities annually were certainly patting themselves on the back for their excellent ratings in the magazine. How many times did a university miss an opportunity to take a real view of its leadership while depending on rankings by *U.S. News and World Report* that lacked validation?

In the United States there are six regional accrediting agencies for public and private elementary, middle, and high schools: Middle States Association of Colleges and Schools; New England Association of Colleges and Schools; North Central Association of Colleges and Schools; Northwest Association of Colleges and Schools; Western Association of Colleges and Schools; and the Southeast Association of Colleges and Schools (SACS). The accrediting agencies determine if K-12 schools meet accrediting standards, which determines if the students are eligible for colleges and scholarships. The standards are established, of course, by the accrediting agencies and are based on little research or established best practices. Some of the regional agencies serve a very large area. SACS, for example, accredits schools and school districts throughout the United States and overseas. It is one of the most powerful groups in all of public and private education, and some would argue that it is the most powerful. SACS is a voluntary, nongovernmental entity. SACS is approved by the United States Department of Education as an entity that enforces educational standards; however, the United .States. Department of Education has no standards or assessment criteria that measure the effectiveness of SACS or any other accrediting agency. SACS dominates the field. It has virtually no competition, so what is the United States. Department of Education suppose to do except approve SACS. SACS is so dominate that it has taken over other accrediting agencies. SACS issues reports on which schools are exemplary, need improvement and whose accreditation might be in jeopardy. Since 2006, SACS has operated under the umbrella of AdvancED, a global accrediting group that assesses 23,000 public and private schools in 65 countries. SACS accreditation is used as a banner of quality by schools and colleges. SACS can put schools and colleges on probation or remove their accreditation because of the organization's failure to meet SACS standards in areas such as academic or financial stewardship and governance.

It is interesting to note that only a few public school districts, private schools and colleges have lost SACS accreditation in the last 40 years. Despite all of the problems in public education, including all of the many articles in local newspapers on a regular basis about local governing board problems, plus all of the schools that are on the No Child Left Behind Needs Improvement list (some for eight years or longer) because of student academic underachievement and schools that have had safety issues, only a few have lost accreditation and only a small percentage of school districts have even been put on probation. But let's not stop the discussion with public schools. Accrediting agencies that accredit private schools answer to no one or any other authority either. It can be difficult to determine how they assess private schools for quality or safety, or the effectiveness of the leaders and governing boards.

How do accrediting agencies and other entities such as bond rating companies assess the quality of leadership in those organizations that they claim to know so well? The fact of the matter is they seldom address leadership. Yet, there is a public impression and belief that the assessors are assessing leaders and governing boards. Also, there is a generally held belief that they each have some positive standing from some unnamed authority that sanctions the quality of their assessments. Even more troubling is the fact that organizations, both public and private, gloat over the ratings of their respective organizations by these outside assessors. Consequently, many dysfunctional organizations hide behind the assessors' ratings and rankings, and equally important, many of these same organizations do not take a true internal view of their own strengths and weaknesses. Instead, they focus on being compliant – complaint with the requirements of the assessor organizations – basic levels of compliance.

In an article for the *Guardian*, Marc Joffe said that Moody's, Standards and Poor, and other credit rating agencies deserve a failing grade. The same is implied from a study at Stanford University that was reported in *The Ratings Game* by the Stanford Social Innovation Review. The authors studied the three primary groups that rate non-profit charities. The authors wrote,

We conducted a detailed study of the agencies to determine how useful

a service they provide. The results were sobering: Our review of their methodologies indicates that these [entities] individually and collectively fall well short of providing meaningful guidance for donors who want to support more efficient and effective nonprofits. Based on our study, the major weaknesses of the ratings agencies are threefold: they rely too heavily on simple analysis and ratios derived from poor-quality financial data; they overemphasize financial efficiency while ignoring the question of program effectiveness; and they generally do a poor job of conducting analysis in important qualitative areas such as management strength, governance quality, or organizational transparency.

How many private school, public school and business leaders would be replaced if they were found to be ineffective based on reliable ratings and rankings by outside assessing entities? How many businesses that failed during the recession could have been saved if the bond rating companies were held accountable for their assessments? How many governing boards would have been held more accountable had outside assessors and accrediting agencies done a better job of measuring effectiveness?

Antidote

There is an old saying that what gets measured gets done. However, it is not very likely that the United .States Department of Education is going to conduct an in depth study of SACS and the other school and school district accrediting agencies to determine what they do, how they do it and whether what they claim to do is effective. It is also unlikely that accrediting agencies and bond rating companies will change their methods. Additionally, an entity such as Charity Navigator that reviews non-profits is not likely to overhaul its methods either. Furthermore, the private school accrediting agencies will not change, and it is certain that the bond rating companies will continue to operate without significant oversight. Therefore, it is imperative that organizational leaders and especially governing boards take the outside assessments from these organizations for what they are worth, and develop strong internal methods and mechanisms for assessing their organization's health. Every organization goes through periods of difficulty and has to contend with challenges at all levels. Sometimes it is just growing pains, but in other situations the organization does not have a clear, objective view and understanding of its own internal and external operations. Or, it may be the challenge of insufficient resources or misaligned or poorly allocated resources, and sometimes it is related to trying to do something new or make a significant change without making the necessary preparations. The reasons for organizational difficulties are multifaceted. And because so many things can go wrong, or so many challenges can occur, it is highly beneficial for organizations to have the ability to accurately diagnose the source(s) of their difficulties in order to quickly correct course and optimize the use of scarce resources. Even when it seems that the organization is functioning efficiently, there is a need for an assessment of performance.

Some organizations contract performance assessments from external vendors, and there are times and circumstances when that is appropriate and necessary, but much can be learned through an organizational self-assessment, too. In fact, an honest internal review can often reveal more than an external-based review. There are numerous self-assessment models that an organization can use, or it can develop its own, with assistance. According to the Center for Non-Profit Management (CNPM), organizational self-assessment should focus on things that are changeable, that the organization can control, that directly impact performance, and that are related to the goals of the organization. Good organizational assessment will identify "cause and effect" relationships, helping insure that whatever corrective actions put in place will produce meaningful change. CNPM says organizational self-assessment has additional benefits as well. It helps bring focus to the organization's improvement efforts and it helps optimize the use of organizational resources and functions. Self-assessment emphasizes opportunities for improvement, not "fixing blame" and it looks at the total organization, not just one or two aspects. An informative self-assessment is performance focused, not just people focused.

Organizational self-assessment does not have to be an overly formal, heavily structured, painstaking process to produce highly useful information. The Baldrige Performance Excellence Program provides a proven approach to meaningful self-assessment through the use of its Criteria for Performance Excellence. The self-assessment criterion from Baldrige applies to many different types of organizations and provides effective and useful feedback. Baldrige offers several examples of when a self-assessment is appropriate, such as when customers/clients are driving a need to change; the industry or environment is changing; the organization is among the best and it wants to stay that way; the leaders want to enhance organizational learning; the organization sees a connection between key issues and pressure on organizational performance; and when an organization is underperforming.

CNPM offers excellent resources for organizational self-assessment, as does the Annie E. Casey Foundation. Additionally, organizations should look at similar organizations that have proven to be successful over time and inquire to determine if and how those organizations self-assess.

Genuine improvement in any and every organization depends heavily on an accurate assessment of its internal strategies, methods, mechanisms, policies, procedures, management of resources, and staffing in order to maintain success and identify weaknesses.

An organization that depends solely on external assessment entities and does not carefully consider internal data or that depends on external evaluators that do not take the time or have the expertise to conduct an effective and useful evaluation will not fully understand its strengths and weaknesses and, therefore, will not make adjustments or significant changes that could benefit the organization and its future. There are times when trust is not high enough between the leadership and the governing board to allow for an internal assessment of the organization, or if there is one the results may not be accepted. This situation, however, should not preclude an organization from carefully and thoroughly and periodically planning an internal assessment. It can be insidiously poisonous to rely only on outside assessments as the sole means of feedback on effectiveness and efficiency.

CHAPTER 9

CABINETS OF CURIOSITIES

People who enjoy meetings should not be in charge of anything.

—*Thomas Sowell*

Poison: One of the most crucial responsibilities of a leader in any organization is the development of an excellent leadership team that functions at the highest levels. No matter how talented the leader may be, there are few organizations that can be successful without a leadership team that works in tangent with the leader and that is supportive of each other, a team that can be open and honest with each colleague and with the leader. A leadership team made up of sycophants will offer nothing to the organization and in fact will inevitably become liability. A dysfunctional leadership team is poison to an organization and can jeopardize current organization operations and the future of the organization.

If the public knew what goes on in executive leadership meetings of public school districts, corporations, non-profit agencies, higher education, and other organizations, they would not know whether to be impressed, cry, or laugh. Many such meetings are commonly referred to as "cabinet" meetings. The term comes from antiquity where a cabinet was a small room that was off-limits to all except a privileged few with connections to monarchs during the 16th century. The famous Oxford Dictionary credits Sir Frances Bacon with the version of the word that extended its meaning beyond that of a small room when he used the description "Cabinet Council," but it was Charles I that actually turned the term into a functionally working entity. Its original use by Charles I and Bacon were in negative terms describing the worse of "foreign" practices.

Over time the term cabinet has come to mean a body of people that serve in an official capacity to advise an organization's leader. If only cabinets served that purpose, it would be useful. Far too many cabinet members merely rubberstamp the leader's ideas, and do not offer true advice. Cabinet meetings are varied and if dominated by the leader who does not understand operational functions, the needs of the organization and the importance of positive human relations and a positive workplace climate they are probably dysfunctional meetings.

Most leaders schedule regular meetings with their top administrators regardless of the size of the organization. Cabinet meetings serve an essential function in any type of organization whether it is public education, non-profit, religious, higher education, or business. The cabinet provides the CEO with information on the complexities and issues of the organization's operations, and it provides reports about the various components of the organization, to trouble-shoot existing or possible problems, and to plan. Also, it is the cabinet in large part that determines the culture, workplace climate, strategic plans, and productivity of the organization, or at least mirrors the leadership style of the CEO. The CEO typically has an agenda for the cabinet meetings that includes items of importance to the organization, such as strategic planning items, budget items, problem-solving situations and items that will be brought to the next governing board meeting, but most CEOs provide time for the cabinet members to provide department updates, also. At least that is how cabinet meetings should operate, more or less. Too often, however, the cabinet agenda is dominated by whatever is fresh on the CEO's mind. It is obviously very important to know what is pressuring the CEO, but not at the expense of knowing what operational issues and challenges exist within the organization.

I worked for a CEO who was not offended by cabinet members who disagreed with him. He enjoyed a lively debate, and encouraged them. He would say, *"Tell me where my thinking is wrong; I need to better understand."* Afterwards, the cabinet would leave the room more often united than divided. He also wanted to hear from every department head and he did not want the glossy version; he wanted the truth. The cabinet meetings were long but productive. The CEO learned many things about the operations of the organization and cabinet members learned from him and from other members of the cabinet.

If a CEO wants cabinet meetings to be effective, he will follow the purpose of meetings that was included in Patrick Lencioni's book, *Death by Meeting,* where he noted that meetings should be productive instead of being used to intimidate and even frighten staff members either by direct confrontation, by ambiguity, and/or by downright misrepresentation, threats and embarrassment. Unlike CEOs that followed him, the effective CEO I worked with understood the value of respect and made an effort, therefore, to encourage a climate of respect. If the CEO of an organization and his top staff members do not respect each other enough to be honest and supportive, the organization will suffer.

In his book, *Counsel to the President,* the former counsel to six presidents, Clark Clifford, describes the varying dynamics in the cabinet of each president he worked for. According Clifford, Truman's cabinet was dominated by a couple of staff members; nevertheless, it was clear that Truman was in charge. Contrast that with the Eisenhower cabinet where there was very little structure, the president was not always engaged in the conversation, and when he was engaged the members of the cabinet listened without much interaction with the president's thoughts and opinions. President Johnson encouraged debate among his cabinet members, but he infrequently followed their advice. Those three different types of cabinet meetings fairly represent how different cabinets operate. Several times in different situations, Clifford said that the interaction and utility of cabinets depended on the leader's understanding of the function and purpose of the cabinet.

Stephen Covey's book, *Speed of Trust*, points out the value and necessity of developing trust between and among colleagues. Covey wrote that organizations are much more productive when trust is at the heart of the enterprise and at the core of the organization's leadership team. Trust and respect are interrelated. Covey wrote that *"Strategy times execution multiplied by trust equals results."* Trust and respect are essential elements of an effective leadership team.

The effectiveness and relevance of cabinet meetings also depends in large part on the relationship between the CEO and the governing board. Some CEOs are so dominated or intimidated by members of the governing board that cabinet meetings center more on concerns of the governing board than the operations of the organization. Many of the governing board issues are localized or so narrow that they have little or no impact on the rest of the organization, or the governing board member's issues are so insignificant that it only wastes the time of the cabinet.

In one cabinet meeting of a non-profit organization, the CEO was perturbed because a governing board member complained about how employees were dressed on Fridays. This particular governing board member did not approve of business casual dress at anytime, and he clearly intimidated the organization's CEO. At the cabinet meeting following the governing board member's tirade about casual dress on Fridays, the CEO spent almost three hours with his cabinet discussing the Friday dress code, despite the fact that his organization was trying to deal with shrinking revenues, employee retention issues, increases in healthcare costs, and many other pressing issues. Additional time was then spent after the cabinet meeting working on an employee dress code that essentially applied to one day a week.

In another organization, according to an accrediting agency report, the hostility among the top level administrators during cabinet meetings spilled over into the discussions and aborted decision making. If, for example, a department within this organization was having issues, such as delivering services in a timely fashion, the cabinet members blamed each other, showed no trust or respect for each other or the CEO and consequently the issues were not resolved. The true business of the organization consequently was not addressed, because the CEO did not use the cabinet effectively.

In too many situations cabinet members chose sides. It can happen even at the highest levels. At one time in President Eisenhower's cabinet, according to Clark Clifford, two of the cabinet members aligned with each other at the expense of the others; consequently the cabinet became divided and dysfunctional. There simply was very little trust and respect in the room. As Covey wrote, *"Trust always affects two outcomes – speed and cost. When trust goes down, speed will also go down and costs will go up."*

One of the most bizarre cabinet meetings I ever witnessed was with a leader who was mercurial. The cabinet typically met in the governing board room because it was spacious, but one day during a cabinet meeting we heard a buzz from one of the speakers that were used during the public information section of the monthly governing board meeting. Technology staff members were working on the system because it had developed a lot of static. But the CEO was convinced that someone had bugged the room so he moved the cabinet meetings to a tiny room that could not comfortably accommodate the cabinet. He had become so paranoid that governing board members were going to find out what was discussed during cabinet meetings that he had the entire building swept for bugging devices. That was silly. We were not exactly talking about a new method for splitting the atom, but he was determined that the cabinet discussions should remain a secret.

The CEO's philosophy about the role of the cabinet was fairly clear; he ruled over the cabinet like a king in his court. He lectured, he chastised, he criticized, he charmed, he pontificated, he raged, he cried, he laughed and sometimes all in the same meeting. To his credit, however, he wanted his cabinet members to keep up with the latest trends and research on best practices and decision making. Some of the books he discussed and recommended that the cabinet read included sections about leadership methods and styles that were ironically contradictory to his own. For example, he liked to quote Robert Greenleaf about *"Servant Leadership,"* but he seldom modeled that type of leadership; in fact, he modeled authoritarianism, almost the polar opposite of Greenleaf's leadership theory. At each cabinet meeting he wanted someone to report on a book or article. He did not give out reading assignments, but he clearly expected everyone to read and to report on what they had read. Most of the cabinet members complained behind his back about the reading requirement, because they would not dare say anything during the cabinet meeting. So it went like this at several consecutive cabinet meetings. The CEO would ask, *"Okay, who read something interesting this week? Okay, someone read something."* No one would say a word. Then he would ask again, *"I know somebody read something."* Eventually, I would raise my hand. *"Okay, go ahead,"* he would say to me. So, I would give a brief synopsis of what I had read and then he would make a brief comment about it. Then he would say, *"Okay, anybody else?"* Everybody would avoid eye contact with him. It became a joke, because I was about the only one reporting. I was on a dissertation committee at a local university so I was expected to remain abreast of research, so the reading expectation was not a problem for me; and frankly should not have been a problem for any of the cabinet members. It was not an unreasonable expectation. Eventually when he asked, *"Okay, who read something?"* everybody looked at me. It became a source of irritation to the CEO when I was the only one volunteering to report. One week he said everybody had to give a book report the next week and he said to me, *"And you keep your mouth shut; you're just showing off."* He really thought I was reporting just to irritate him. At the next cabinet meeting no one reported, not even his favorite sycophants. After an uncomfortably long period of silence he said to me in an attitude of capitulation, *"Okay, tell us what you read."* After a few more months, he abandoned this routine. It was curious that he did not reprimand or require reports from each cabinet member, but I realized that his top staff members, the ones that he brought with him to the organization were not reporting either. I think he recognized that their passive-aggressive behavior was tough to overcome. What he failed to recognize was that his leadership style, his philosophy about cabinet meetings and his demeanor did not invite or encourage respect at any level, which prevented his cabinet from being fully engaged in any conversation for fear of his reactions. Nor did he ever show any indication that he knew the purpose of cabinet meetings and how those meetings could be a productive use of time. Additionally, his cabinet meetings were seldom absent some intrigue. At one time, he was convinced that someone on his cabinet was telling the governing board everything that was discussed during cabinet meetings. He said repeatedly to the cabinet, *"I have to trust you people that what we talk about in here remains in here. I can't have you talking to the board members."* He claimed that governing board members would call him the same day of the cabinet meetings or shortly thereafter and ask him about something that was said or discussed during the cabinet meeting. Understandably, this upset him and it was clearly inappropriate for a cabinet member to call a governing board member and equally it was inappropriate behavior for a governing board member to get involved in those topics. Consequently, he repeatedly yelled at the entire cabinet about it. It was never clear if governing board members were actually being told about cabinet meetings or if that was paranoia of the CEO.

A non-profit agency with a national reputation had a dynamic CEO who was always off saving the world and providing virtually no leadership within the organization. He delegated almost all leadership responsibility to the organization's vice president. The vice president was later described as a charming, skillful, and intelligent Machiavellian who did not respect anyone on the executive team, because of his narcissistic belief that the organization centered on him and no one could compete with his leadership prowess. The CEO started each cabinet meeting with a review of his most recent travels and his impression of how the organization was thriving under his leadership. He said it was important for the team to know about the rich, famous and/or influential people he was hanging around with, for the benefit of the organization. He seldom asked for reports from cabinet members about the successes or problems within the organization. In fact, he normally left the cabinet meetings after he recounted his travels in grand details. Consequently, he missed much of the important information that had direct impact on the organization. There was no doubt he was good at raising money for the organization, or so it seemed, but he was not attuned to the daily operations of the organization. During a critical time for the organization a cabinet member, the finance director, said he needed the CEO and the cabinet to see the trajectory of the budget and the services provided to clients, because he had some concerns. The CEO was not at the cabinet meeting and in his typical fashion the vice president dominated the conversation during the meeting, talking about everything that was not important to the internal operations of the organization. Toward the end of the cabinet meeting, the vice president turned to the finance director who had concerns about the direction of the budget and services and said, *"Nathan here has some issues with the rest of you guys. He claims that you're not pulling your weight, so revenues are down and our services to clients are diminishing."* He did not give time for a discussion; he did not allow the finance director to give a report on the circumstances, and he embarrassed him so that he would not bring the subject up again, which he did not. The organization's decline was somewhat insidious over several months, but then it became clear that they were in serious financial trouble. When the organization's CEO realized what was going on, he immediately fired the vice president and realigned his leadership team. The once promising vice president was out of the organization and the traditionally excellent community service-based organization would struggle to regain its stature in the community, because services were reduced due to declining donations. An effectively run cabinet and the presence of the CEO during cabinet meetings could have prevented the organization's decline.

Cabinet meetings are critically important and to a large extent can determine how an organization operates. However, when governing board members, community members, or executive search firms are asked to develop questions for prospective leaders they seldom include questions about the role of the cabinet in the mission and goals of the organization. How leaders utilize the cabinet varies, depending on the style of the leader and the needs of the organization. But many successful leaders try to build a collaborative cabinet team, and in doing so the cabinet meetings become an open dialogue that benefits the organization. In her book, *Tough Choices*, Carly Florina describes this style: "*Collaboration requires more consultation and agreement among peers. It requires acceptance of accountability while sharing resources. It means trusting others to their job while knowing that others must trust you to do the same.*" The challenge, however, is that it can be difficult for a leader to develop a cabinet; it is a real skill and a rare skill. Jon R. Katzenbach, author of *Teams at the Top*, wrote, "*With a culture of individual accountability and self-reliance pervading executive suites, few senior executive groups even function as real teams.*"

One of the best resources for understanding dysfunctional executive leadership and team building comes from Patrick Lencioni's book, *The Five Dysfunctions of a Team: A Leadership Fable*. There are lessons from the book that are important for any leader or governing board to understand. The first dysfunction is the *absence of trust*. Experts such as Stephen Covey emphasize the strong link between trust, respect and effective and efficient leadership. Lencioni describes *lack of trust and respect* as an unwillingness to be vulnerable within the executive leadership group, such as a cabinet. The leader has to address this by making the cabinet meeting environment safe for everyone to make comments and safe for members of the cabinet to be wrong. Members of the cabinet must not be made to feel that being wrong is unforgiveable. The second dysfunction is the *fear of conflict*. Constructive conflict is essential for teamwork; that is how problems are resolved and worked out; that is how the best ideas emerge; and that is how potentially disastrous decisions are halted. The third dysfunction is *lack of commitment*. The cabinet members need to know that their opinions matter; that they will be heard and taken seriously. An ineffective leader wants his cabinet to have only opinions that mimic and support his. Without feeling their opinions are at least listened to, the cabinet will not make comments and will not be fully committed; they will not work their hardest to ensure positive results. The fourth dysfunction is *avoidance of accountability*. The ineffective leader will hold all cabinet members accountable, but only when things do not go well; and the leader takes credit when things go well. Sometimes this is played out during cabinet meetings, where the leader embarrasses certain members of the cabinet if not the entire cabinet when something does not go right, without acknowledging his own decision making role. It is essential for all members of the cabinet to be accountable and for each member of the team to hold each other accountable. Otherwise, the cabinet members will not speak up even when they see that another member is not working in an effective manner or is being a detriment to the organization. The fifth dysfunction is *inattention to results*. This is when the leader allows members of the cabinet to let their desire for status, personal achievement and recognition, and their ego circumvent what is best for the organization. John Wooden, the legendary college basketball coach and leadership expert, wrote, *"It's the little details that are vital. Little things make big things happen. Every success is team-dependent, not individually driven."*

Antidote

When reviewing applicants for leadership positions, governing boards should consider many qualities that the perspective leader must possess in order to be selected. That is obvious. What is not so obvious is the importance of teambuilding. The list of qualities must include an exploration of how the prospective leader builds teams and how he utilizes and manages the leadership team. In a study by Marie McIntyre, *Building An Effective Management Team,* she studied more than 500 members of 72 management groups in both business and government. The teams were surveyed using the Team Effectiveness Assessment for Management instrument. Teams rated in the top 25 percent on team effectiveness measures were compared with teams rated in the bottom 25 percent on team effectiveness. The study found five success factors differentiated the most successful teams from unsuccessful ones:

1. *To focus activity and effort, management teams need a clear understanding of their purpose and the goals they intend to accomplish.*
2. *To make informed decisions, management teams must access critical information from both inside and outside the organization.*
3. *To cooperate in achieving team goals, management team members must be able to develop positive, supportive relationships.*
4. *To make good decisions, management teams must effectively process the information available to them – the research found that the leader of a management team has more influence over this aspect of team effectiveness than any other.*

5.   *To accomplish results, management teams must make the transition from discussion to action. A brilliant decision that is implemented poorly will be of no benefit to the organization.*

These factors can be put into practice by an effective leader and by governing boards. McIntyre said, *"Trust is knowing that when a team member does push you, they're doing it because they care about the team."* The degree of respect required to reach levels of effectiveness that benefits the organization is almost completely determined by the leader's ability and willingness to build an effective team and structure cabinet meetings in such a way to maximize the potential for dynamic discussions and effective decision making.

Leaders that do not know how to build an effective team or how to manage what could be an effective cabinet are poison to an organization. Leaders who understand and acknowledge this and are willing to look to team building experts to learn more about the dynamic possibilities of team building and effective cabinet meetings should consider the following resources: John Maxwell *(The 17 Indisputable Laws of Teamwork: Embrace Them and Empower Your Team)*; Patrick Lencioni *(Five Dysfunctions of a Team)*; Arbinger Institute *(The Anatomy of Peace)*; Spencer Kagan *(Cooperative Learning)*; John Newstrom *(The Big Book of Team Building Games: Trust-Building Activities, Team Spirit Exercises, and Other Activities)*; Price Pritchett *(The Team Member Handbook for Teamwork)*; and Thomas Kayser *(Building Team Power: How to Unleash the Collaborative Genius of Teams for Increased Engagement, Productivity, and Results)*.

If a leader has an epiphany and wants ideas on how to quickly start positive team building, with the understanding that long-term strategies will come from the team, Bradley Sugars' book, *Instant Team Building,* is a good way to kick-start the effort to build an effective team and manage cabinet meetings.

CHAPTER 10

SQUEEZE THE LEMON: A STORY OF LEADERSHIP, TRANSITION AND COLLAPSE

All my life, I always wanted to be somebody. Now I see that I should have been more specific.

—*Jane Wagner*

Poison: *A new leader in an organization comes in with high expectations and the governing board has even higher expectations. There are a number of issues many of which relate to communications that can make the transition to new leadership successful or a failure. The failure of a governing board to prepare the new leader and the existing staff for change that comes with new leadership threatens the success of the transition. The breakdown in communication and a disconnection between expectations and outcomes poisons the work environment. Consequently, the entire organization suffers and the new leader's tenure could be short lived.*

The person selected as the next CEO of the organization was an insider, who had worked for years in the same organization. He was a smooth, friendly, smart, and talented person who had worked at various levels of administration. For his chief of staff he selected a smart, intuitive career administrator with a good heart and a sharp mind. His second appointment was a friend that he put him in charge of a multi-million dollar building program with no experience with that type of work. He had been an excellent mid-level manager and was bright, but he did not know anything about the multi-million dollar construction business. Consequently, the organization later became embroiled in litigation with a contracted construction oversight company that at last count had cost the organization millions of dollars just in legal fees over construction project overruns and late project completions.

The CEO made other appointments and one day thereafter called me to serve in an administrative role. When I was asked to move to a higher level in the organization, I was very content with the job I had at the time and I could have probably continued in that position for several more years, but to be named to a top level position appealed to my pride and I had the illusion or delusion that maybe I could make a difference. When the call did come, the CEO was very gracious and charming. I accepted the position and moved to a different level of responsibility, power, prestige, and political intrigue and chaos. During his first year in the job, the CEO liked to quote Jack Welch, the legendary CEO of General Electric and author of *Winning*. In speech after speech, the CEO read what Welch wrote: *"Look, anyone can manage for the short-term just keep squeezing the lemon. And anyone can manage for the long-term just keep dreaming. You were made leader because someone believed you could squeeze the lemon and dream at the same time."*

The new CEO saw himself as savior and champion who could squeeze the lemon and dream at the same time. Actually, it was more like squeezing a fuzzy lemon and scheming at the same time. Leaders have to have courage to make difficult decisions, as does any governing board member. And being the leader of an organization is a very difficult job. That is why it is difficult to understand why a leader would want to create situations that make his job even more difficult, and why a leader would ignore the advice of this staff, at least until the staff is eventually filled with sycophants. The CEO, who some took to calling "Lemon" because of his constant reference to the squeezing the lemon quote, needed to stabilize an organization that had suffered through two and half years of turmoil under the previous dictatorial CEO and before him several years of status quo slippage under a laissez-faire CEO. Additionally, the budget needed a long-term strategy because economic hard-times were clearly marching toward the organization and community. Also, the reorganization started under the previous CEO needed to be retooled. The central office staff had been wisely reduced under the previous administration and more reorganization needed to take place. Reorganization was necessary to protect essential functions and resources, but even with a reduced staff it could be done. Additionally, the facility construction funding account and mechanism that funded new construction and renovation of old facilities was being poorly run and wasting thousands if not millions of dollars, so it obviously needed immediate attention. If confidence was lost in the use of the funds, the source of the support for generating such funds would shrink or be lost.

At the same time the governing board continued to meddle in the organization's operations and the needs of the clients continued to shift and change rapidly. Businesses were moving out, immigrants and refugees were moving in, pockets of poverty and high need were growing in checkerboard fashion all over the service area. A performance malaise had taken hold during the leadership vacuum caused by the fighting between the previous dictatorial CEO and the governing board. There was a lot of work to be done and the governing board thought the new CEO could succeed where the previous CEO had failed. There were many other organizational needs, but the one thing that the organization needed more than anything was leadership stabilization, thoughtful long-term strategic planning, and the restoration of trust, respect, and pride.

Instead, what they got was more construction controversy, a poorly organized strategic plan and consolidation plan, a larger central office staff, wasteful spending, a budget crisis, a negative style of leadership, lost opportunities, negative news stories, and finally scandal and corruption. After a short period of time under the CEO's leadership, organizational morale was so negative that it became a debilitating factor in organizational performance. The vast majority of people working in such organizations are good people who are genuinely interested in what is best for their clients. Poor decisions are made, of course, in any organization, but often those come out of a lack of information or the unpredictable nature of life and unforeseen circumstances. There are, however, decisions that are made because of either arrogance or ignorance from the leadership position, and sometimes it is difficult to tell the difference.

One of the tasks I inherited was putting the names to the organizational chart created by the new CEO. I just happened to have the software that made that task easy, so by default the task of updating the organizational chart fell to me. During his first three years as CEO, there were 40 different versions of the organizational chart and the number of staff members added to his central office eventually grew to the point that it required several legal size papers and small print to fit everyone onto the organizational chart. The previous CEO had reduced the central office staff from 28 to 19 staff members, representing an annual savings of well over $1 million. During his transition as leader the new CEO added all of the positions back with different titles, of course, and then created more positions until finally the central office staff grew from 19 to 35, which added almost $2 million to the annual costs to operate the organization. This occurred despite the fact that revenue for operations continued to decline due to serious economic conditions and despite the dire warnings by the chief financial officer of deteriorating future economic conditions. To make matters even worse, he seemed oblivious to growing organizational morale issues, and his condescending attitude did not help.

In an article about leadership transition by Antoinette LaBelle, *Transition to New Leadership*, she reported on a survey of 630 nonprofit leaders throughout the United States that focused on transitioning to a new leadership position. LaBelle states, "*A new hire at the top of the organization signals to the world that everything is up for grabs – all options for change are on the table. Prior research on leaders and change tells us that new hires feel a need to make an immediate impact – to both establish credibility and legitimize their hiring…it is of interest that few leaders in our study underwent a formal orientation or on-board programs.*" According to LaBelle, many if not most new leaders are not prepared to understand how change in leadership will blend with existing conditions of the organization. Also, the leadership team is not prepared for the change brought by new leadership – how to adjust to the change while continuing to run the organization; and seldom has a governing board done anything to prepare the new leader or the existing staff for the transition. Thus, there is the potential for a complete breakdown in communications and the possibility that the new leader will not listen to the advice of staff members. This is especially critical during the first few months of a new leader's tenure.

Michael Watkins, author of *The First 90 Days*, states, "*The actions you take during your first three months in a new job at the top will largely determine whether you succeed or fail. Transitions are periods of opportunity, a chance to start afresh and to make needed changes in an organization. But they are also periods of acute vulnerability, because you lack established working relationships and detailed understanding of your role.*" John Maxwell, author of *Everyone Communicates Few Connect*, believes that people and especially leaders must *connect* and not just *communicate*. In fact, he states that a leader, especially a new leader, is communicating at all times, whether he intends to or not. Virtually everything a leader says or does or does not do communicates something. Maxwell opines that new leaders must connect to increase their influence in every situation; connecting is related to learning about others; connecting goes beyond words; connecting requires a great deal of energy; and connecting is more skill than natural talent.

As referenced in *Everyone Communicates Few Connect*, the article *To Achieve or Not: The Manager's Choice* by Jay Hall created a communication and success rubric for new leaders:

> **High Achievers** care about people as well as success.
> **Average Achievers** concentrate on production.
> **Low Achievers** are preoccupied with their own security.

High Achievers *view subordinates optimistically.*
Average Achievers *focus more on their own status.*
Low Achievers *show a basic distrust of subordinates.*

High Achievers *seek advice from subordinates and others.*
Average Achievers *are reluctant to seek advice from subordinates.*
Low Achievers *don't seek advice.*

High Achievers *listen well to others.*
Average Achievers *listen only to supervisors and rely on self, policy and organization manuals.*
Low Achievers *avoid communication.*

Perhaps this explains in part the findings of research by the Alexcel Group and the Institute of Executive Development. They found that 68 percent of failed new leaders lacked interpersonal and leadership skills; 45 percent lacked personal skills; and 41 percent failed due to goal conflicts between the leader and the organization. In other words, what we have is a *"failure to communicate."* Cindy Kraft summarized the study with the following findings:

Global leader turnover is approximately 15 percent according to a 2007 study by Booz Allen, a decade–high number. Other studies suggest 40 percent of new leaders fail within the first 18 months. And Aon Consulting reports a 50 percent chance an executive will quit or be fired within his first three years. Ninety two percent (92 percent) of respondents said it takes 90+ days to reach productivity and 62 percent said over six months. And even after making it through the first 90 days and the first 180 days, a significant percentage of executive hires are gone within two years. While not as long as with external hires, 72 percent of respondents said internal executives need more than the first 90 days to get up to speed, and 25 percent said over six months were needed. Thirty percent of external hires fail to meet expectations in two years and the failure rate of internal senior executive transitions is 20 percent, representing millions of dollars in losses at the executive level.

The public would not appreciate a circumstance where a chief financial officer is telling the CEO to look at ways to cut spending so that the coming financial turbulence will not bankrupt the organization only to have the CEO ignore the advice and continue to add central office positions. What would clients think if they knew that an organization's own attorney warned the CEO about a conflict of interest involving a staff member and he ignored that, too, only to have that staff member later investigated by the organization's attorney because of a conflict of interest that may have costs the organization hundreds of thousands if not millions of dollars? How would the public react to a non-profit agency that serves the mental health needs of the community but the governing board shifts money from transporting underserved citizens to its own travel budget? What would the reaction be if a financially strapped business spent over $100,000 on staff development activities? Those situations actually happened and were the result of transition to weak or self-centered leadership.

Antidote

The transition to new leadership can be an exciting time for the new leader and the organization, if there is a transition plan that is centered on communications, essential management functions, strategic planning, team building, improving morale, and sound decision making. Governing boards should ask the finalists for leadership positions how they plan to make the transition, including how they plan to communicate (or connect) with the staff in the organization, how they will handle staffing decisions and appointments, and how they will communicate with the governing board. Governing boards should tell the finalists about the challenges facing the organizations; only an honest assessment of the organization will prepare the potential leader to address those issues that need the most attention quickest. However, the governing board cannot be divided in its assessment of the organization, where one governing board member tells one thing while undermining the opinion of other governing board members. A review or assessment of the finalists' communication skills and communication plans may help determine if the finalists have what it will take to make the transition successful. John Maxwell wrote, "*It's difficult to find common ground with others when the only person you're focused on is yourself.*" Michael Myatt states, "*The moral of the story is leaders need to be honest, have a demonstrated track record of success, be excellent communicators, place an emphasis on serving those they lead, be fluid in approach, be focused, and have a bias for action. If these traits are not possessed by your leader and leadership team, you will be in for a rocky road ahead.*"

The advice of Maxwell and Myatt stands strong for leaders who also must improve staff morale, one of the most overlooked aspects of new leadership. Louis Gerstner, Jr. was keenly sensitive to the morale of his IBM employees when he took over IBM. He came to his new job when the organization was struggling in many ways, but addressing morale was one of his first priorities and thus improving morale became one of his most urgent strategies. He said this to the organization: "*It is not helpful to feel sorry for ourselves. I'm sure our employees don't need any rah-rah speeches. We need leadership at all levels and a sense of direction and momentum, not just from me but from all of us. I don't want to see a lot of prophets of doom around here. I want can-do people looking for excitement.*" Gerstner went on to say that the organization did not have time to focus on who created the problems, "*We have little time to spend on problem definition. We must focus our efforts on communications, solutions and actions.*"

Rosabeth Moss Kanter said that leaders, especially new leaders, must energize depressed employees, passive teams or sluggish organizations, and she offered guiding principles to accomplish that.

1. *Believe in people and their power to make a difference.* Show them they are worth it by investing in things that matter to them, and show sincerity by taking the time to find out want matters to employees.

2. *Direct the energy tied up in negativity (resentment, rivalry, or disrespect) into positive actions.* If people seem petty, make them noble by focusing them on a bigger cause and giving them a chance to contribute to it. Negativity inevitably leads to rampant rumors and spreading dissatisfaction which compromises the effectiveness of the leader and organization outcomes.

3. *Make initiative possible and desirable.* Awaken creative thinking by opening real opportunities to contribute new ideas. Seek them, find them, fund them, praise them, and provide a support system. It is also critically important to provide feedback to employees about their work and ideas.

4. *Start with small wins – things that people can control.* Look for even small successes, good ideas, and other things that can be praised. While this is important, it must also be sincere, because false praise of mediocrity can portray the new leader as naïve or worse.

When governing boards are interviewing candidates for the leadership position, they should conclude by asking the candidates this question suggested by Marcus Buckingham: "*What is the difference between chess and checkers?*" Most prospective leaders will respond that chess is more difficult and requires more strategic thinking. While that is true, the most insightful answer is this: the pieces in checkers move in only two directions while the pieces in chess move in multiple directions. As Buckingham said, "*Thus, if you want to excel at the game of chess you have to learn how each piece moves and then incorporate these unique moves into your overall plan.*

The same is true for the game of leading. Mediocre new leaders play checkers with their people. They assume that their employees will be motivated by the same things and driven by the same goals." The effective new leader understands the dynamic fact that employees are different and cannot be managed like pieces on a checker board.

In his book, *The New Boss: How to Survive the First 100 Days*, Peter Fischer states that new leaders that are successful *"recognize and develop key relationships, deal adroitly with hidden rivals and predecessors, build networks in the organization, show that they are team oriented, communicate with senior management on strategy and style of leadership and impart confidence and trust."*

CHAPTER 11

RUMORS RULE

Life is simple; it's just not easy.

—Anonymous

Poison: The decision making process has been reviewed ad nauseam by researcher for decades, particularly in reference to how leaders make effective decisions and under what circumstances. Arrogance and rumor are impediments to effective decision making. These two elements separately are poison to an organization, but if they both exist an organization's health is seriously compromised. Interestingly, arrogance can actually fuel rumors. Arrogance can impact decisions by distorting the perceptual screen of leaders, so that a leader ignores sound advice, data, and probabilities and instead makes decisions based more on self-preservation and perhaps even in response to rumors. Rumors can be a fast-spreading poison that permeates an organization before the leader can implement damage control, if the CEO is oblivious to the needs of the organization's staff members and governing board to receive information in a timely and consistent manner.

Typically, when a leader loses his humility, hard and difficult times are inevitable. In his book, *What Got You Here Won't Get You There*, Marshall Goldsmith discusses several weaknesses that can doom a leader. Though he listed several weaknesses, Goldsmith says that the root cause of all of the weaknesses are ego issues: the ego that tells the leader that he knows everything and is always right and, therefore, there is no need to learn or grow; the ego that tells the leader that he is better than all others and is especially smarter and wiser than any subordinates or governing board member. The ego tells the leader that any and all rules do not apply to him and that his role is not defined by anyone or any limitations. Alone, however, it is difficult for the leader to sustain this state of ego; therefore, he will occasionally recruit co-ego conspirators to re-inflate his ego and reassure him that his ego and leadership style are healthy while all those around him are either incompetent or are well meaning stooges who need a leader to tell them what to do. Sometimes the sycophants will start well placed rumors to discredit members of the leadership team who do not always agree with the leader. Then the leader can use those rumors to justify his decisions.

Over the years I have seen leaders twisted and shaped by rumors and by sycophants that whisper in their ears about other people for the sole purpose to curry favor. Unfortunately, rumors are a part of any organization; however, some rumors are simply the nature of people while others are part of a deliberate effort to undermine members of a leadership team or even a governing board. In his book, *Manager's Guide to Understanding and Combating Rumors*, Allan Kimmel writes: *"Rumor. Think about this word. Say it out loud. Rumor. It has such ugly connotations, doesn't it? A statement that cannot be proved or disproved. Rumor. Rhymes with tumor."* Kimmel notes that rumors spread quickly, are difficult to manage, and can have a detrimental impact on an organization. The impact of rumors and the motive for rumors vary. Rumors about colleagues can damage reputations. Rumors started by governing board members to discredit a CEO can be devastating and usually poison the work climate for everyone. Rumors about a non-profit organization can impact donations. Rumors about a business can impact sales. Rumors about inappropriate use of funds can have political implications for community CEOs. Rumors that a new learning program in another school district increased test scores can lead a school district to spend money on an untested product. Rumors that a school has mold can result in parents needlessly keeping their children out of school. Rumors that building a school near a power line will cause brain damage can cause a school district to spend more money on more costly property. Rumors that an employee at a non-profit organization has a "history" can cause the organization to reassign him unnecessarily. Rumors that a chief financial officer may have personal financial problems may cause a governing board to press for his removal.

Rumors can create behaviors and reactions that are not based on facts and a well placed rumor can damage reputations and lead to terrible decisions within any organization. Therefore, rumor control is a significant function and responsibility of a leader. Anyone who works in any organization for any length of time will soon learn that rumors and gossip are a regular part of working with people. Yet, very few if any leaders are ever trained on the origins of rumors, the potential harm of rumors or on rumor or gossip control. And seldom are governing boards trained in rumor control. Too often leaders succumb to rumors and gossip, and sometimes fuel them. In his article for *Small Business*, Alex Saez, states that rumors and gossip can hurt an organization's reputation, decrease morale and damage productivity. There is danger for a leader who encourages rumors in the mistaken belief that he will somehow benefit from the rumor, because once rumors start they can rage out of control. Stephen Leigh, author of *Speaking Stones*, said, *"Rumors are like lightning on summer tinder, producing flames that dance in flickering brilliance from person to person, sometimes flaring in great conflagrations of exaggeration."*

One of the biggest mistakes a leader can make is to listen to and start believing rumors. Leaders who are struggling in their role, particularly ones who are under fire from the governing board, are very susceptible to the temptation to believe and encourage certain rumors. It is a very dangerous game. Over time a leader that listens to and starts believing rumors will eventually become a source of rumors and eventually the target of rumors. The tragedy is that some good ideas, strategies and programs are sacrificed at the altar of rumors. It is a fact that leaders in every organization will have to at some time address issues related to rumors, but they must understand that they may be intentionally or unintentionally feeding rumors.

There are many definitions of rumors, but the definition used in this context is the one most commonly used in sociological research of rumors: an account or explanation of events, persons, places or things circulating from person to person that are not based on fact or accuracy. The worst rumors are those that seem valid, based on either the messenger or the content. These types of rumors often spread very quickly and are therefore difficult for a leader to manage or respond to in an effective manner.

According to research by Susan Pendleton, *Rumor Research Revisited and Expanded*, rumors originate primary due to one of three circumstances. The first is *wish fulfillment rumors* that reflect what people want to happen – what they want to hear. For example, staff members may be under the leadership of a tyrannical boss who rules by intimidation and fear. A staff member mentions to another staff member that he wishes the boss would find another job. In the course of this conversation the evolution of a rumor begins with a statement that the boss is *"most likely"* looking for another job and that *"most likely"* to the next person changes to the boss is *"probably"* looking to move. It then becomes shortened during a brief conversation to, *"Have you heard that the boss is looking for another job?" "Well, no, I haven't heard that; where is he going?" "I don't know, but wouldn't you think it would be another state since no one likes him around here?" "Yea, it's probably another state."* And the rumor spreads. Sometime later the leader gets a phone call from a governing board member, asking, *"Why are you looking for another job and why didn't you tell us?"* The leader is completely puzzled, but the stammering denial only fuels the governing board member's suspicion. Before the leader can contemplate how such a rumor was started, the rumor has spread to all parts of the organization;

thus, disrupting the operations of the organization.

The second type of rumor Pendleton describes is the *bogie man or fear rumors* that reflect feared outcomes, either motivated by a need to prepare for the worse or portray the situation as helpless or hopeless. There are situations where a leader started a rumor in a misplaced attempt to manage expectations. Sometimes these types of rumors accompany bad news or a negative event, making the situation worse. As an example, the CEO of a non-profit organization looked at budget challenges and determined that the budget would have to be scaled down, so he announced this to the staff members. He simply said that the budget for each department will need to be reduced. The CEO said nothing about layoffs or furlough days (unpaid days off). Yet, a department head called a meeting to relay the CEO's message about being frugal, and added, *"I hope this doesn't mean layoffs in the future."* Afterwards, the rumor started that the organization was in such serious financial trouble that layoffs might be considered. As rumors circulate, they tend to become more succinct and incorrect, so this rumor became, *"We're going to have layoffs."* But that is not where it ended. It's only natural to ask, *"When we will have layoffs?"* This rumor had energy and substance to move rapidly across the organization in this form: *"We're in such bad shape it's only a matter of time before they start laying off employees."* The rumor may have seemed innocuous, but rumors like this can spread quickly and have the emotional force to take staff members' concentration away from their jobs. The CEO, upon hearing the rumor, tried to reassure staff members that layoffs were not part of the solution, *"yet."* He did not intend to add the word *"yet"* at the end of his statement, but he did because he did not want to limit that option in the future if that decision had to be made. Therefore, all of his efforts to stem the rumor were compromised. Leaders need to remember that any effort to control or counteract a rumor must be carefully planned and executed. A wrong word in the wrong place at the wrong time can change an interpretation of the meaning of the message, to make it worse or spin it off into another series of rumors.

The third type of rumor, according to Pendleton, is the *malicious intent rumor*. Divisive rumors are often by design, so that a staff member can, for example, cut off competition for a promotion or drive a wedge between and among staff members in order to manipulate social messaging and workplace interaction, perhaps to one's advantage at the expense of another employee. An employee, for example, determines that another employee is his competition for any future promotion in the organization. Consequently, the manipulative employee, Zach, asks a staff member if he has heard anything about another employee, Joe, suggesting that he was unhappy and might consider giving up his job to go back to college. Of course, the rumor starts and Joe initially is oblivious to the rumor. One day someone asks Joe if it was really true that he was leaving the organization to go back to school. Joe, quick to dismiss the rumor without being cautious of his words says, *"No, I have to work, even though I would like to go back to college and finish my MBA."* Joe has just inadvertently confirmed the contents of the rumor by acknowledging in an off-hand manner that he would like to go back to college. That innocent spark is all that is needed to spread the rumor throughout the organization that Joe is leaving to go back to college. Joe, consequently, moves to quell the rumor but fragments of the rumor remain for months and even enter into internal discussions about whether or not Joe should be considered for a promotion.

Malicious rumors are used by organizations in competition with other organizations. Some organizations seem to use rumors as standard operating procedures with competitors. Two organizations, for example, in competition for the same grant may be dependent on receiving the grant to maintain prestige and/or programs. One of the organizations resorts to rumors about fiscal mismanagement of the other organization to scare off the grantors. More often this is found in businesses. One of the earlier, widespread examples was when a competitor started a rumor in the mid-1970s that McDonald's hamburgers were made with worm meat, in order to save money. What appeared at first to be a silly rumor found traction and negatively affected sales in Atlanta, Georgia stores. In fact, McDonald's held a press conference with a regional United States Department of Agriculture officer present to assure the public that the rumors were *"unfounded"* and *"unsubstantiated"*. In 1989, over seven million people heard a rumor that Coca Cola contained carcinogens; a rumor that was rumored to have been started by a Coca Cola competitor.

According to many studies, rumors arise in situations that are ambiguous or threatening in some way. Ambiguous situations in organizations include primarily leadership issues, either from the organization's leader or from the governing board. Based on research by E.K. Fiske, *Research on Gossip: Taxonomy, Methods and Future Directions*, it is only natural for people to react to unsettled or unsettling situations by a core need to understand and to act in some manner when a situation is chaotic, unorganized, or rifled with a lack of trust, particularly when the leader of an organization is ineffective. He further noted that as rumors spread, the information in the rumor is truncated so the message becomes more precise and therefore spreads more rapidly across the organization and to more employees. According to Fiske, *"About 70 percent of details in a rumor are lost in the first five to six person-to-person (verbal to verbal) transmissions."* He cited research of William Stern who set up experiments on the chain of rumors and chain of subjects. Stern found that the rumor was shortened and changed significantly by the time it reached the end of the line of people. Gordon Allport, a student of Stern, discovered that negative rumors were much more likely to be disseminated to others than positive rumors; concluding that it is only human nature to more quickly pass along a negative rumor than it is a positive rumor. In their book, *Switch: How to Change Things When Change is Hard,* Dan and Chip Heath note a study that found people are much more likely to share and remember negative information, pictures, and images than positive ones.

Leaders of organizations must understand the dynamic nature of rumors and become more familiar with this dynamic phenomenon, instead of dismissing rumors as a paltry nuance that should be ignored. The belief that rumors are inevitable and will eventually go away is misdirected. This is a naïve and risky attitude toward rumors.

Prashant Borida and Nicholas DiFonzo's article *Problem Solving in Social Interactions on the Internet: Rumor as Social Cognition* described rumor transmission as a *"collective explanation process."* This is a means of explaining why dysfunctional organizations are rift with rumors, because within a vacuum created when leadership has drifted away from the organization's vision, mission, objectives and initiatives staff members create and find their own explanation process. Rumors fill the communications and leadership vacuum. Additionally, rumors can become such a controlling factor in a leadership vacuum that it will be difficult for a leader or governing board to manage them or counter them. Rumors are more likely to arise in circumstances where there is lack of formal communications or reliable communications, because the need for information is not being met during times of uncertainty. Leaders can make this worse by focusing on the wrong things during times of change. When the communication of change and the purposes and goals of change are not shared with staff members that are hungry for information and a modicum of assurance rumors will increase.

The new CEO of a small foundation roared into his new job with change on his mind. During every meeting with staff members and executive staff, the new CEO reminded them that he was hired to make changes in the organization, but when he was asked about the changes he had in mind he demurred. He refused to offer any indication of what the changes might include and who they might affect. He once told his executive team, *"I'll tell you what you need to know when I decide that you need to know it."* People cannot function in that type of work environment by quietly going about their work; it's not normal human behavior to act as if everything is the same when the threat of change is being tossed around recklessly by an organization's CEO. So, there was fertile ground for dissent and therefore rumors. A rumor started that the new CEO was going to dismiss many staff members, so out of fear some staff members started slipping anonymous notes to the new CEO disparaging other staff members. Competent staff members started looking for other jobs. At first it was limited to just two people, each being afraid to lose their salary and job standing, who started malicious rumors of deception and deceit that led to accusations each and the other were trying to undermine the new CEO. The CEO was in a difficult situation, though most of it was due to his lack of control, because he soon realized that he really needed both talented staff members. But what was he to do about the rumors? Were they true, fully or partially? How accurate were the rumors that two of his top staff members were at each other throats? The CEO was faced with a situation where, being new on the job, he had to sort out the facts from rumor while trying to acclimate to his new job. Wisely, he called upon his former mentor for advice. The mentor listened patiently while the CEO discussed the dilemma about the rumors and how he was perplexed because he did not know if the rumors were true about his two top assistants. His mentor listened very carefully but offered no comment. The CEO became very frustrated with his mentor's silence. Finally, he said, *"Well, what should I do?"* The mentor walked around the CEO's office with his hands folded behind back in a thoughtful pose. Then the mentor stopped abruptly and said, *"In ancient Greece, Socrates was considered the wisest of his wise peers. One day Socrates was called upon suddenly by a friend who ran up to him excitedly and said, 'Socrates, my teacher, do you know what I just heard about one of your students?' 'Wait a minute,' Socrates replied. 'Before you tell me about the rumor I'd like you to pass a little test. It's called the Triple Filter Test.' Socrates continued despite an impatient and puzzled look from the messenger, and said, 'That's right; it's called the Triple Filter Test, and before you talk to me about my student let's take a moment to filter what you're going to tell me. First, have you made absolutely sure that what you are about to tell me is true?' 'No,' the man said. 'Actually I just heard about it and...' 'All right,' said Socrates. 'So you don't really know if it's true or not. Now let's try the second filter. Is what you are about to tell me about my student something good?' 'Well, no,' the man said, 'on the contrary....' 'So,' Socrates said, 'you want to tell me something bad about him, even though you're not certain it's true?' The man shrugged his shoulders. Socrates continued, 'You may still pass the test because there is a third filter – the filter of usefulness. Is what you want to tell me about my student going to be useful to me?' The man said, 'Ah, not really, no.' 'Well,' Socrates concluded, 'if what you want to tell me is not true, good or useful why tell me at all?'*

The CEO seemed puzzled and said to his mentor that he did not understand the relevance of that story and his own situation because he was hearing the rumors from more than one person. The mentor said simply, *"Why do you listen to the rumors and why would you react to the rumors? You don't know if they are true; you know they are negative; and how are they useful to you? Be the leader; look at what you're doing that fosters an atmosphere that is ripe for rumors. How much of this are you responsible for?"* Then the mentor moved closer to the CEO and asked, *"And have you spread the rumors, too?"* Taken aback, the CEO first said he had not, but the mentor suspected differently, so, he pressed him. Finally, the CEO said to his mentor, *"Well, yes, I did share the rumors with a couple of governing board members, but only because I wasn't sure what to make of the rumors. Don't worry, I'll go back to those board members and tell them what I heard was probably not true."* The mentor said, "Read the *Parable of the Feathers."* The CEO asked about the parable, but the mentor told him to find it on his own. They parted ways and the CEO went back to work. He tried to concentrate on his work, but the *Parable of the Feathers* haunted him, so finally he pushed his work aside and searched for the parable. This is what he found.

Once upon a time a man went to the town monk. *"Monk,"* he confessed, *"I have been slandering you to my neighbors. I have thought about it and I regret doing it. I am truly sorry for what I've said and how I've treated you and talked about you behind your back, spreading rumors. I take back all the bad I have said. How may I find penance?"* The monk nods then sagely offers these instructions: *"Go pluck 3 chickens. Stuff a bag with the feathers, then place one feather on every doorstep where you have slandered me. Return to me when you complete your task."* Scurrying away, the villager meticulously complies. He returned to the monk the next day. *"Monk,"* he said, *"I have completed your instruction. What should I do now?"* *"Now,"* said the monk, *"go collect every feather that you placed on the doorsteps."* *"But, but,"* splutters the villager, *"that's impossible; it has been an entire night and the wind has blown the feathers in all directions."* The monk nods in agreement, turns, and walks away. The CEO leans back in his chair and feels the pain of guilt and remorse. He instantly understood why his mentor told him to read the parable– one cannot so easily take back the harmful words of rumors. He made a decision that he later said probably saved his career. In fact, he said he grew as a person and a leader that day, because he took a different and honest view of himself. He did not like what he saw. The CEO called each of the top executives in and told them about the rumors he had heard, but he focused primarily on their skills and how much he will depend on them in their respective leadership roles. He admitted that the rumors distracted him and even troubled him until he realized that he was part of the problem; his failure to communicate and interact with his staff had created conditions for rumors. He said the organization will only survive and thrive if they all work together. Thereafter, as a team they worked on an organizational plan and vision and shared that with all staff members and the governing board the same week it was concluded. The organization's plan was implemented successfully and the organization grew steadily for several years. The CEO became a mentor to both top executives. One of them became a successful CEO in another organization and the other top executive is in line to succeed the current CEO. The CEO is now grooming him to take his place, and he has already told his successor the *Parable of the Feather* and about Socrates' Three Filters.

Antidote

Arrogance and rumors poison organizations. David Hume wrote, *"When men are most sure and arrogant they are commonly most mistaken, giving views to passion without that proper deliberation which alone can secure them from the grossest absurdities."* The research on arrogance indicates clearly that arrogant leaders are seldom effective over time, and the research on rumors, which indicates that a leader's effectiveness can be hampered by rumors, have not been convoked. The outcomes from an arrogant style of leadership include the vacuum of effectiveness that is going to be filled by something, and rumors too often fill the void. The combination of arrogance and the lack of communications create the conditions for a negative work climate. Arrogance makes a debilitating impact on trust and respect, and the lack of thereof is at the core of an organization that suffers from unrelenting rumors. Rumors fill a trust and respect void caused by leaders that do not communicate effectively with staff members because they do not think staff members are worthy of the time it takes the leader to communicate or the leader lacks effective communication skills. Rumors fill a respect void caused when leaders do not understand and do not make any effort to understand the needs of staff members. In *The Trust Factor*, written by Bob Whipple, an expert on leadership, he states, *"Trust and rumors are incompatible. If there is low trust, it is easy for someone to project something negative for the future. When trust is low, these sparks create a roaring blaze....of rumors."* There are times when a leader has to address rumors, regardless of whether he wants to or not, and then there are times when a leader inherits a work climate that is rife with rumors. Whipple offers possible antidotes for the poison of rumors:

1. *Intervene quickly when there is a rumor and provide solid, believable, truthful information about what is really going to happen or has happened.*

It is best to plan this type of intervention before the rumor even starts, but the main point is that it is essential to nip the problem as soon as it is detected. It is also wise to check with key staff members to make sure the communications information from the leader has actually been received by employees. This is also a key moment for the leader in another regard. He must take the time necessary to make an honest self-assessment. Has he spread rumors and gossip? Has he intentionally or unintentionally encouraged gossip and ignored rumors? Has he quickly quashed some rumors but allowed others to fester?

2.   *Coach the worst offenders to stop.*
Usually it is not difficult to discern the people in a group who like to stir up trouble with rumors. They are easy to spot in the break room, in the hallway, and other places where work does not take place. One interesting way to mitigate a group of gossipers is to get to know them better - sit at the lunch table with them, for example. This may feel uncomfortable at first, but it can be very helpful at detecting rumors early, and it gives the staff the opportunity to talk to the leader, which can quell rumors. Just as in fighting poison, the sooner the antidote can be applied, the easier the problem is to control. If the same employees continue to be the genesis of rumors, a more direct approach to them may be in order to stop the rumor-generating behavior. Those employees must understand that rumors negatively affect the work and integrity of the organization.

3.   *Double communications in times of uncertainty.*
There are times when the genesis of a rumor is easy to predict. Suppose all the top managers have an unusually long, hastily called closed-door meeting. People are going to wonder what is being discussed. Suppose the financial reports indicate that continuing on the present path is impossible - that operational changes will have to be made? What if there are outsiders walking around the organization with tape measures? What if all travel has been cancelled and purchase orders limited? All these things, and numerous others, are bound to fuel speculation on what may be happening, and from that rumors are born. When this happens, smart leaders get out of the office and interface more with the staff. Unfortunately, when there are unusual circumstances, too many leaders like to hide in their offices or in meetings to avoid having to deal with pointed questions. That is exactly the opposite of what is needed to prevent rumors from taking control and poisoning the work environment.

4. *Find multiple ways to communicate the truth.*

   Sometimes people need to hear something more than once to start believing it. According to the *Edelman Trust Barometer for 2011*, nearly 60 percent of people indicate they need to hear organizational news (good or bad) at least three to five times before they believe it. It is important to utilize all available means of communicating with staff members – small or large group meetings, memorandums, emails, conference calls, webinars, etc. and keep the communications flowing. Rumors can be persistent and resistant to facts.

5. *Reinforce open dialog.*

   Leaders can find themselves in a precarious situation when engaging in dialog with staff members. Leaders should encourage questions to make sure all of the areas fertile for rumors are addressed. One of the most counterproductive reactions to questions and comments is to be defensive or critical of the staff members asking questions. Criticizing and discouraging questions is a quick path to the rumor mill. It is critically important to remember that increasing the trust level is the best way to subdue the rumor agents.

6. *Model a no-gossip climate.*

   People pick up on the tactics of a leader and mimic them throughout the organization. If the leader is prone to intentionally leaking out juicy bits of unsubstantiated speculation, then others in the organization will be encouraged to do the same thing. Conversely, if a leader refuses to discuss or acknowledge information that is incorrect, then he models the kind of attitude that will be picked up by many staff members. The key to modeling a no-gossip work climate is to develop a no-gossip expectation – not necessarily a policy, but an expectation, which can be encouraged and clarified through guidelines for staff members when they hear a rumor. This may include a definition of rumors and advice on how to respond to rumors (e.g., Ask one's immediate supervisor about rumors, gossip or other information that might be misinformation). A good resource is the *Respectful Workplace Guidelines* developed by the Human Resources Division of the University of Virginia.

7. *Extinguish gossip behavior.*

   This may mean breaking up a clique of busy-bodies or at least adding some new objective blood into the mix. It may get to the point that staff members that are consistently and persistently at the center of rumors are too poisonous to continue employment. Rumors are serious. If they continue because of the behavior and attitude of the same staff members each time, those staff members should be referred to the organization's department of human resources.

It is clear that rumors in the workplace can poison the environment, reduce productivity, threaten careers, and create animosity between and among staff members. An important leadership function is to prevent and control rumors, and it is imperative for leaders to identify and correct those elements that make rumors more likely to occur and spread, such as poor or ineffective communications.

CHAPTER 12

CIRCLE OF SYCOPHANTS

When a man is wrapped up in himself, he makes a pretty small package.

—John Ruskin

Poison: Successful organizations are built from the quality of work done by its employees, and the quality of work from competent employees is not possible if a leader hires employees who are more loyal to the leader than to the organization. A leader's failure to select quality employees and instead promote and select sycophants will lead to a poisonous work environment that compromises the organization's mission and progress. Malcolm Forbes said, "Never hire someone who knows less than you do about what he's hired to do."

An essential component of leadership is the leader's ability and willingness to hire good people. In Stephen Covey's book, *The Speed of Trust*, he points out how important it is for a leader to select people he can trust, but he warns about blind trust. Hiring people a leader can trust does not mean hiring relatives, friends, relatives of friends, or staff who will always tell the leader what he or she wants to hear, despite knowing that the truth may save the leader or more importantly may save the organization from future problems. That is not trust, nor is that loyalty. Trust and loyalty come from people who support the leader but who also are honest with the leader and other managers and who have the best interests of the organization in mind. It does not help the organization or its leader if the *"trusted"* support staff will not warn him about poor decisions, inconsistencies, or poor choices.

In Mrunal Belvalkar's article, *Dangers of Misplaced Loyalty*, he asks important questions: *"Have you ever found it difficult to report on someone or report something negative to someone about him? Have you found it difficult to stand up against someone because doing that made you feel like you were betraying your relationship with that person? If the answers are yes to both questions, then yours, my friend, is misplaced loyalty. Misplaced loyalty is when you are loyal to a person…and your loyalty makes you biased so that you are defensive for all the wrong reasons."*

In his book, *The One Thing You Need to Know*, Mark Buckingham warns leaders that the employee selection process is critical to the success of the leader and the organization. It sounds so obvious, but it is not practiced as if it is obvious. Another complicating factor is what a leader said or did or promised on his or her way to the top. Was some deal-making part of the promotion? Did the leader weaken his position from the outset by making promises to take care of someone's friend or relative by selecting them to an important job? What was the role of the governing board? Did the leader make overt or implicit promises to governing board members about hiring certain people to important positions in the organization in return for the leadership job? These types of situations will almost certainly lead to failed leadership and poison the organization from the top down.

In many organizations the human resources department defines the culture of the organization based on hiring practices. Is it the practice to hire relatives, friends, friends of relatives, relatives of friends, college buddies, sons and daughters of vendors, sons and daughters of other organizations, for example? Or does the organization have internal policies prohibiting such practices?

Patronage was rampant in one of the organization where I worked, but it had not always been that way. The sons and daughters of governing board members were hired in a number of positions, some of which were open and some of which were created just for the purpose of patronage and influence. Additionally, many central office staff member's children were hired over more qualified applicants. In one family the husband and wife worked for the same organization as did all three of their children. If a person who is qualified applies for a position, the selection process should be allowed to run its course. When applicants are not given the same opportunities simply because they are not "connected", it becomes poisonous for the work environment. It becomes an even more serious issue when the relative of a governing board member, a CEO or other high ranking staff member does not perform well. To counter this, some organizations have developed a nepotism policy.

In his book, *Winning*, Jack Welch said, *"Nothing matters more in winning than getting the right people on the field. All the clever strategies and advanced technologies in the world are nowhere near as effective without great people to put them to work."* It is very difficult to find the right person for essential jobs in any organization. That is what a good leader knows and works on relentlessly each time a job opens, and that is the message he conveys throughout the organization. Welch says that hiring the right person is so important to an organization that during his successful career he devised three "acid tests" for selecting the right person: integrity, intelligence, and maturity. Integrity is based on telling the truth – taking responsibility for past actions, admitting mistakes, and correcting them. "*They play to win the right way, by the rules.*" Welch's concept of intelligence as a prerequisite for hiring is not in the traditional IQ sense of intelligence, rather it is what a good job candidate possesses that denotes his knowledge of work, of people, of how to make things work, how things work, how to motivate people, how to communicate and how to learn. Welch's third test for selecting a candidate is maturity – not age, but maturity. There are some long-term employees who never mature and yet there are some young candidates for jobs that show ability and skills to handle pressure, stress, and failure and yet know how to enjoy their job and career. The mature person also knows what is appropriate behavior at all times – when to be high task and low relationship oriented and low task and high relationship oriented. That takes a presence of mind that only comes with a certain level and type of maturity. Winston Churchill was asked once why he promoted a junior military officer over a more veteran officer who had over 20 years of experience. He said, "*Yes, he has worked 20 years, but he has been doing the same thing for 20 years in the same way. We need new ideas.*" Churchill was talking about maturity of ideas and maturity of motivation.

Employees that are hired only because of favoritism seldom possess integrity, intelligence and maturity. They may possess one of the three or even two of the three, but seldom all three. There is a good example of this in the following case study.

A non-profit organization had three critical positions to fill after a new CEO of the organization was hired by the governing board. One of the positions became vacant when the incumbent was not selected for the CEO position. Another position opened because the new CEO was told by the governing board to get rid of him. And the third vacant position was created when a popular and very effective employee retired. The new CEO was pressed to fill these three key positions, because they were top level positions that had very significant operational functions. While time was of the essence in filling the positions, the new CEO could have been more deliberate and discerning, relying on interim staff in the meantime; instead, he used time as an excuse for quickly and hastily filing the positions. As it was revealed later, each hire was not vetted carefully and each one had connections with various members of the governing board. This does not mean that governing board members cannot and should not help get the word out in professional circles about job openings, but it does mean that governing board members should not be advocating for hires that are clearly not ready for, qualified for or in any way mature enough and experienced enough to handle critical jobs. In this non-profit organization, unfortunately, that is what happened. A person with only a few years of experience in finance was named to be the chief finance officer, because his mother was a close friend of a governing board member. The experienced and very effective human resources officer was replaced with someone who had no human resources experience, except for hiring a few people in a small office, but his father was a friend of the organization's new CEO. And the person selected for the top communications officer position was a governing board member's relative. All three of the new hires were enthusiastic, smart and clearly over their heads from the first day. The new chief financial officer had never prepared a budget for an organization. He had an idea of what needed to be done, but he did not know how to do it. He also had no operational sense of the daily strains on the budget such as cash flow. In less than six months, an organization that was solid and sustainable, but never blessed with a large endowment, started paying its bills late and was in danger of finishing the fiscal year in a deficit. The human resources officer was smart, energetic and committed, but he could not or would not make decisions. He was the type of leader that always told his staff that he would get back with them after he has time to think about the issue. Many times decisions needed to be made without delay. Jack Welch called this type of leader the *"Last-one-out-the-door boss."* Those delays repeatedly hurt the organization, because the unresolved issues begin to compile into a quagmire of unresolved problems. The communications officer was responsible for fund raising and communicating with clients and the community. He was full of great ideas, was articulate, was thoughtful and in general a very delightful person. Everyone who worked for him and with him immediately liked him. That is why it became a puzzle when so many sound and well developed projects started by him never came to fruition. He could not finish what he started. He did not have that part of maturity that helps a leader cross the finish line despite problems, issues, and other challenges. He could not cope; he could not navigate disruptions, and he could not execute a plan to complete a project. Welch said, *"Being able to execute is a special and distinct skill. It means a person knows how to put decisions into action and push them forward to completion, through resistance, chaos, or unexpected obstacles."*

Stephen Covey, author of *The Seven Habits of Highly Effective People*, said that leaders who are dependent or independent seldom find success at the highest levels of success, because it takes *interdependence* – the ability to combine one's own efforts with the efforts of others to achieve success, and that takes integrity, intelligence and maturity. From the previous case study - because he was not effective in hiring, the CEO's effectiveness was diminished before he was even two years into his leadership role. The same governing board that meddled in the selection of the top positions turned against the CEO after signs of mismanagement, low morale, diminishing contributions and fewer clients. Apparently, it never occurred to the governing board that its selection criterion and selection process was flawed.

Other examples of the CEO's capitulation to the whims of the governing board and his own self-destruction included providing staff members favored by the governing board with promotions and pay raises during times when the organization was facing budget reductions, when programs were being eliminated or reduced that provided direct services to clients, when employees were being furloughed to save money, and when salaries were frozen. This blatant disregard for employees had a devastating impact on morale and productivity. Instead of reconsidering his management decisions and his style of leadership and instead of listening to members of his immediate staff that warned him about nepotism, budgets, fair play with employees, and other issues, the organization's CEO continued to jeopardize the little humility and sense of purpose that remained. His character was being shaped by power. He blamed staff members instead of accepting responsibility for hiring incompetent people based on favoritism.

This arrogance and failure to recognize the importance of hiring and promoting competent employees is not limited to any particular type of organization. In a mid-size business, a vendor was upset with the company for supposedly not making payments on time. Because this was a business that advertised efficiency as a cornerstone of its existence, the vendor went to the news media to "*expose this myth of efficiency.*" The news media reported the accusation based on the vendor's records. The business' audit division thoroughly investigated the complaint and the business' attorney looked into the accusations. From all accounts, the business had done nothing wrong. Those findings were shared with the news media, but apparently the reporter had already prepared his story and he was not going to let facts get in the way, so he aired a negative report. Even though the story was weak and was not supported by facts, and even though there was no public outcry or even concern by the business governing board of directors, nevertheless, the CEO went berserk. He told governing board members that some staff members had "*planted*" the story; that they had contacted the reporter, and that they were trying to make the business look bad. His top staff did not always agree with him but that did not mean that they would stoop so low as to call a news media outlet. That was only one of many situations that suggested to his competent staff members that it was time to leave, and many did. But there was another angle to the story. As it turned out, the CEO himself planted the story for the purpose of discrediting the business' chief financial officer and his staff, because the CEO wanted to replace him and others in the finance division with his friends and a friend of one of the members of the governing board. This all became apparent when the CEO continued to fabricate financial issues. Employees in the finance office became suspicious and an internal investigation discovered the plot. One year that same business CEO demanded and received a $15,000 raise, plus $2,500 for monthly "expenses." He took the $15,000 raise during the worst financial crisis in the history of the organization. At the time, his salary was over $250,000. He took this raise during a time when employees were being furloughed, programs were being cut, and salaries were being reduced.

In a much publicized public organization, a school district CEO did the same thing. He hired friends and colleagues when the school district was in financial chaos, and he demanded and received a $10,000 raise from the governing board, primarily because he was hiring their friends and relatives, too. The outrage from teachers was felt throughout the school district. Teachers expressed their frustration and anger publicly and across the school district morale sank to an all-time low. The teachers expressed their outrage in many ways without walking off the job. They called governing board members. They spoke out at governing board meetings. The only thing the CEO said was that he deserved the raise. It was unimaginable what a selfish act this was on his part. He knew but did not care about the impact on morale and the negative community perception of his actions. It so outraged some citizens and local politicians that a bill was introduced in the next state legislative session that prohibited school administrators from receiving a raise when teachers are furloughed. But there was no public demand to remove him from office and the governing board made no effort to curb his greed; they simply fed it, because they were a part of it. For years, he continued to hire unqualified employees who were loyal to him and consequently all performance measure outcomes continued to decline.

In an article in BusinessKnowledgeSource.com, *Advantages and Disadvantages of Hiring Friends and Relatives*, the writers state that a friend or family member may take advantage of their status, knowing that it is more difficult to fire someone who is close to the leader or member of the governing board. Also, other employees may feel jealous when a friend or family member is hired, thinking it is favoritism, which often it is. This may especially be the case when a family member or friend is given a promotion over a non-relative/friend, or when a position is created that previously did not exist. Additionally, personal family problems or disagreements between friends may be brought to the workplace and the leader may be tasked with trying to resolve the issues, which takes his time away from the organization. This may make it uncomfortable for other employees and difficult for work to get done. It may be more difficult to create a necessary change in the workplace when it might negatively affect a friend or relative that works for the leader.

There are many examples of what can happen when a friend or relative who is incompetent is hired in an important job. There was a school district that found itself in the newspaper almost every day for accusations of mismanagement related to many things, such as an on-going investigation by the county district attorney of the Special Purpose Local Option Sales Tax (SPLOST) manager. The CEO had been warned about this manager by the governing board attorney and staff members on more than one occasion, but the manager was a friend of the CEO. At the same time, it was revealed that the school district had been fined $30,000 for a mud run-off from a new school construction site. That was bad enough, but the construction manager who was also the chief operations officer (COO) knew about the mud runoff and refused to do anything about it to the satisfaction of the local county inspector. The inspector did not want to burden the school district, but the COO was too arrogant to do anything and he knew the CEO would not hold him accountable because of their friendship. When the CEO was contacted about the situation, he dismissed the whole thing and told the inspector, "*Talk to my COO.*" To make matters even worse, the COO, with the approval of the CEO, told the governing board attorney to fight the fine. That decision costs the school district $30,000 in attorney fees. Despite the efforts of the attorneys, the fine was enforced, so the total bill for this blunder, show of arrogance and disinterest or unwillingness to control his friend, as well as the CEO's own behavior and attitude cost the school district $60,000. The same amount as a veteran teacher's salary for a year. In the meantime, the COO, who was under investigation by the county district attorney, continued to receive his $200,000 salary and was allowed to keep his secretary who was making $70,000. The interesting and at the same time disturbing part of this saga is that while the COO was being investigated the CEO asserted that the COO was doing a great job and soon thereafter renewed his contract at full salary for another year. So picture this: the county district attorney accuses the COO of wrong-doing; the CEO covers for his friend; the COO says no one can tell him what to do; the school district is in financial trouble, and the CEO renews the COO's contract for $200,000 and keeps his secretary. The CEO refused to speak to the news media and he refused to speak to the public. But he did speak to the local district attorney; the local district attorney made sure of that. One has to ask, where was the governing board during all of this? There was no righteous indignation from the governing board, because their friends and relatives were being hired.

Another example of this type of leadership poison can be found in a non-profit organization that was bereft with the CEO and governing board hiring friends and relatives. The organization had a long standing policy regarding equipment. When the organization's equipment reached the end of its effectiveness, to the point that the repairs cost more than the worth of the equipment or when equipment could not be fully restored, that equipment was considered "surplus" and could be auctioned to the public. The money from these auctions went into the organization's general operations fund. As part of his employment contract with governing board, the CEO received a "company" vehicle. Some organizational CEOs keep those vehicles for several years and some are replaced every two years, at donor's expense. This particular CEO wanted a new car, so his two year old vehicle was sent to the organization's service center and was supposed to be added to the auction inventory. At the same time, the CEO received a new vehicle. An auditor later found that the "old" vehicle was in good shape and was purchased by the CEO instead of going to auction so he could give the vehicle to one of his children. However, since the old vehicle was not sold at auction, the CEO bought it for $10,000 under resale value. The auditor found that the CEO purchased the old company car that was supposedly put in surplus by his friend; consequently, the non-profit's annual audit was compromised. In their book, *The Arrogance Cycle*, Michael Farr and Edward Claflin, state that, "*It's a fundamental characteristic of an "Arrogance Cycle" - the assumption that 'consequences won't happen to me.'*"

There was a tip to authorities that a public organization's CEO was using his business credit card inappropriately to purchase gasoline for his family's vehicles. When he was being interviewed by the district attorney's office investigators he thought he could push the attention away from himself by shifting the discussion to the organization's chief operations officer (COO), his friend. The CEO had a very difficult time explaining how his business credit card was used three times in the same day at the same gas station for gasoline. His explanation was so unreasonable that it was laughable. He said he traveled as much as 340 miles a day visiting clients - 340 miles per day! When asked why he used the same gas station, he said it was convenient, which made him appear to be driving around in circles. But the best story was the reason why he was later nicknamed "*High Octane.*" He claimed that during one of those fill ups he realized he had put the wrong grade of gas in his vehicle and he panicked. He said he got some unnamed person to siphon the gas out of the vehicle so he could refill it with the right grade of gasoline.

After that story, much of whatever credibility he had left was gone. He and the organization became a laughing-stock. The damage to the morale of employees across the organization was staggering. But that was only the beginning. A few weeks later, several police cars showed up one morning at the central office headquarters of the organization. The district attorney investigators had a search warrant for all computers and other materials that might be related to the investigation of the CEO and the COO. His friend, the COO, had turned on him when he learned that the CEO blamed his discretions on the COO. What shocked employees and the public, however, was that at the same time the central office was being searched, another set of police officers and investigators went to the CEO's home to conduct a search of his home computer. They also had a warrant to review his personal financial records. During the following chaos, the governing board asked him to temporarily resign so that they could appoint an interim CEO during the investigation. He continued to receive his full salary, as did the COO. Only a few weeks later, when everyone was hoping that the controversies would abate, the governing board received word that the investigation against the CEO was based on some strong evidence; consequently, the investigation would prolong the agony, so they fired him. Then two months after that came even more shocking news that the CEO and the COO were indicted by a grand jury for racketeering and other charges. The indictment included allegations of misappropriation of millions of dollars; misuse of credit cards for personal use; and many others violations. He and his codefendants were also alleged to have received thousands of dollars worth of sports events tickets from vendors.

Long before the district attorney started an investigation and long before the actions of the COO became possibly criminal, the CEO had been warned by some of his senior staff members. But the senior staff members who tried to warn him years before and who advised him all left the organization within a few months of each other three years before the indictments because of the fear of what was becoming of the CEO and the organization. It was painfully obvious to those senior staff members that the CEO was not listening to any critical or constructive comments, which meant that his "advisors" were the staff members that were indebted to him to the point of blind loyalty. The position of leadership and the power and influence that went with it inflated their egos. With a transition to an ego-based leadership style, comes an unfettered need to surround oneself with sycophants who only hastened the CEO's demise by inflating his ego and distorting his view of leadership responsibility.

In an article titled *Obsequious Sycophants*, Doug Blackie refers to blind loyalty subordinates as an "*obsequious sycophants*".

> *Blind followership is not a good thing – especially when combined with the fallacy of executive infallibility.... I call it the fallacy of executive infallibility because, let's face it, executives are fallible. They're people just like you and me. They put they pants on one leg at a time and, yes, they make mistakes.*

It is incumbent upon leaders to make a choice: do they slavishly implement potentially bad or misinformed executive decisions or do they demonstrate their loyalty and integrity by questioning the wisdom of the decision? Effective leaders are skilled at walking the fine line between ensuring they have the confidence of their leaders – and being able to objectively assess whether the latest orders handed down from above are indeed wise and well thought out. I believe it's a leader's responsibility to ensure that executive decisions are made with the best information. If decisions are flawed -or simply don't make sense- there is no harm in respectfully seeking clarification from their leader. What was the basis for the decision? Have they considered the unintended consequences? Are they aware of this alternative approach? I have found that an executive may reconsider their decision when presented with better information or the risks of a certain course of action. Or they may not. At least you've made your case. Challenging an executive decision involves risk, requires a lot of courage and a significant amount of social capital with the executive leadership.

In the end, the leaders that engage in padding their egos at the expense of the organization by hiring sycophants instead of qualified staff members totally lose any semblance of humility. Their actions severely hurt the organization. An organization's credibility, focus on services and staff, morale, financial stability, ability to attract and retain competent and gifted staff members, and the confidence of its clients and community can be lost for a long time. In one of the cases described above the CEO's clearly unqualified hire was selected to run a million dollar fund-raising and renovation program, not because he had any background that prepared him for the job, but only because he was the CEO's friend. He was an excellent salesman but he had no experience in fund-raising or the construction or financing business. Yet, he was one of the CEO's favorite people. That was all that mattered, and that was okay with the governing board. The renovation project started on borrowed funds with collateral centered on a history of donations. When the fund-raising activities collapsed due to mismanagement, the CEO blamed staff members, but not his friend. When costs overruns, construction delays, construction site management issues, and other problems occurred on a regular basis, the CEO always came to his defense and blamed the construction management firm and others. The non-profit floundered and almost lost everything before the governing board was forced to change CEOs and top management, as well as change their own ways of managing oversight duties and selecting leaders.

A widely recognized expert in leadership studies, Warren Bennis, wrote in his book *On Becoming a Leader* that effective leaders do not dwell on making mistakes because they know they will learn from them. On the other hand, those leaders who make excuses for mistakes, or blame others for the mistakes, and who listen only to those subordinates that agree with them on all matters without offering a counterpoint do not learn from their mistakes and therefore make even more blunders. That was the case with the CEOs mentioned in this chapter. They reached a point in their leadership where the organization was only a means that served their ego. They lost their purpose; they lost their focus; they lost good people willing to tell them the truth; they lost their moral compass; and their circle of sycophants became a larger and tighter group. And the governing board was not held accountable until it was too late.

There are tragic stories of the demise of talented and experienced leaders, but the additional story is the damage that was done to once successful, proud organizations and the thousands of people who were impacted by the decisions and the subsequent embarrassment brought on each organization and community. The leaders abused their powers. They did not want to be questioned and their personal needs were more important than the needs of the organization. Hiring friends and relatives was more important than selecting competent staff applicants. In the face of growing issues about their judgment and their arrogant attitude about hiring, they each continued to make incredibly narrow-minded, self-serving decisions with the encouragement of sycophants.

Warren Bennis speaks of the leader's journey as "*the process of becoming an integrated human being.*" In her book about Winston Churchill, Celia Sandys wrote that one of the most important *Churchillian Principles* is magnanimity, because "*magnanimity breeds trust and loyalty among subordinates and partners.*" The magnanimous leader wants subordinates and other staff members who encourage the leader but who also question the leader when they think he is wrong. The irony with many unsuccessful leaders is they surround themselves with those that agree with them and who build them up with false praise. Then that same leader will turn on his sycophants and treat them like the abused spouse who is too terrified to stay and too afraid to leave. These seeds of dysfunction become the harvest of organizational chaos. In Ira Chaleff's book, *The Courageous Follower*, the author states that if the abusive leader is not confronted by staff then the staff is in collusion with him and the climate of the organization can be irreparably harmed.

It is understandable from the leader's perspective to be cautious about surrounding himself with a cadre of staff members who question and criticize to the extent that nothing is accomplished. That is a legitimate and realistic concern. Subordinates can question his decisions, but not to the point of disrespect. But the leader sets the tone for the entire organization. A caring, strong, organized, strategic and thoughtful leader can have such a positive and profound impact on the entire organization that it filters down through all levels and the organization ultimately benefits. There are many leaders who have devoted their entire career and life to ensuring that their organizations met the needs of their clients. They are engaged in community work; they are at countless activities and events; they manage by walking around asking for feedback from staff and clients; they make a monumental effort to include all sections of the community, and they take the time that is necessary to cultivate a healthy, working relationship with local government officials, businesses, charities, and the local legislative members for the sole purpose of benefitting the clients through the good deeds and effectiveness of the organization, but more importantly, they select the right people to the get the job done effectively and efficiently.

Peter Drucker, a legendary expert in leadership wrote: "*The leaders who work most effectively, it seems to me, never say "I." And that's not because they have trained themselves not to say "I." They don't think "I." They think "we"; they think "team." They understand their job is to make the team function. They accept responsibility and don't sidestep it, but "we" gets the credit. This is what creates trust, what enables you to get the task done."*

Antidote

There are leaders whose power derives from their position and yet they mistakenly think that their power comes not from position but from their personality, talents, and/or intelligence; consequently, the selection of employees must first come from loyalty to the leader. The employee's talent or fit for the job is secondary to loyalty to the leader; at least that is what the ineffective leader thinks. This leads to a cadre of employees who are not independent thinkers and who would never advise the leader that he is wrong or that another course of action would be more prudent or beneficial. The leader's way is the right way; no questions asked. Governing boards have to be mindful of this when selecting a leader. In fact, it behooves governing boards to ask candidates for the organization's top leadership position how they select staff, what history they have in selecting quality staff in important positions. It may be useful to learn how many previous subordinates ascended to leadership positions. Perhaps a look at the candidates' subordinate retention rate would be informative, too. Also, a selection committee should take the time and put forth the effort to ascertain if the candidates for the leadership position have a history of hiring friends and relatives or competent staff members. Governing boards should make it clear that the organization's leadership should fill positions with quality candidates who are loyal first to the organization and its mission. Additionally, the leader should be expected to provide a path to success not only for those with leadership promise but for all employees. An effective leader absolutely has to create a working environment that values people, creativity, independent thought, and collegial relationships between and among employees. This type of work environment naturally leads to loyalty to the organization because the employees feel vested in its mission and operations. There is a critical difference between loyalty to the organization and loyalty to the leader. Ideally, a governing board wants to see both types of loyalty, but certainly not one at the expense of the other. There is an ironic outcome for leaders hiring employees who are loyal to them at the expense of the organization. Those employees do not respect or trust the leader; therefore, they are not productive which only serves to jeopardize the leader's standing with the governing board.

This is not to imply that hiring quality people for the right job is easy; it can be very difficult. And there are times when a relative or friend may actually be qualified for a job. Therefore, it is extraordinarily important for every organization to follow precise steps when trying to match the right person for the right job. *Entrepreneur, Inc.* suggests a progressive process starting with developing accurate job descriptions and compiling a "success profile" to indicate what skills a person would need to be successful in each job. Considerable time and effort, with the help of experts, should be spent on developing a series of questions for both applicant screening purposes and for later interviews with the finalists. It is important to take a jaundiced view of resumes. Bo Bennett wrote: "*Resume: a written exaggeration of only the good things a person has done in the past, as well as a wish list of the qualities a person would like to have.*" Resumes must be carefully scrutinized and time must be given to verifying references. Applicant interviews should have a formal and an informal component. First, the interview should start with a structured interview format with pre-developed questions. It is important to structure and follow the questions in much the same way for each applicant, so that fair comparisons of the applicants can be made. Secondly, the structured interview should be followed by a more informal format of questions that are based on reality where the interviewers ask the applicants how they would handle case scenarios. These case study scenarios can reveal applicants' abilities or weaknesses in many domains and situations.

The governing board has to be a role model for the CEO in the selection of qualified employees. Governing boards who advocate friends, business partners, relatives or those affiliated with others in any way for positions in the organization are putting the CEO in a very difficult situation; plus, the message is loud and clear that loyalty to people overrides loyalty to the organization and its mission.

CHAPTER 13

DATA-DOMINATED DECISIONS

"In God we trust. All others must bring data."

—*W. Edwards Deming*

Poison: Data is the language that leaders use to make decisions in many organizations, or so it is said. The phrase "data-driven decisions" has moved from a catchy phrase to an expectation of leaders and governing boards. Vision statements, mission statements, objectives and even motives now must be "data-driven". Platforms for change are built on data-driven planning and data-driven strategies. But are decisions really data-driven? Leaders and governing boards are often misled by this emphasis on data-driven decisions. Any statistician will say that "unscrubbed" data (cleaning the data set for accuracy) is unreliable; unrelated data is pointless; masses of data is unmanageable, and decisions made from unscrubbed, unrelated and unmanageable data are potentially detrimental to any organization. Data must provide information to the organization that is useful. Many fool-hearty decisions are made because of an overreliance on or a misunderstanding of data, and many organizations pick and choose data to meet their needs and thereby risk making erroneous assumptions that precede poor decisions. Governing boards and leaders should be very precise in how data is collected and used for planning and decision making purposes. If a prospective leader or candidate for a governing board position states that decisions should be data-driven, that assertion should be challenged, for it can be poisonous.

A non-profit agency's leadership team, including the governing board, decided to move completely to "data-driven decision-making". All of the organization's goals, strategies and objectives were going to be tied to data. No major decision was to be made without data to guide those decisions. One problem became immediately obvious – where would all of the data come from? A Request for Proposals was published for data vendors to submit development proposals for a data platform. The organization settled on a vendor that was expert in researching, developing and reporting data in virtually every category deemed important by the organization's leadership team. The vendor went to work and soon thereafter, mountains of data became available to the CEO, his top staff and the governing board. It did not take long for the leadership team to realize that the data was different from previous data retrieval systems by the sheer volume and scope of the data. The governing board started asking the CEO for a report on the data, as it was excited about the prospect of making data-driven strategies and planning decisions.

The CEO soon recognized that the data company did not provide a blueprint for data interpretation and data analysis tied to strategic use of the data. The accepted proposal addressed only data collection and data delivery. Neither the CEO nor his leadership team had the expertise to decipher the data in a way that could be tied to the organization's strategic plan and performance measures. The CEO learned that the data company could provide data interpretation and analysis service for the organization, but at considerable additional cost, and there was no budget for that additional cost. So, decisions were made from the data, as best the leadership team could understand the data, until conflicting data started to appear. For example, some data showed that the service delivery model that the organization had spent a significant amount of money on was not as effective as indicated in annual reports. Instead of making changes to the delivery model, the organization only referred to the sections of the data that supported at least some component of the service delivery model. That is what the governing board heard about, not a full report of the data.

The organization was so excited about data-driven decisions that little thought was given to the impact of these decisions, the reliability of the data entry, and conflicting outcomes. Too often, decisions are impacted almost immediately by incoming data, without first considering longitudinal data for trends or trajectory or without taking the time to consider the source of the data. Data can be extremely valuable for every organization, regardless of type or size, but leaders and governing boards should be thoughtful and careful before they plunge into "data-driven" decisions, and they should not be careless in the use of that term.

In a book that all leaders and governing boards should read, *The Signal and the Noise*, by Nate Silver, the author takes the reader through many examples of how data can be fatally flawed, overused, misinterpreted, and yet many times useful, if the signal can be found within the noise. Silver finds that all data tell a story, but, *"The story data tells us is often the one we'd like to hear, and we usually make sure it has a happy ending.*" He explains that data is considered wonderful when it supports a leader's theory, practice, or expectations and, yet, it is viewed as irrelevant or suspicious if it does not support the leader's story. Silver makes the point that data can make leaders and governing boards lazy, if not irresponsible, because it is so readily available and because it removes tough decision-making, or so they think. If a leader can make decisions based only on data, the thinking goes, then poor decisions are less likely to occur, and if they do make a blunder it can be blamed on the data; it is not his fault; he was relying on data. Blame the data, not the leader. Silver wrote, *"Before we demand more of our data, we need to demand more of ourselves."* Data can make a leader careless, plus there is a temptation to mislead others with data, such as a governing board, stockholders, employees, clients, contributors and other stakeholders. There are many examples, from misleading data about political trends, energy consumption, weather, birth rates, service delivery models and a thousand other topics.

In recent years, non-profit organizations and others have followed the data trend started by business leaders, to say all decisions are data-driven. Non-profit and education leaders are often pressured by the public and business leaders in particular to run all organizations like a business, even though research shows that 80 percent of new businesses fail within the first two years and even though most of the Fortune 500 companies from 30 years ago do not exist today. Nevertheless, non-profit leaders and educational leaders do often adopt business practices, so the jump to data-driven decisions seemed logical. For example, some leaders jumped at the chance to hire high-powered and expensive consultants to implement a data analysis and decision-making concept called the "Balanced Scorecard", developed by Bob Kaplan and David Norton in a *Harvard Business Review* paper in 1992. The original concept of the Balanced Scorecard was grounded in business financial management, but it took a turn toward data collection and cataloguing data in many types of organizations as a means of determining if goals and objectives are met and to guide decision making. It is interesting to note that the Balanced Scorecard concept that relies on data was not the subject of any research to determine if it was effective until 2008, sixteen years after it was introduced, when Andrew Neely of the Cranfield School of Management published a research paper, *Does the Balanced Scorecard Work: An Empirical Investigation.* In his study Neely explored the performance impact of the Balanced Scorecard by employing a quasi-experimental design. He collected three years of financial data from two separate electrical wholesale divisions within the same company. One of the divisions used the Balanced Scorecard and the other did not. Neely found that the division that implemented the Balanced

Scorecard saw improvements in sales and gross profit, but so did its sister division. There was no difference between the divisions in the number of sales and the gross profit; thereby, the author of the study wrote, "*Hence the performance impact of the Balanced Scorecard has to be questioned.*" Despite this finding and others like it, businesses and other organizations continue to use the Balanced Scorecard, even though some leaders and workers, as well as governing board members, often feel overwhelmed with the data, and populating the data cells can be painstaking slow and laborious.

Educators have followed the lead of businesses by adopting the moniker that all decisions are data-based, with many public school districts implementing data development systems overlaying the Balanced Scorecard. But educators are no different than others that are enamored with data and its lure of simplifying decision making, and educators also turn a blind eye to data that does not support what they want it to support. There are actually many examples, but we will focus on just one for the purpose of making a point. The use of middle schools, grades 6-8, was adopted by educators without any research indicating that students in the middle school age range of 11-13 benefit from the middle school concept, being separated from the so-called negative influences of high school students and the so-called overbearing influence of supportive elementary school climates. And every year school districts across the country advocate the use of middle schools while at the same time claiming data-driven decision making. A Harvard research project by Guido Schwerdt, Harvard Institute for Economic Research, and Martin West, Harvard Graduate School of Education, titled *The Impact of Alternative Grade Configurations on Student Outcomes through Middle and High School*, questions the promises made about the middle school concept and the industry that it has created. The authors used statewide data from Florida school districts to estimate the impact of attending public schools with different grade configurations on student achievement through grade ten.

Based on an instrumental variable estimation strategy, we find that students moving from elementary to middle school suffer a sharp drop in student achievement in the transition year. These achievement drops persist through grade 10. We also find that middle school entry increases student absences and is associated with higher grade 10 dropout rates.

Apparently, data-driven decisions do not apply to data about middle schools. That is the fallacy; data driven decisions only apply when data supports those decisions.

An article in *Wired* magazine by Brian Christian, *The A/B Test: Inside the Technology That's Changing the Rules of Business*, addresses the dangers of data-driven decisions and introduces the world to a new term, HPPO (Highest Paid Person's Opinion). The HPPO usually makes the decisions in organizations that do not know how to read the data and make data-driven decisions. According to Christian, the data-driven decisions typically start with the HPPO and move to the fast-track down the organizational chart to a hard landing on the employees who are central to the day-to-day operations. The staff of *Intercom* wrote in an article, *The Problem with Data Driven Decisions,* that data-based decisions are only useful when applying the right methods. They indicate that data is one perspective, and only one perspective, and therefore should not be the only driving force that guides decisions.

For example, if Apple were data driven, they would release a $400 netbook or shut down their Genius Bar. If Zappos were driven by data, they would abandon their generous returns policy. Just because data is objective by definition, it doesn't mean that it guides you to the right decision. Just because (data) can be precise, it doesn't follow that it's valuable. Data is a false god. You can tag every link, generate every metric, and run split tests for every decision, but no matter how deep you go, no matter how many hours you invest, you're only looking at one piece of the puzzle.

It is important for leaders and governing boards to realize that everything that can be counted counts but not everything that counts can be counted.

This is another story about data. In this non-profit organization after three consecutive years of declining revenues, staff positions were furloughed five days each year, equipment purchases were delayed, and services were trimmed. The governing board became convinced that the declining economy was not the main problem, so they discerned that their problems rested with the CEO and his management style. One governing board member described the CEO as "lackluster", meaning that the contribution declines were probably tied to that. One governing board member was convinced that mining all sorts of data would turn the organization around, because nothing was better than data-driven decision making. The CEO explained that the organization did not lack for data; there were mounds of data, and making all decisions based just on the data could be risky. Nonetheless, the organization converted to a *"data-driven decision making machine,"* as one governing board member so proudly proclaimed. Data was coming in from every source possible and dozens of charts and graphs were developed to convince the governing board that decisions could and would be made according to the data. The governing board even insisted that the organization should create a "Data

Wall" in every office. As Silver would say, it was becoming increasingly difficult to separate the *signal* from the *noise* of data. Data indicated, for example, that aging equipment was affecting productivity, but only marginally. So the governing board determined, contrary to the opinion of the organization's CEO, new equipment needed to be purchased. The CEO said the organization could not offer the equipment, yet, and besides the needs of the clients were changing so it would be prudent to delay the purchases until new technology was developed. The governing board said the data was more important, so the CEO was forced to put the already financially challenged organization further in debt with the purchase of computer upgrades and software, as well as related purchases. Silver wrote, *"Extrapolation is a very basic method of prediction – usually, much too basic."* Data taken in isolation from other factors and influences can give a misleading impression and lead to false assumptions. After the organization went into receivership, a performance and financial audit revealed that the organization did not have sufficient strategies or skills to decipher the important and relevant elements of the data fields. Consequently, the data sent the leadership decision-making in the wrong direction for the wrong reasons with the wrong expectations and ultimately with the wrong outcomes.

In an article for *Foreign Affairs* entitled "*Big Data*," the authors express optimism about the large amount of data available to organizations, but they also offer many precautions.

> *...knowing the causes behind things is desirable. The problem is that causes are often extremely hard to figure out, and many times, when we think we have identified them, it is nothing more than a self-congratulatory illusion. Behavioral economics has shown that humans are conditioned to see causes even where none exist. So, we need to be particularly on guard to prevent our cognitive biases from deluding us; sometimes, we just have to let the data speak... this requires a new way of thinking and will challenge institutions and identities. In a world where data shape decisions more and more, what purpose will remain for people, or for intuition, or for going against the data?*

Perhaps too many leaders follow literally what leadership guru, Edwards Deming, said about data, *"In God we trust. All others must bring data."*

Antidote

There is no doubt that data is essential to all leaders, governing boards and organizations. Without data, there are no measures of effectiveness, no indications that strategic plans and objectives are working, and no way to tie the organization's budget to initiatives. Without data, an organization is operating in the blind. However, leaders and governing boards need to understand the purpose and the potential of data and manage expectations. Data that does not provide relevant information is only data, and information from data is only useful if it provides insight that can be applied to the organization in a constructive manner. Atul Butte, a Stanford University professor, said, "*Hiding within those mounds of data is knowledge that could change so many things.*" Nate Silver wrote in *The Signal and the Noise,* trying to determine what data is useful and how it is useful requires recognition that data can be a lot of noise with a signal embedded in the noise. It takes skill at the data entry level, skill at the data retrieval level, skill at the data mining level, skill at the data interpretation level, and skill at the data relevancy level to make data work for an organization in an accurate and productive way. As mentioned earlier, however, there is the temptation to cherry pick data to support favorite strategies, products, or services. Ronald Coase, Nobel winning economist, said, "*Torture the data, and it will confess to anything.*"

How does a leader use data? Many data experts recommend that the leader and his staff develop several questions related to the vision, mission, strategies and objectives of the organization. Additionally, the leader can ask the governing board and other stakeholders to do the same thing. The purpose of data then becomes clear; it is to answer those questions. Too often, the questions are developed after the data is available, which then become data-driven questions rather than organization-driven questions. This method is more likely to gleam information from the data that is relevant to the organization and makes the mounds of data manageable. Additionally, this method has the potential to disaggregate data so that specific information relevant to specific components of the organization can be reviewed for program and service delivery model effectiveness measures, based on the questions and the data.

Author of *Five Rules for the Data-Driven Business,* Patricio Robles, offers very practical advice for organizational leadership determined to be data-driven:

1. Remember that organizations can collect too much data. "*... collecting as much data as they can find...is not only distracting, it can reduce the quality of the data-driven decisions.... When too much data is collected, there's a greater likelihood that the wrong analyses will be performed.*"
2. Key metrics derived from data should be tied to goals. "*Numbers*

in and of themselves are often of limited use. Metrics should be associated with goals."

3. Context helps. "*When setting goals, context is your friend. Tying key metrics to goals are meaningful.*"

4. The past and present are not the future. "*Data is inherently limited to yesterday and today. Predictions, no matter how sophisticated, are still just predictions. The data-driven business uses data to make educated decisions; it doesn't naively believe that data is a crystal ball.*"

5. Do not dismiss the qualitative. "*If you're only paying attention to the hard data, you're missing out on a huge part of the big picture. What matters most to your organization? That question has to be asked.*"

Leaders must understand that there is no data that will fully replace any of the skills that make them and governing boards effective. There are many essential facets of leadership that cannot be found in a data spreadsheet. So, for those leaders and governing boards that hope to simplify decision-making by depending solely on data, they need to know that they could be drinking poison while believing that the elixir called data is medicinal. John Naisbitt, the author of the *Megatrends* books, wrote, "*Intuition becomes increasingly valuable in the new information society precisely because there is so much data.*"

CHAPTER 14

POISON AND ANTIDOTES

The only difference between medicine and poison is the dose…and intent.

—Oscar G. Hernandez, MD

If I had known the difference between antidote and anecdote, my friend might still be alive.

—Steven Wright

Leadership and governance are very difficult. Reaching levels of competence and mastery as the leader of an organization or when serving on a governing board is challenging. That is why effective leaders and governing board members are so difficult to find and even more difficult to keep. Leadership and governance are both difficult to teach, because so much of effective leadership and governance is intuitive and relies on qualities that cannot be easily taught, such as courage, integrity, insight, humility and a good heart. There are, however, ways to make leaders and governing boards more effective - by example, illustration and discussion. The difference between effective and ineffective leadership and governance is not easy to discern and can be like medicine and poison – the difference is the dose and the intent. The areas of potential poison include: handling criticism; handling bad news; roles of leaders and governing board; selecting new leadership; work climate and safety; leadership style; organizational assessment; planning for the unexpected; developing a leadership team; transitioning to new leadership; rumors; hiring competent employees; and using data.

The following is a summary of leadership poison and antidotes and the lessons for leaders and governing boards.

Handling Criticism

The effective leader will be skilled in handling criticism in order to discern valid criticism from invalid criticism, and be able and willing to move past self-serving reactions and instead determine what is best for the organization. The effective use of constructive criticism can strengthen a leader and ultimately the organization.

<u>Poison:</u> Effective leaders have the ability to handle criticism while ineffective leaders take any criticism as attempts to limit their power or persuasion. Additionally, effective leaders and governing boards let subordinates make hard decisions and support those decisions even during difficult times. There is a belief among ineffective leaders making difficult decisions that they must above all else protect themselves from governing board criticism. He believes he will become the target of criticism and thereafter works in a climate of mistrust and blame. The ineffective leader is defensive when the implementation of one of his concepts, projects, or initiatives runs into obstacles. He will not concede that his idea was flawed in design or was doomed by a lack of resources or ineffective strategies; instead, the leader blames others and may convince the governing board that he is not responsible.

<u>Antidote:</u> There are effective governing boards that understand their role in the organization and do not try to influence the organizational leader's decision regarding personnel and other operational matters. This understanding is an essential antidote to the poison of governing board interference. Unchecked, governing board interference not only compromises the effectiveness of the leader, it also jeopardizes the outcomes of the organization. Strict attention to the development and implementation of governing board by-laws can counteract the poison of interference and unhealthy responses to criticism. This is not to minimize the role of the governing board, but instead to clarify their role and thus create a climate whereby criticism can lead to constructive change. The organization's leader can share information with the governing board in appropriate ways to keep them informed in order to enhance trust through communications and also to manage expectations. For example, it is appropriate for governing boards to monitor organizational risk through regular, formal reports from the leadership team, but not to the point that the reports interfere with the operations of the organization.

One of the biggest challenges for organizational leaders and governing boards is handling criticism. This is linked directly to the appropriate roles of each, and the failure to handle criticism in constructive ways can damage the relationship between the leader and the governing board. Leaders and members of governing boards can benefit from training on how to handle criticism in constructive ways. Ron Edmondson, an expert in leadership and communications, offers ways to handle criticism that can be an antidote to the poison of criticism-reaction failure:

1. *Consider the source.* If the source of the criticism is from a person or group that never sees anything positive and is a constant source of criticism then that source would be viewed differently than criticism from an individual or group that shares the good with the bad. Also, a source that has facts, figures, etc. instead of rumor should be carefully considered. Too often, a leader or governing board treats any type of criticism the same way; they ignore it or shift the blame, especially if they have been guilty of interference or role confusion in the first place.

2. *Listen.* Leaders and governing boards should carefully and thoughtfully listen to criticism in order to understand and discern possible underlying issues. Leaders sometimes expect the worse, especially if they have made ill-advised decisions, and that's what they hear, even if the critic is offering constructive criticism. It is also possible that the critic has effective ideas on how to remedy the situation or prevent similar poor decisions in the future.

3. *Analyze.* Is the criticism accurate? Is it possible the criticism that leaders are quick to attribute to a subordinate is actually a criticism of top leadership and the vehicle or target of that criticism is the subordinate? Think of the ramifications if this is true. The leader's misanalysis results in a reprimand of the subordinate when the criticism of the subordinate is only an example of the failure of leadership at the top of the organization.

4. *Common themes.* Criticism can be widespread and vague or it can be narrow and specific. An effective leader will look for consistent criticism and thematic criticism, where the same type of criticism comes from different quarters with some of the same specific information. Governing board members who do not think their participation in the operations of the organization is inappropriate may discover, through an honest appraisal of criticism, how disruptive their actions are to the effectiveness of the organization. Leaders and particularly the governing board should look for trends in the criticism, so information can be gathered in order for the leader to help subordinates adjust accordingly to correct problems. Additionally, he needs to share trends with the governing board in case a policy needs to be revisited or if an honest discussion about

the behavior of the governing board is necessary to avoid further organization problems.

5. *Give an answer.* Edmondson states that a criticism is best viewed as someone asking a question; therefore, it deserves a response. Such as, "Why does the governing board participate in personnel decisions when they have selected the CEO to make those decisions?" It is okay to agree to disagree. A leader should not be hasty to agree or disagree and should not give an answer that commits him or the governing board to a certain course of action before he has the chance to analyze the criticism. The leader may want and need a change in the makeup of the governing board, for example, but he cannot and must not state that to subordinates who may be rightfully upset with ongoing governing board interference.

Leaders and governing board members should refrain from openly criticizing each other. There are many antidotes to that type of poison, including working together to improve communications and understanding each person's role through training. This open communication can generate a more open-minded reaction to criticism and a constructive use of criticism.

Handling Bad News

Every leader regardless of the type or size of an organization will have to contend with and respond to bad news. It is often the case that how a leader and organization respond to bad news becomes the focus of attention over time rather than the bad news itself.

Poison: An ineffective leader hides bad news or tries to discredit the source of the bad news. The failure to address bad news typically makes matters worse, sometimes much worse than the original problem. A leader who strives to give the impression that everything is operating fine when in fact it is not has unleashed a poison that will be difficult to contain and counteract. Bad things happen in any organization. Some bad outcomes are self-inflicted through poor decision-making; some are self-inflicted because circumstances were not right or a decision was implemented at the wrong time; and some bad things happen because of circumstances beyond the control of the organization. Regardless of the cause or circumstance, every organization must be prepared for bad news and have a thoughtful and considered way of receiving and managing bad news. Ignoring the symptoms does not make the consequences anything but worse. The same is true with bad news. Leaders have to expect the unexpected, and many times the success or failure of a leader is determined by his reaction to the unexpected. So much depends on the leader's decision-making acumen. Some are known for making quick decisions, and are praised for their decisive response in difficult situations. Other leaders are more deliberate and inquisitive when a decision has to be made, and are admired for taking time to make the best decision. Depending on the situation, a quick decision maker can make a bad situation worse by not collecting all of the facts, elements, and contemplating possible consequences before making a decision. Yet, there are times when a leader can be paralyzed by indecision when a timely decision is essential. The poison of leadership is manifest when a leader either approaches all decisions the same way, with haste or hesitation, or misreads situations with haste when it needs deliberation or with hesitation when expediency is necessary.

Antidote: Tim Berry, a writer on leadership, wrote that a good measure of the type of leadership can be identified by asking this question: "*How quickly does the leader get bad news?*" If the leader is usually one of the first to hear bad news; subordinates don't wait to tell him; the subordinates don't tell each other first; and they don't try to hide bad news from the leader, then the leader is someone who knows how to handle bad news and a crisis. In this chapter, some of the leaders refused to hide the bad news and refused to deny that a crisis was present or pending. In fact, they made it clear to their leadership teams and governing boards that no one was going to hide the facts. The leaders and the their teams calmly and thoroughly identified the essential components of the situation; developed a list of responses and resources; shared the challenge with governing board members and with clients in an appropriate and timely manner, and ultimately implemented a plan with far reaching goals and results.

In an article for CBS News *Money Watch* by Steve Tobak titled, *How to Deliver Bad News*, he offers the following advice: "*The method incorporates elements of crisis management, customer service, effective communication, and even some psychology. And, if you do it with empathy and finesse, I've found that you can actually improve your relationship with the other party in many ways.*" Additionally, Tobak advises leaders to be genuine; be empathetic; develop a plan; and deliver. "*Be honest with yourself about the role you personally played in the outcome. This is critical because, if you played a direct role, i.e. you screwed up, you need to be straight with yourself about that or you'll end up feeling guilty and weird and that will come across negatively. In other words, you need to diffuse your appraisal and come to terms with your own emotional state and the impact of it all on* the organization."

Leaders should think about how they would feel from the perspective of their clients. Leaders must try to understand what clients stand to lose or how they will feel as a result of the bad news. Leaders must make sure they are clear that responsibility and accountability rests with them. Clients appreciate leaders taking responsibility, so do employees and governing boards. When leaders communicate bad news, it can be done in such a way that the leader's empathy and concern for the client is apparent. One of the worst things a leader can do is to play the "poor me" role, at the expense of the ones most impacted by a crisis.

Leaders should consider all the ways they can make the situation better, understandable, or right. This may require creative, innovative ways of thinking beyond anything the leader has attempted before. During times of crisis, in particular, leaders may need to toss out existing plans and start over, or they may need to find the most effective parts of an existing plan and focus more resources on that aspect of the plan. In any case, leaders need to have a clear picture of the options at their disposal and under exactly what conditions the leader and the organization are willing to bring them to bear on the situation.

If a leader is genuine, displays empathy, and develops an appropriate plan, he is ready to deliver. The leader's emotional state will be clear. That means he will be empathetic but not emotionally distraught. And depending on the reaction, leaders may have an arsenal of possibilities to offer to help make things right. Tobak offered a good example of the time that a company could not deliver a key component on time, resulting in a shutdown of one of his customer's production lines.

During the 'bad news delivery' face-to-face meeting with the customer, we held a conference call with my company's head of operations who, seemingly on the fly and under pressure from the customer, committed to an accelerated schedule that would minimize my customer's pain. That was a preplanned contingency to use if necessary. The result was a customer who felt that I would do anything to go to bat for him; my company would pull out all the stops to meet his needs, and he helped to make all that happen by the way he handled the meeting. We all won and our relationship was stronger as a result.

One of the most serious mistakes leaders make in delivering bad news is the emotional build up and the rush to get it over with. They typically do not take the time to diffuse their own emotional state; put themselves in the other person's shoes, and do enough contingency planning to know what can be done to make things right. Bad news and a leader's response can turn into a self-inflected poisoning.

Erika James in her article *Leadership as (Un)usual: How to Display Competence in Times of Crisis*, suggests that there are two types of situations: (1) *Sudden Crisis* and (2) *Smoldering Crisis*. Sudden crises occur without any warning and are beyond the organization's control; consequently, leaders are judged completely on how they respond to the situation within what was even possible, given the circumstances. Smoldering crises are different from sudden because they begin as bad news and escalate into a significant event. James recommends that all leaders create a situational preparation mentality and modality by starting with a signal detection strategy or plan. This can be accomplished at least in part by encouraging staff members to inform leadership when something happens or is happening that may smolder and become worse. In other words, do not hide bad news. Many unexpected and challenging situations can be prevented, but leaders must grow situational skills that include the ability to sift through a lot of information and determine what is important, what can be delayed and what needs to be addressed rapidly. It cannot be said often enough that leaders must develop trust with employees and the governing board members before challenging situations occur. Trust is essential during difficult times. In fact, the lack of trust is perhaps the most compelling obstacle during a crisis. A "bunker mentality" response is not uncommon when the leader, staff and governing board do not trust each other, and no good decisions can come from that climate. Leadership expert, Robert Freeman, once said, *"Character is not made in a crisis it is only exhibited."*

A few weeks after the Katrina storm flooded New Orleans, an editorial cartoon appeared in *Time Magazine* that showed a man standing in waist-deep water holding a sign that pleaded, *"Leadership Please."* In his book, *Crisis Leadership*, Gene Klann wrote:

Nothing tests a leader like a crisis. The highly charged, dramatic events surrounding a crisis profoundly affect the people in an organization and can even threaten the organization's survival. But there are actions a leader can take before, during, and after a crisis to effectively reduce the duration and impact of these extremely difficult situations. At its center, effective crisis leadership is comprised of three things - communication, clarity of vision and values, and caring relationships. Leaders who develop, pay attention to, and practice these qualities go a long way toward handling the human dimension of a crisis. In the end, it's all about the people and the plan.

Ken Sweeny's book, *Crisis Decision Theory*, focuses on three steps of crisis decision making theory: (a) assessing the severity of the negative event; (b) determining response options [instead of repeating what may have worked or not worked in the past]; and (c) evaluating response options. Sweeny wrote, "*Some crises have more consequences than others, but crisis decisions theory recognizes that even relatively inconsequential negative events may require considerable attention at the time they occur.*" There are no precise and exact decision making protocols that will be appropriate for every type of unexpected event. However, at the very least, every organization could build a basic protocol based on questions that should be asked and answered at the onset of an unexpected situation.

1. How serious is the situation?
2. Is the situation unexpected or has it happened before?
3. What components of the organization are most affected by the situation?
4. What are the response options?
5. What are the pros and cons of each response option?

Organizations can then combine those questions and answers with the concept of Strengths, Weaknesses, Opportunities, and Threats analysis, sometimes referred to as SWOT. For example, identify the strengths of each response option; identify the weaknesses of each response option; does a response option have opportunities for making the situation a valuable learning experience for the organization and can the decision response possibly strengthen the organization's standing by illustrating its ability to respond effectively to an unexpected situation? Rahm Emanuel, the former chief of staff for President Obama, once said, "*You never let a serious crisis go to waste. And what I mean by that it's an opportunity to do things you think you could not do before.*"

Roles of the CEO and the Governing Board

In many organizations there is considerable role confusion between the leader and the governing board. Unless those roles are clearly distinguished, the organization will suffer. Some leaders resist working with governing boards which causes internal conflict and instability, while other leaders capitulate to the whims of the governing board. Some governing board members intentionally attempt to become involved in the daily operations of the organization. This role confusion creates problems for the organization.

Poison: Governing board members that interfere with the daily operations of the organization have a detrimental effect on the entire organization, from top to bottom and all directions inside and outside the organization. Governing board members that are self-focused, narrowed-minded, self-serving and that sacrifice the best overall interests of the organization can contaminate an organization. It can be deadly to an organization's efficiency. An organization's leader that capitulates to this type of governing board has sacrificed his effectiveness and loses the confidence and trust of employees and others. This double dose of poison jeopardizes the future of the organization by leading to decisions that may cost the organization in untold ways for many years. The leader must have the courage to say no to the governing board, and they in turn, must trust his judgment and respect the purpose and operations of the organization. The lack of trust and courage poisons many aspects of the organization, regardless of the type of organization, because the primary goal of the organization is compromised by leadership chaos.

Antidote: In his book, *The Speed of Trust*, Stephen Covey states that an effective leader must have the trust of everyone in the organization in order to reach maximum efficiency. He conveys that micromanaging comes from a lack of trust and over self-indulgence from the leader. Covey asks the questions: *Do people trust their boss and does their boss trust them*? If that trust of leadership is diminished it reverberates across the organization. Of course, trust works both ways and any discussion about trust or the lack therein must be an honest appraisal of the behavior of employees and leadership. Leadership based on trust means that employees can trust that leaders are dependable and honest, while leaders can trust that employees are doing their jobs and are not falsifying records or stealing from the organization, for example, and that governing board members are fulfilling their role instead of trying to manage the operations of the organization. Covey's emphasis on trust focuses on leaders that do not trust any employee to do anything without intrusive supervision, even when there is no indication that employees are doing anything wrong. This applies to the behavior of governing boards that do not trust the CEO. This approach to leadership minimizes production and leads to employee turnover. In organizations with a history of employee misbehavior, the CEO and governing board cannot be naïve about the leader-employee relationship. Trust is earned and is not an entitlement. In the book *The Twelve Absolutes of Leadership*, Gary Burnison suggests that the lack of trust and the forfeiture of leadership develop when an organization loses its purpose which can be the result of governing board interference.

In this chapter, there are examples of governing board members replacing the purpose of the organization with their own purposes and agendas. When the CEO abdicates his role in order to please governing board members the purpose of the organization is sacrificed. The antidote to this type of poison is an absolute, unbreakable devotion to purpose and commitment to purpose. Burnison writes: *"To be a leader is to be passionate about purpose – authentically and genuinely. Leaders make purpose their North Star and continually lead the organization toward it. Embody purpose – people will watch you and follow your lead; personally shape and continually deliver the message about purpose; walk the talk of purpose in everything you do – if you don't, purpose is just the slogan du jour; be grounded in purpose over time."*

Governing board members, CEOs, and communities must maintain the purpose of the organization and protect it, because the insidious effects of even the smallest amount of self-purpose can ruin it. They must understand their role as leader and governing board members. Carlo Corsi, Guilherme Dale, Julie Hembrock Daum and Willi Schoppen list essential things governing board members should be thinking about.

The effective functioning of a board depends on a number of factors, including the mix of knowledge and experience among them, the quality of information they receive and their ability to operate as a team. The [governing board] chairman's role...is pivotal in managing the group dynamic, playing to the board's strengths and maintaining regular contact with organizational directors between meetings. High-functioning boards rotate meetings around...locations.... Boards not only evaluate the performance of the CEO, but take the formal assessment of their own work seriously and use the findings to develop — and hold themselves to — objectives for improvement. Transparency and trust prevail.

An effective governing board should take the time for self-evaluation, using the role of the governing board and the mission of the organization as cornerstone indicators of effectiveness. The effective governing board member stays focused on the purpose of the organization and each governing board member's role in protecting and encouraging the purpose of the organization.

Effective boards put their companies [organizations] at a distinct advantage; nowhere is this more evident than in the way they address strategy, from formation through to execution. The conventional delineation of responsibility is that the executive team develops the strategy and the governing board fine tunes it and then oversees its execution by management, measuring the CEO's performance against a set of agreed-upon objectives. (Corsi, et al.)

The distinction is clear – an organization's leader and her executive team create the strategy and execute the strategy. The governing board offers support and holds the leadership accountable, but governing board members should not be involved in the daily operations of the organization. It cannot be stated too often how disruptive governing board inference is to the operations of an organization. The long-term impact can compromise the quality of work and jeopardize staff morale. Also, there are other ramifications of role confusion.

Ultimately, it is sustainability that is the measure of success. There are many organizations and businesses that found short-term success at one time but do not even exist now. Take for example, the Fortune 500 list. In the 1980s it took five years for one-third of the Fortune 500 to be replaced; in the 1970s it took a decade to replace the Fortune 500, and prior to the 1970s it took two decades. Jim Collins, author of *Built to Last*, notes that only 71 companies on the original 1955 Fortune 500 list are there today. Sustainability should be a major concern to governing board members, which means for example that constant changes in an organization's leadership because of the failure of the governing board to understand its proper role jeopardizes sustainability of the organization. It can be a challenge to get governing boards and CEOs of organizations to understand and accept this. An organization's governing board or a CEO that focuses on self-interest and role confusion has no real goal or plan for sustainability and therefore focuses only on the short-term. Chip Heath wrote in *Made to Stick*, "*Many armies fail because they put all their emphasis into creating a plan that becomes useless ten minutes into the battle*." Some organizations have recognized that sustainability is too important to depend solely on whatever quirks of board governance might jeopardize them, so they are developing sustainability managers. These managers work with the organization's CEO and the governing board to point out how decisions and the behavior of governing board members may impact the future of the organization in positive or negative ways.

Selecting New Leadership

Transitioning to new leadership is a major issue in all organizations. A successful organization may lose momentum under a new leader, if his skill set and needs of the organization do not match. If the new leader was selected more for political reasons than organization efficiency, it is only a matter of time before negative results will surface. Thoughtful and careful consideration must be given to leadership selection and transition.

Poison: The selection of a leader based on personal agendas of the governing board or on perceived short-term needs of the organization can poison critical components of the organization. This is toxic when the leader aims to maintain the status quo and when the leader relinquishes leadership functions and lets the organization drift on its own. Equally destructive is totalitarian leadership because an overbearing, bullying leader does not work well in problem-solving situations and typically creates morale issues within the organization. No organization can survive or thrive with those types of leaders. The laissez-faire leader is often controlled by the governing board, thus, decisions such as personnel decisions are driven more by the leader's desire to please the governing board than by the needs of the organization. The totalitarian leader tries to control everything and ends up controlling very little. Without the right type of leader, one who has effective communication skills, understands the value of trust and good support staff, and seeks independence from the governing board, a once successful organization can decline rapidly and irreversibly.

Antidote: In the book *Influencer: The Power to Change Anything* the authors note that the attraction of short-term strategies is to make short-term progress. There is something positive to be said about immediate success to build motivation and morale and to let everyone inside an organization and outside know that a new leader is in place and the governing board is taking care of business, as Louis Gerstner did when he first joined troubled IBM. However, there is a dynamic chain of events that spiral downward from the selection of a leader by a governing board based on short-term needs, and most of those events are not good for the organization. Governing boards must be very thoughtful about the selection of the organization's leader and refrain from the overwhelming temptation to select for the short-term or select based on a desire to maintain the status quo. It behooves the governing board to take the time to review its strategic plan; conduct a self-assessment; survey the employees; determine the future needs of clients and the organization, and conduct a "Gap Analysis" to determine the gap between the organization's goals and the outcomes. From that thoughtful approach, the governing board can create attributes that the next leader must possess in order to move the organization toward short-term and long-term goals. Also, the governing board should annually sign an Assurance of Governance that compels each governing board member to refrain from nepotism. The organization's leader should also sign an Assurance of Governance. This is a commitment on part of the governing board and the leader to stay true to their different roles in the organization and focus on selecting and promoting talented employees.

Contrary to many of the myths and assumptions surrounding the selection of new leaders, experts such as James Citrin and Julie Hembrock argue that the process of choosing a leader should begin with a deep understanding of the organization's needs and the kind of person who will both fit into its culture and bring the right experience and skill-set to get the job done — and only then seek the person who best matches those needs. This may seem like common sense, yet in practice this represents a different way of thinking for many organizations.

Contrary to many opinions, research by LaBelle found that the first hundred days do not comprise a sufficient indication of how the leadership transfer has succeeded. The key is communications. LaBelle wrote,

To keep the organization steering in the right direction requires constant and constructive communication between the leader and the governing board. Open communication links should allow the leader to bring both good news and bad news to the governing board. In turn, the governing board needs to listen appropriately and give honest feedback. Change in leadership is hard. Support from the governing board is imperative. The new leader's personal successes will serve as an encouragement; the governing board's recognition of the new leader's results will reinforce and strengthen the process and outcomes.

Research by the Hay Group and reported by Gilmore, has found that if a new leader is following a well liked leader it is important for him to avoid falling into a popularity contest in an effort to fit in and be liked by everyone. Gilmore recommends that the new leader,

Simply put, you need to be yourself and follow your own vision and communicate effectively. In establishing credibility and a loyal following amongst the team it is important that they see you for yourself and not a mold of the previous leader. You have to let them all know that you are not your predecessor, but you have your own talents and motivation.

New leaders that pressure themselves or that feel pressure by governing board members to protect the status quo are not following sound advice. The new leader needs to let the organizational staff members and the governing board know what he stands for and communicate that effectively and often, and maintaining the status quo should be quickly dismissed. New leaders must recognize and develop key relationships and build networks in the organization in order to convey the clear message that they are team-oriented and not status quo oriented. Additionally, according to Goodyear and Golden, "*It is important that a new leader convey trust in the organization from the beginning, through delegation. Focused discussion between leaders and followers about successful outcomes and accountability mechanisms can result in focused and successful implementation.*"

Climate and Safety in the Organization: A Leadership and Governance Function

Effective organizations and competent leadership will understand the importance of workplace climate, not only for employee morale but also for workplace safety and productivity. The nexus for safety and efficiency is the climate of the organization and the role the leader shares with employees in developing a positive workplace climate that can respond effectively to almost anything that challenges or threatens the organizations, including emergencies and change.

Poison: The leadership requirements of any organization are very complicated, and the leader must never forget that each organization has basic needs that must be met before it can expand or excel. Too often, leaders and governing boards fail to understand that organizations have work climates that live and breathe, and must, therefore, be protected and nurtured. The complexity of the work climate requires an understanding of what motivates employees. Leaders and governing boards must strive to identify and meet the basic needs of employees. This is especially true in two vitally important areas: change and safety. Organizations have to be prepared for change and must take safety seriously. Some of the dynamics related to change also apply to safety, because both are directly related to the workplace climate. Many organizations do not have a plan to manage change nor do they have a clearly defined and fully developed safety plan until after something happens or fails. Research shows that employees and clients in every part of society are acutely aware of change and safety and there is a full expectation that every organization understands the importance of both and, consequently, have plans in place that includes all of the essential elements for managing change and safety, based on functions of the organization. The lack of change and safety planning and training of employees is poisonous to leaders, employees, governing board, clients, and ultimately to the organization.

Antidote: An effective leader must understand the dynamics that can negatively impact workplace climate and an organization's ability to effectively handle change. Leaders must also understand the relationship between leadership, change, conditions for change, and how all of these link to workplace climate. A safe work climate is a basic and essential requirement of every organization, but many organizations are finding it more difficult to provide safety because of continued budget cuts and because safety is not a top priority to some governing boards and CEOs. No one's health or safety should be at risk because of budget issues or a lack of safety planning and preparation. Also, most courses and books on leadership or governing, whether it is directed to schools, colleges, non-profit organizations or business environments do not address the need for a safety plan nor do they establish the link between the organization's climate, managing change, leadership and productivity. This is a major oversight. Every organization, regardless of mission and size, must take the time to develop a positive workplace climate and safety management plan. Studies have found that organizations that understand the dynamic nature of workplace climate find that respect for the climate through actions such as safety awareness and planning create conditions for success, transitions, and change in the workplace. Leaders and governing boards can seek assistance on the development of a safety plan from the local emergency management agency and from the Federal Emergency Management Agency (FEMA). A crisis can occur at any time, change is inevitable, and it is unlikely that any organization will escape the necessity of responding to a crisis or deal with change. A comprehensive approach to workplace climate places a strong emphasis on prevention, using strategies which range from building design to policies and programs which improve the organization's climate. One example of this is the Atlanta branch of Ernst and Young, an international accounting firm. The workplace design was changed to eliminate the dreaded work cubicles. They were dehumanizing, created social isolation, discouraged creative interaction, and created a mob scene during evacuation drills. The redesign opened up the floor space to allow interaction between and among employees, and the redesign offered a more open design for safety and emergency evacuations. In a short period of time, the workplace improved substantially, as measured by improved employee productivity and attendance.

Crisis management is that part of an organization's approach to safety and change which anticipates potential problems and establishes a coordinated response to minimize stress and disruptions in the organization; thus, it is both prevention and management. It is not possible, however, to anticipate all events. Crisis management functions as a time-limited, problem-focused intervention designed to identify, confront and resolve the crisis, restore equilibrium, and support adaptive responses. Developing safety-related policies provides both a foundation and a framework for action and a climate of support and care for employees and clients.

Leadership is necessary to ensure effective implementation of plans and maintenance of preparedness and a positive workplace climate. The essential and basic components of a plan can be used for any type of crisis, as well as for significant changes in the workplace.

There are four major components of planning that are essential to a workplace that is safe, positive, and prepared: *Crisis Response Team*; *Critical Management Plan*; *Critical Incident Management Plan* and *Training for Preparedness*.

Crisis Response Team - A Crisis Response Team can be a highly effective organizational unit for dealing with a variety of crises. Well-functioning teams provide a network that can support action whenever crises arise. *Crisis Management Plan* – An organization that is prepared before a crisis occurs will be much more likely to deal with it effectively during and after a crisis. The plan should be designed to result in a differentiated, coordinated response to crises. *Critical Incident Management Plan* - A critical incident management plan focuses more narrowly on situations that involve imminent danger to life and limb and require a coordinated response involving public safety resources and public health resources. *Training for Preparedness* – Preparation for and response to crises rely on people understanding policies and procedures and knowing what they are to do during a crisis. These are achieved through training. Maintaining preparedness is an ongoing process which involves debriefing following crises, periodic review, updating, table-top (practice) exercises, and ongoing training. When a crisis occurs, effective communication is essential within the organization, with the governing board, with all stakeholders and clients, and with the media. Effective communication can speed the restoration of equilibrium; poor communication (i.e., lack of communication, incorrect information, etc.) can make a bad situation much worse.

All organizations must focus on workplace climate and develop plans based on strategic needs and aims. The failure to do so jeopardizes the organization's effectiveness and ultimately its purpose. A comprehensive workplace plan should lay the foundation for a positive work climate, effective response to change, safety, and crisis management. All of this is directly related to the organization's leadership.

Leadership Style

Many case studies and research findings have reached the same conclusion – leadership style does matter. More specifically, it is fairly well established that certain types of leaders do not fare well when their leadership style and personality clash with the organization's needs and the productivity of its employees and expectations of the governing board.

Poison: There are many leadership traits and styles that are poison to an organization. Leadership that does not match the needs of an organization, regardless of good intentions makes for an unsuccessful present and future. The organization can lose precious momentum and ineffective selection of support staff can actually jeopardize the future of the organization. This situation, however, is quickly exacerbated by a governing board's decision to hire a leader who is either already arrogant or who becomes arrogant with the bestowed and perceived power of the position. This arrogance of power and position becomes a poison that spreads throughout an organization.

Antidote: Arrogance, the need to "win" at the expense of the organization, according to Grady Bogue in his book, *The Enemies of Leadership,* is an enemy of leadership in the extreme, primarily because the collateral damage to the organization can be significant. The authors of *In Search of Excellence,* Thomas Peters and Robert Waterman, noted the importance of treating people right: *"Treat people as adults; treat them as partners; threat them with dignity; threat them with respect."* All leaders and all governing boards are selected by someone who has the authority to make such selections or by a public that has the power of the vote. Those in position to make these decisions, no matter the type of organization, must give more attention to the future of the organization and base selections of leaders on their ability to hold the future in mind while developing short and long-term strategies. That is not possible in the minds and actions of arrogant leaders. Therefore, arrogance must be avoided at all levels, from the CEO to the lowest level manager; an arrogant leader cannot lead and should not be selected for any leadership position. According to the Society for Industrial and Organizational Psychology, the angst of arrogance is clearly illustrated by one former CEO at American International Group (AIG), Joe Cassano.

Cassano was the president of AIG's financial products unit and is credited by some as single-handedly bringing about the downfall of AIG. Many accounts describe Cassano as a quintessential arrogant CEO. Former coworkers report that in stark contrast to his predecessors, Cassano had penchants for yelling, cursing, bad-mouthing others, and belittling colleagues, as well as little tolerance for opposing viewpoints. In the absence of Cassano's persistent arrogant behavior (and unwillingness to tolerate dissent regarding his management practices), it is possible that AIG's crisis would have been considerably less severe or altogether avoided. However, despite the fact that it was the practices he sanctioned that led AIG to be regarded as one of the most notable examples of excess associated with Wall Street, Cassano remains unapologetic about his role and blames others for the crisis.

Can an arrogant leader change? Robert Greenleaf opines in his book *Servant Leadership* that leaders can be taught how to lead effectively. If that is true, then staff development in every organization should include training on treating employees, clients and each other with respect.

In an article for *Inc. Magazine*, the magazine's staff compiled leadership pointers from experts that were categorized into several components:

1. Focus on employee happiness rather than employee motivation. *Inc.'s* researcher, Max Chafkin, interviewed successful business CEOs and found that many of them focused on the happiness factor of employees and customers. He found that working environments that include humor were strong on camaraderie and production. Customers that felt pleased with the employees' treatment reinforced the positive behavior by giving positive feedback.

2. Set a good example. *"A leader's attitude is contagious. Communication is a key to making members of the organization's team feel included in major decisions. Employees are more motivated when they feel needed, appreciated, and valued."*

3. It is important to make sure employees share in the organization's success. *"Employee performance, productivity, and motivation can all be tied to how invested a worker feels in his or her company (or organization)."*

4. It is also important to create a culture of support and collaboration. In his book *Drive: The Surprising Truth About What Motivates Us*, author Daniel H. Pink writes that the crash of Wall Street is a striking example of the peril of motivating employees strictly with cash. He advises that instead, companies and organizations should create conditions for employees to find the joy in work itself. That can mean giving workers the autonomy to choose what they do and with whom, which can help foster a desire for mastery of tasks and skill sets and simply doing more, better.

5. Leaders should encourage workers to voice complaints. *"When Dell amassed an online 'anti-fan club,' excoriating the PC maker across the blogosphere, it not only acknowledged criticism, but also actually fixed things,"* according to Jeff Jarvis in his book, *What Would Google Do.*

There are scores of reasons why employees are reluctant to offer critiques of management or their company's culture. However, it is important to remember, as *Inc.*'s Leigh Buchanan writes, "*When the heat's not lowered, steam escapes.*" One motivational strategy that works well in some organizations is to take on volunteer assignments. A significant way to improve morale and motivation is to encourage and then provide ways for employees to do volunteer work in the community where they live or in the community near the workplace. This becomes even more powerful when the leader of the organization also participates in volunteer events. This may be supported by compensatory work time, by public recognition of the volunteers' work during an organization's meeting, and/or by articles in the organization's eLetter, newsletter, etc. The volunteer work itself can be so rewarding that the benefit is a happier and more productive employee. These types of projects not only help charities, but also help employees create some of their most inspired work.

Another motivational consideration is to appeal to the creative spark in employees – there is a distinct energy in start-up companies that can be captured in any organization or business. Some businesses and organizations operationalize this practice by periodically gathering employees in small clusters at the office and for about 15-30 minutes in a very informal way, with laughter and banter, collaborate by brainstorming ideas. Some call this "controlled chaos," but it can energize an organization.

There is poison for all when an organization's leader pays scant attention to the needs of the employees and organization. People will attempt to change and will accept change such as new ideas about work, new strategies, and new expectations if they believe it will be worth it and they can do what is required. This response to change is consistent with those essential components specified in the *Three Cs of Implementing Strategy* that Scott Edinger insists are necessary for strategies to be implemented successfully: Clarify the strategy to all employees; communicate the strategy to all employees and stakeholders; and cascade the strategy so that employees and others know how the strategies are related to their daily jobs/work. With these in place, and with the motivation and good will of its leader, most individuals will at least try to enact the change.

Organizational Assessment

Assessment in organizations and assessment of organizations are wholly different but equally important. Assessments are a useful way for leaders and organizations to measuring effectiveness and identify changes that are necessary for the health of the organization. Effective assessment can guide strategic planning, but organizations do not have to depend solely on external assessors, and probably should not totally depend on outside evaluators. Self-assessment can be very valuable.

Poison: The assessment of leadership is critical to the success of an organization. In many circumstances, the assessment comes from an outside source, such as the Better Business Bureau, non-profit rating institutions, bond rating organizations, accrediting associations, popular news magazines, and others. Are these organizations held accountable for how they assess organizations? Does a "good score" or "negative score" actually mean that an organization and thus its leadership are truly good or bad? If there is a poison, it comes insidiously from assessments that go easy on organizational leadership which in reality is not effective. An organization can be poisonous and no one knows until problems erupt that could have been dealt with much earlier and much more effectively had it been revealed honestly. Organizations that aim for success or that desire to continue successfully, must contemplate how to best assess its operations and not depend solely on organization whose existence is dependent on its evaluation of other entities. An organization and its leadership can die from the poison of false or misleading assessments.

Antidote: There is an old saying that what gets measured gets done. However, it is not very likely that the United .States Department of Education is going to conduct an in depth study of SACS and the other school and school district accrediting agencies to determine what they do, how they do it and whether what they claim to do is effective. It is also unlikely that accrediting agencies and bond rating companies will change their methods. Additionally, an entity such as Charity Navigator that reviews non-profits is not likely to overhaul its methods either. Furthermore, the private school accrediting agencies will not change, and it is certain that the bond rating companies will continue to operate without significant oversight. Therefore, it is imperative that organizational leaders and especially governing boards take the outside assessments from these organizations for what they are worth, and develop strong internal methods and mechanisms for assessing their organization's health. Every organization goes through periods of difficulty and has to contend with challenges at all levels. Sometimes it is just growing pains, but in other situations the organization does not have a clear, objective view and understanding of its own internal and external operations. Or, it may be the challenge of insufficient resources or misaligned or poorly allocated resources, and sometimes it is related to trying to do something new or make a significant change without making the necessary preparations. The reasons for organizational difficulties are multifaceted. And because so many things can go wrong, or so many challenges can occur, it is highly beneficial for organizations to have the ability to accurately diagnose the source(s) of their difficulties in order to quickly correct course and optimize the use of scarce resources. Even when it seems that the organization is functioning efficiently, there is a need for an assessment of performance.

Some organizations contract performance assessments from external vendors, and there are times and circumstances when that is appropriate and necessary, but much can be learned through an organizational self-assessment, too. In fact, an honest internal review can often reveal more than an external-based review. There are numerous self-assessment models that an organization can use, or it can develop its own, with assistance. According to the Center for Non-Profit Management (CNPM), organizational self-assessment should focus on things that are changeable, that the organization can control, that directly impact performance, and that are related to the goals of the organization. Good organizational assessment will identify "cause and effect" relationships, helping insure that whatever corrective actions put in place will produce meaningful change. CNPM says organizational self-assessment has additional benefits as well. It helps bring focus to the organization's improvement efforts and it helps optimize the use of organizational resources and functions. Self-assessment emphasizes opportunities for improvement, not "fixing blame" and it looks at the total organization, not just one or two aspects. An informative self-assessment is performance focused, not just people focused.

Organizational self-assessment does not have to be an overly formal, heavily structured, painstaking process to produce highly useful information. The Baldrige Performance Excellence Program provides a proven approach to meaningful self-assessment through the use of its Criteria for Performance Excellence. The self-assessment criterion from Baldrige applies to many different types of organizations and provides effective and useful feedback. Baldrige offers several examples of when a self-assessment is appropriate, such as when customers/clients are driving a need to change; the industry or environment is changing; the organization is among the best and it wants to stay that way; the leaders want to enhance organizational learning; the organization sees a connection between key issues and pressure on organizational performance; and when an organization is underperforming.

CNPM offers excellent resources for organizational self-assessment, as does the Annie E. Casey Foundation. Additionally, organizations should look at similar organizations that have proven to be successful over time and inquire to determine if and how those organizations self-assess. Genuine improvement in any and every organization depends heavily on an accurate assessment of its internal strategies, methods, mechanisms, policies, procedures, management of resources, and staffing in order to maintain success and identify weaknesses.

An organization that depends solely on external assessment entities and does not carefully consider internal data or that depends on external evaluators that do not take the time or have the expertise to conduct an effective and useful evaluation will not fully understand its strengths and weaknesses and, therefore, will not make adjustments or significant changes that could benefit the organization and its future. There are times when trust is not high enough between the leadership and the governing board to allow for an internal assessment of the organization, or if there is one the results may not be accepted. This situation, however, should not preclude an organization from carefully and thoroughly and periodically planning an internal assessment. It can be insidiously poisonous to rely only on outside assessments as the sole means of feedback on effectiveness and efficiency.

Developing a Leadership Team

Successful organizations are not "One-Man Shows." An organization may have a skilled leader, someone with a powerful personality and an advanced set of skills, but even that type of leader cannot possibly make an organization successful without an effective, dependable, and hardworking team.

Poison: One of the most crucial responsibilities of a leader in any organization is the development of an excellent leadership team that functions at the highest levels. No matter how talented the leader may be, there are few organizations that can be successful without a leadership team that works in tangent with the leader and that is supportive of each other, a team that can be open and honest with each colleague and with the leader. A leadership team made up of sycophants will offer nothing to the organization and in fact will inevitably become liability. A dysfunctional leadership team is poison to an organization and can jeopardize current organization operations and the future of the organization.

Antidote: When reviewing applicants for leadership positions, governing boards should consider many qualities that the perspective leader must possess in order to be selected. That is obvious. What is not so obvious is the importance of teambuilding. The list of qualities must include an exploration of how the prospective leader builds teams and how he utilizes and manages the leadership team. In a study by Marie McIntyre, *Building An Effective Management Team,* she studied more than

500 members of 72 management groups in both business and government. The teams were surveyed using the Team Effectiveness Assessment for Management instrument. Teams rated in the top 25 percent on team effectiveness measures were compared with teams rated in the bottom 25 percent on team effectiveness. The study found five success factors differentiated the most successful teams from unsuccessful ones:

1. *To focus activity and effort, management teams need a clear understanding of their purpose and the goals they intend to accomplish.*
2. *To make informed decisions, management teams must access critical information from both inside and outside the organization.*
3. *To cooperate in achieving team goals, management team members must be able to develop positive, supportive relationships.*
4. *To make good decisions, management teams must effectively process the information available to them – the research found that the leader of a management team has more influence over this aspect of team effectiveness than any other.*
5. *To accomplish results, management teams must make the transition from discussion to action. A brilliant decision that is implemented poorly will be of no benefit to the organization.*

These factors can be put into practice by an effective leader and by governing boards. McIntyre said, "*Trust is knowing that when a team member does push you, they're doing it because they care about the team.*" The degree of respect required to reach levels of effectiveness that benefits the organization is almost completely determined by the leader's ability and willingness to build an effective team and structure cabinet meetings in such a way to maximize the potential for dynamic discussions and effective decision making.

Leaders that do not know how to build an effective team or how to manage what could be an effective cabinet are poison to an organization. Leaders who understand and acknowledge this and are willing to look to team building experts to learn more about the dynamic possibilities of team building and effective cabinet meetings should consider the following resources: John Maxwell *(The 17 Indisputable Laws of Teamwork: Embrace Them and Empower Your Team)*; Patrick Lencioni *(Five Dysfunctions of a Team)*; Arbinger Institute *(The Anatomy of Peace)*; Spencer Kagan *(Cooperative Learning)*; John Newstrom *(The Big Book of Team Building Games: Trust-Building Activities, Team Spirit Exercises, and Other Activities)*; Price Pritchett *(The Team Member Handbook for Teamwork)*; and Thomas Kayser *(Building Team Power: How to Unleash the Collaborative Genius of*

Teams for Increased Engagement, Productivity, and Results).

If a leader has an epiphany and wants ideas on how to quickly start positive team building, with the understanding that long-term strategies will come from the team, Bradley Sugars' book, *Instant Team Building,* is a good way to kick-start the effort to build an effective team and manage cabinet meetings.

Transitioning to New Leadership

Poison: A new leader in an organization comes in with high expectations and the governing board has even higher expectations. There are a number of issues many of which relate to communications that can make the transition to new leadership successful or a failure. The failure of a governing board to prepare the new leader and the existing staff for change that comes with new leadership threatens the success of the transition. The breakdown in communication and a disconnection between expectations and outcomes poisons the work environment. Consequently, the entire organization suffers and the new leader's tenure could be short lived.

Antidote: The transition to new leadership can be an exciting time for the new leader and the organization, if there is a transition plan that is centered on communications, essential management functions, strategic planning, team building, improving morale, and sound decision making. Governing boards should ask the finalists for leadership positions how they plan to make the transition, including how they plan to communicate (or connect) with the staff in the organization, how they will handle staffing decisions and appointments, and how they will communicate with the governing board. Governing boards should tell the finalists about the challenges facing the organizations; only an honest assessment of the organization will prepare the potential leader to address those issues that need the most attention quickest. However, the governing board cannot be divided in its assessment of the organization, where one governing board member tells one thing while undermining the opinion of other governing board members. A review or assessment of the finalists' communication skills and communication plans may help determine if the finalists have what it will take to make the transition successful. John Maxwell wrote, *"It's difficult to find common ground with others when the only person you're focused on is yourself."* Michael Myatt states, *"The moral of the story is leaders need to be honest, have a demonstrated track record of success, be excellent communicators, place an emphasis on serving those they lead, be fluid in approach, be focused, and have a bias for action. If these traits are not possessed by your leader and leadership team, you will be in for a rocky* *road ahead."*

The advice of Maxwell and Myatt stands strong for leaders who also must improve staff morale, one of the most overlooked aspects of new leadership. Louis Gerstner, Jr. was keenly sensitive to the morale of his IBM employees when he took over IBM. He came to his new job when the organization was struggling in many ways, but addressing morale was one of his first priorities and thus improving morale became one of his most urgent strategies. He said this to the organization: "*It is not helpful to feel sorry for ourselves. I'm sure our employees don't need any rah-rah speeches. We need leadership at all levels and a sense of direction and momentum, not just from me but from all of us. I don't want to see a lot of prophets of doom around here. I want can-do people looking for excitement.*" Gerstner went on to say that the organization did not have time to focus on who created the problems, "*We have little time to spend on problem definition. We must focus our efforts on communications, solutions and actions.*"

1. Rosabeth Moss Kanter said that leaders, especially new leaders, must energize depressed employees, passive teams or sluggish organizations, and she offered guiding principles to accomplish that.

2. *Believe in people and their power to make a difference.* Show them they are worth it by investing in things that matter to them, and show sincerity by taking the time to find out want matters to employees.

3. *Direct the energy tied up in negativity (resentment, rivalry, or disrespect) into positive actions.* If people seem petty, make them noble by focusing them on a bigger cause and giving them a chance to contribute to it. Negativity inevitably leads to rampant rumors and spreading dissatisfaction which compromises the effectiveness of the leader and organization outcomes.

4. *Make initiative possible and desirable.* Awaken creative thinking by opening real opportunities to contribute new ideas. Seek them, find them, fund them, praise them, and provide a support system. It is also critically important to provide feedback to employees about their work and ideas.

5. *Start with small wins – things that people can control.* Look for even small successes, good ideas, and other things that can be praised. While this is important, it must also be sincere, because false praise of mediocrity can portray the new leader as naïve or worse.

When governing boards are interviewing candidates for the leadership position, they should conclude by asking the candidates this question suggested by Marcus Buckingham: "*What is the difference between chess and checkers?*" Most prospective leaders will respond that chess is more difficult and requires more strategic thinking. While that is true, the most insightful answer is this: the pieces in checkers move in only two directions while the pieces in chess move in multiple directions. As Buckingham said, "*Thus, if you want to excel at the game of chess you have to learn how each piece moves and then incorporate these unique moves into your overall plan. The same is true for the game of leading. Mediocre new leaders play checkers with their people. They assume that their employees will be motivated by the same things and driven by the same goals.*" The effective new leader understands the dynamic fact that employees are different and cannot be managed like pieces on a checker board.

In his book, *The New Boss: How to Survive the First 100 Days*, Peter Fischer states that new leaders that are successful "*recognize and develop key relationships, deal adroitly with hidden rivals and predecessors, build networks in the organization, show that they are team oriented, communicate with senior management on strategy and style of leadership and impart confidence and trust.*"

Rumors

Poison: The decision making process has been reviewed ad nauseam by researcher for decades, particularly in reference to how leaders make effective decisions and under what circumstances. Arrogance and rumor are impediments to effective decision making. These two elements separately are poison to an organization, but if they both exist an organization's health is seriously compromised. Interestingly, arrogance can actually fuel rumors. Arrogance can impact decisions by distorting the perceptual screen of leaders, so that a leader ignores sound advice, data, and probabilities and instead makes decisions based more on self-preservation and perhaps even in response to rumors. Rumors can be a fast-spreading poison that permeates an organization before the leader can implement damage control, if the CEO is oblivious to the needs of the organization's staff members and governing board to receive information in a timely and consistent manner.

Antidote: Arrogance and rumors poison organizations. David Hume wrote, "*When men are most sure and arrogant they are commonly most mistaken, giving views to passion without that proper deliberation which alone can secure them from the grossest absurdities.*" The research on arrogance indicates clearly that arrogant leaders are seldom effective over time, and the research on rumors, which indicates that a leader's effectiveness can be hampered by rumors, have not been convoked. The outcomes from an arrogant style of leadership include the vacuum of effectiveness that is going to be filled by something, and rumors too often fill the void. The combination of arrogance and the lack of communications create the conditions for a negative work climate. Arrogance makes a debilitating impact on trust and respect, and the lack of thereof is at the core of an organization that suffers from unrelenting rumors. Rumors fill a trust and respect void caused by leaders that do not communicate effectively with staff members because they do not think staff members are worthy of the time it takes the leader to communicate or the leader lacks effective communication skills. Rumors fill a respect void caused when leaders do not understand and do not make any effort to understand the needs of staff members. In *The Trust Factor*, written by Bob Whipple, an expert on leadership, he states, *"Trust and rumors are incompatible. If there is low trust, it is easy for someone to project something negative for the future. When trust is low, these sparks create a roaring blaze....of rumors."* There are times when a leader has to address rumors, regardless of whether he wants to or not, and then there are times when a leader inherits a work climate that is rife with rumors. Whipple offers possible antidotes for the poison of rumors:

1. *Intervene quickly when there is a rumor and provide solid, believable, truthful information about what is really going to happen or has happened.*
   It is best to plan this type of intervention before the rumor even starts, but the main point is that it is essential to nip the problem as soon as it is detected. It is also wise to check with key staff members to make sure the communications information from the leader has actually been received by employees. This is also a key moment for the leader in another regard. He must take the time necessary to make an honest self-assessment. Has he spread rumors and gossip? Has he intentionally or unintentionally encouraged gossip and ignored rumors? Has he quickly quashed some rumors but allowed others to fester?
2. *Coach the worst offenders to stop.*
   Usually it is not difficult to discern the people in a group who like to stir up trouble with rumors. They are easy to spot in the break room, in the hallway, and other places where work does not take place. One interesting way to mitigate a group of gossipers is to get to know them better - sit at the lunch table with them, for example. This may feel uncomfortable at first, but it can be very helpful at

detecting rumors early, and it gives the staff the opportunity to talk to the leader, which can quell rumors. Just as in fighting poison, the sooner the antidote can be applied, the easier the problem is to control. If the same employees continue to be the genesis of rumors, a more direct approach to them may be in order to stop the rumor-generating behavior. Those employees must understand that rumors negatively affect the work and integrity of the organization.

3. *Double communications in times of uncertainty.*
   There are times when the genesis of a rumor is easy to predict. Suppose all the top managers have an unusually long, hastily called closed-door meeting. People are going to wonder what is being discussed. Suppose the financial reports indicate that continuing on the present path is impossible - that operational changes will have to be made? What if there are outsiders walking around the organization with tape measures? What if all travel has been cancelled and purchase orders limited? All these things, and numerous others, are bound to fuel speculation on what may be happening, and from that rumors are born. When this happens, smart leaders get out of the office and interface more with the staff. Unfortunately, when there are unusual circumstances, too many leaders like to hide in their offices or in meetings to avoid having to deal with pointed questions. That is exactly the opposite of what is needed to prevent rumors from taking control and poisoning the work environment.

4. *Find multiple ways to communicate the truth.*
   Sometimes people need to hear something more than once to start believing it. According to the *Edelman Trust Barometer for 2011*, nearly 60 percent of people indicate they need to hear organizational news (good or bad) at least three to five times before they believe it. It is important to utilize all available means of communicating with staff members – small or large group meetings, memorandums, emails, conference calls, webinars, etc. and keep the communications flowing. Rumors can be persistent and resistant to facts.

5. *Reinforce open dialog.*
   Leaders can find themselves in a precarious situation when engaging in dialog with staff members. Leaders should encourage questions to make sure all of the areas fertile for rumors are addressed. One of the most counterproductive reactions to questions and comments is to be defensive or critical of the staff members asking questions. Criticizing and discouraging questions is a quick path to the

rumor mill. It is critically important to remember that increasing the trust level is the best way to subdue the rumor agents.

6. *Model a no-gossip climate.*

People pick up on the tactics of a leader and mimic them throughout the organization. If the leader is prone to intentionally leaking out juicy bits of unsubstantiated speculation, then others in the organization will be encouraged to do the same thing. Conversely, if a leader refuses to discuss or acknowledge information that is incorrect, then he models the kind of attitude that will be picked up by many staff members. The key to modeling a no-gossip work climate is to develop a no-gossip expectation – not necessarily a policy, but an expectation, which can be encouraged and clarified through guidelines for staff members when they hear a rumor. This may include a definition of rumors and advice on how to respond to rumors (e.g., Ask one's immediate supervisor about rumors, gossip or other information that might be misinformation). A good resource is the *Respectful Workplace Guidelines* developed by the Human Resources Division of the University of Virginia.

7. *Extinguish gossip behavior.*

This may mean breaking up a clique of busy-bodies or at least adding some new objective blood into the mix. It may get to the point that staff members that are consistently and persistently at the center of rumors are too poisonous to continue employment. Rumors are serious. If they continue because of the behavior and attitude of the same staff members each time, those staff members should be referred to the organization's department of human resources.

It is clear that rumors in the workplace can poison the environment, reduce productivity, threaten careers, and create animosity between and among staff members. An important leadership function is to prevent and control rumors, and it is imperative for leaders to identify and correct those elements that make rumors more likely to occur and spread, such as poor or ineffective communications.

Building a Support Team

Poison: Successful organizations are built from the quality of work done by its employees, and the quality of work from competent employees is not possible if a leader hires employees who are more loyal to the leader than to the organization. A leader's failure to select quality employees and instead promote and select sycophants will lead to a poisonous work environment that compromises the organization's mission and progress. Malcolm Forbes said, "Never hire someone who knows less than you do about what he's hired to do."

Antidote: There are leaders whose power derives from their position and yet they mistakenly think that their power comes not from position but from their personality, talents, and/or intelligence; consequently, the selection of employees must first come from loyalty to the leader. The employee's talent or fit for the job is secondary to loyalty to the leader; at least that is what the ineffective leader thinks. This leads to a cadre of employees who are not independent thinkers and who would never advise the leader that he is wrong or that another course of action would be more prudent or beneficial. The leader's way is the right way; no questions asked. Governing boards have to be mindful of this when selecting a leader. In fact, it behooves governing boards to ask candidates for the organization's top leadership position how they select staff, what history they have in selecting quality staff in important positions. It may be useful to learn how many previous subordinates ascended to leadership positions. Perhaps a look at the candidates' subordinate retention rate would be informative, too. Also, a selection committee should take the time and put forth the effort to ascertain if the candidates for the leadership position have a history of hiring friends and relatives or competent staff members. Governing boards should make it clear that the organization's leadership should fill positions with quality candidates who are loyal first to the organization and its mission. Additionally, the leader should be expected to provide a path to success not only for those with leadership promise but for all employees. An effective leader absolutely has to create a working environment that values people, creativity, independent thought, and collegial relationships between and among employees. This type of work environment naturally leads to loyalty to the organization because the employees feel vested in its mission and operations. There is a critical difference between loyalty to the organization and loyalty to the leader. Ideally, a governing board wants to see both types of loyalty, but certainly not one at the expense of the other. There is an ironic outcome for leaders hiring employees who are loyal to them at the expense of the organization. Those employees do not respect or trust the leader; therefore, they are not productive which only serves to jeopardize the leader's standing with the governing board.

This is not to imply that hiring quality people for the right job is easy; it can be very difficult. And there are times when a relative or friend may actually be qualified for a job. Therefore, it is extraordinarily important for every organization to follow precise steps when trying to match the right person for the right job. *Entrepreneur, Inc.* suggests a progressive process starting with developing accurate job descriptions and compiling a "success profile" to indicate what skills a person would need to be successful in each job. Considerable time and effort, with the help of experts, should be spent on developing a series of questions for both applicant screening purposes and for later interviews with the finalists. It is important to take a jaundiced view of resumes. Bo Bennett wrote: *"Resume: a written exaggeration of only the good things a person has done in the past, as well as a wish list of the qualities a person would like to have."* Resumes must be carefully scrutinized and time must be given to verifying references. Applicant interviews should have a formal and an informal component. First, the interview should start with a structured interview format with pre-developed questions. It is important to structure and follow the questions in much the same way for each applicant, so that fair comparisons of the applicants can be made. Secondly, the structured interview should be followed by a more informal format of questions that are based on reality where the interviewers ask the applicants how they would handle case scenarios. These case study scenarios can reveal applicants' abilities or weaknesses in many domains and situations.

The governing board has to be a role model for the CEO in the selection of qualified employees. Governing boards who advocate friends, business partners, relatives or those affiliated with others in any way for positions in the organization are putting the CEO in a very difficult situation; plus, the message is loud and clear that loyalty to people overrides loyalty to the organization and its mission.

Using Data

Poison: Data is the language that leaders use to make decisions in many organizations, or so it is said. The phrase "data-driven decisions" has moved from a catchy phrase to an expectation of leaders and governing boards. Vision statements, mission statements, objectives and even motives now must be "data-driven". Platforms for change are built on data-driven planning and data-driven strategies. But are decisions really data-driven? Leaders and governing boards are often misled by this emphasis on data-driven decisions. Any statistician will say that "unscrubbed" data (cleaning the data set for accuracy) is unreliable; unrelated data is pointless; masses of data is unmanageable, and decisions made from unscrubbed, unrelated and unmanageable data are potentially detrimental to any organization. Data must provide information to the organization that is useful. Many fool-hearty decisions are made because of an overreliance on or a misunderstanding of data, and many organizations pick and choose data to meet their needs and thereby risk making erroneous assumptions that precede poor decisions. Governing boards and leaders should be very precise in how data is collected and used for planning and decision making purposes. If a prospective leader or candidate for a governing board position states that decisions should be data-driven, that assertion should be challenged, for it can be poisonous.

Antidote: There is no doubt that data is essential to all leaders, governing boards and organizations. Without data, there are no measures of effectiveness, no indications that strategic plans and objectives are working, and no way to tie the organization's budget to initiatives. Without data, an organization is operating in the blind. However, leaders and governing boards need to understand the purpose and the potential of data and manage expectations. Data that does not provide relevant information is only data, and information from data is only useful if it provides insight that can be applied to the organization in a constructive manner. Atul Butte, a Stanford University professor, said, *"Hiding within those mounds of data is knowledge that could change so many things."* Nate Silver wrote in *The Signal and the Noise,* trying to determine what data is useful and how it is useful requires recognition that data can be a lot of noise with a signal embedded in the noise. It takes skill at the data entry level, skill at the data retrieval level, skill at the data mining level, skill at the data interpretation level, and skill at the data relevancy level to make data work for an organization in an accurate and productive way. As mentioned earlier, however, there is the temptation to cherry pick data to support favorite strategies, products, or services. Ronald Coase, Nobel winning economist, said, *"Torture the data, and it will confess to anything."*

How does a leader use data? Many data experts recommend that the leader and his staff develop several questions related to the vision, mission, strategies and objectives of the organization. Additionally, the leader can ask the governing board and other stakeholders to do the same thing. The purpose of data then becomes clear; it is to answer those questions. Too often, the questions are developed after the data is available, which then become data-driven questions rather than organization-driven questions. This method is more likely to gleam information from the data that is relevant to the organization and makes the mounds of data manageable. Additionally, this method has the potential to disaggregate data so that specific information relevant to specific components of the organization can be reviewed for program and service delivery model effectiveness measures, based on the questions and the data.

Author of *Five Rules for the Data-Driven Business,* Patricio Robles, offers very practical advice for organizational leadership determined to be data-driven:

1. Remember that organizations can collect too much data. *"... collecting as much data as they can find...is not only distracting, it can reduce the quality of the data-driven decisions.... When too much data is collected, there's a greater likelihood that the wrong analyses will be performed."*

2. Key metrics derived from data should be tied to goals. *"Numbers in and of themselves are often of limited use. Metrics should be associated with goals."*

3. Context helps. *"When setting goals, context is your friend. Tying key metrics to goals are meaningful."*

4. The past and present are not the future. *"Data is inherently limited to yesterday and today. Predictions, no matter how sophisticated, are still just predictions. The data-driven business uses data to make educated decisions; it doesn't naively believe that data is a crystal ball."*

5. Do not dismiss the qualitative. *"If you're only paying attention to the hard data, you're missing out on a huge part of the big picture. What matters most to your organization? That question has to be asked."*

Leaders must understand that there is no data that will fully replace any of the skills that make them and governing boards effective. There are many essential facets of leadership that cannot be found in a data spreadsheet. So, for those leaders and governing boards that hope to simplify decision-making by depending solely on data, they need to know that they could be drinking poison while believing that the elixir called data is medicinal. John Naisbitt, the author of the *Megatrends* books, wrote, *"Intuition becomes increasingly valuable in the new information society precisely because there is so much data."*

EPILOGUE

Leadership expert, Peter Drucker, pointed out many years ago and it still holds true today that leaders are the basic and the scarcest resource of any enterprise. Most organization failures, including businesses, are due to ineffective leadership. Many organizations face an almost continuous search for persons who have the skills necessary to lead effectively and efficiently. The source of leadership influence varies. Some leadership stems from hierarchy position in the organization, where authority is vested in the title and the leader has no other influence. This is viewed as legitimate power, but the leader's influence can be limited unless the leader also has effective leadership skills. Leadership influence stemming from expertise can be very effective, because employees respect the leader's knowledge, but this influence is also compromised if expertise is the sole source of influence. Leadership based on coercion seldom works effectively for any type of organization; there is ample research to prove that. Even effective organization leaders face multiple difficult tasks almost daily, and the governing board can be useful and powerful ally or a destructive force. That balance is a delicate and awkward dance.

The difference between effective and ineffective leadership and governance is often leadership style, expectations, communications or other more subtle things that poisons what otherwise could be and perhaps once was an effectively run organization. Or, perhaps it's an ingredient that is missing that has turned the leadership and governance poisonous, such as trust. The different roles and responsibilities of leaders and governance boards are not clearly articulated in some organizations, particularly the role differences in the operations of an organization. The relationship between leadership and governance is essential to any organization, large or small. It can be a healthy relationship grounded in trust and respect and common purpose. It can be a strengthening relationship supported and encouraged by the success of the organization. An organization's sustainability can be ensured by a strong bond between the leader and the governing board. There are organizations where the governing boards evaluate themselves, based on factors such as advising the leader rather than dictating to him; setting organizational goals and objectives with the leader rather than despite him; receiving operational reports rather than interfering with operations of the organization, and collaborating with each other and the leader rather than dominating and controlling him and quarreling among and between each other. These same productive organizations have leaders who respect the governance boards; who understand their role and the role of the governing board; who understand that the governing board has to be aware of the leader's performance as well as the performance of the organization in order to make decisions in the best interests of the organization; who understand that the leader must communicate effectively and routinely with the governing board; and who understand that the relationship between the leader and the governing board members is always a work in progress.

Both the leader and the governing board must remain aware that every organization has a workplace climate, the conditions within the organization that in large part determine the long-term health of the organization. That climate can be poisoned by poor leadership and poor governance. Leaders and governing boards must also understand the group dynamics of each governing board, from governing boards with twenty members to those with only three. That dynamic can and usually does change over time, and it's important for governing boards to understand what changes are taking place in order to remain effective. For example, the change of one governing board member can change the group dynamics of the governing board and its interaction with the leader. That is another reason why governance training is so important for leaders and governing boards.

Our society which is a broad, interacting connection of various types of individuals and organizations cannot live and prosper without effective leadership and governance. The ingredients and the dose determine if they are healthy or poisonous to organizations.

NOTES

Introduction

1. Barbara Kellerman, *Bad Leadership*, Harvard Business Review Press, 2004.
2. Alan Goldman, *A Toxic CEO Manifesto*, Psychology Today, July, 2011.
3. Pamela Mendels, *The Real Cost of Firing a CEO*, Chief Executive, April 1, 2012.
4. National Institute for Occupational Safety and Health, publication #99-101, 1999.
5. Journal of Business, Economics and Finance, *Impact of Workplace Quality on Employee's Productivity*, 2012, Vol 1, Issue 1.
6. Jean Lipman-Blumen, *The Allure of Toxic CEOs*, Oxford University Press, 2006.

Chapter 1

1. Ron Edmundson, *Five Wrong Ways to Respond to Criticism*, Ron Edmundson.com, 2011.
2. Grady Bogue, *The Enemies of Leadership*, Phi Delta Kappa International, 1985.
3. Mortimer Feinberg and Jack Tarrant, *Why Smart People Do Dumb Things*, Simon and Schuster, 1995.
4. Grady Bogue, *Commentary*, KnowNew.com, 2010.
5. Scott Adams, *Informed decision making quote*, Creator of Dilbert Comic Strip, 2008.
6. C.S. Lewis, *Mere Christianity*, Harper Press, re-released 2001.

Chapter 2

1. *Terence's Comedies*, ancient Roman playwright.
2. Carol Love, Jim Redmond, Rick Ammen, *Managing Bad News*, Center for Community Engagement, 2010.
3. David Javitch, *Delivering Bad News*, Entrepreneur, 2008.
4. Dana Britol-Smith, *Overcome Your Fear of Public Speaking, Speak*

for Success, 2003.

5. James Lukaszewski, *Good New About Bad News*, Security Management Magazine, April, 2000.

6. Tim Berry, *How You Handle Bad News is the Ultimate Test of Leadership*, Business Insider, 2011.

7. Steve Tobak, *How to Deliver Bad News*, MoneyWatch, 2011.

8. Erika James, *Leadership as (Un)usual: How to Display Competence in Times of Crisis*, Organizational Dynamics, Vol. 34, No. 2, 2005.

9. Robert Freeman, *Lincoln on Leadership*, Humanities 360, 2009.

10. Gene Klann, *Crisis Leadership*, Center for Creative Leadership, 2013.

11. Ken Sweeny, *Crisis Decision Theory*, Psychological Bulletin, January, 2008.

Chapter 3

1. *Civic Index for Quality Public Education*, Public Education Network, 2008.

2. Frederick Hess, *The Role of the Local Governing board*, Center for Public Education2002.

3. *Local Governing Board Voter Participation Survey*, Iowa Governing Boards Association, 2007.

4. Kent Weeks, *Governing Boards Duties*, State University.com, 2000.

5. Greg Edwards, *Truman Bank Board Member Resigns Cites Interference*, St. Louis Business Journal, September 28, 2011.

6. Stephen Covey, *The Speed of Trust*, Simon and Schuster, 2008.

7. Gary Burnison, *The Twelve Absolutes of Leadership*, McGraw-Hill Education, 2012.

8. Carlo Corsi, Guilherme Dale, Julie Hembrock Daum, and Willi Schoppen, *Five Things Board Directors Should Be Thinking About*, Point of View, 2010.

9. Jim Collins, *Built to Last*, Harper Business Essentials, 1994.

10. Chip Heath, *Made to Stick*, Random House, 2007.

11. Lisa Iannucci, *Dealing with Difficult Board Members*, The Cooperator, 2008.

12. John Jantsch, *The Commitment Engine*, Penguin Group, 2012.

13. Dayton Ogden and John Wood, *Succession Planning: A Board Imperative*, Bloomberg Business Week, March 25, 2008.

Chapter 4

1. Robert Greenleaf, *Servant Leadership*, Paulist Press, 1977 and 2002.
2. George Patton, quote on Leadership, *Patton on Leadership*, Alan Axelrod, Palgrave MacMillan Books, 2007.
3. Dorothy Law Nolte, *Children Learn What They Live*, In *100 Ways to Enhance Self-Concept in the Classroom*, J. Canfield and H.C. Wells, Allyn and Bacon, 1976.
4. Marcus Buckingham, *The One Thing You Need to Know*, The Free Press, 2005.
5. Cooper, B. S., Fusarelli, L. D., & Carella, V. A. *Career crisis in the superintendency? The results of a national survey*, American Association of School Administrators, 2002.
6. *The Great City Schools Survey of Superintendents*, Great City Schools Council, 2003.
7. Steve Denning, *Seven Lessons Every CEO Must Learn*, Forbes Magazine, January, 2013.
8. The Center for Association Leadership, *Succession Planning for Nonprofit CEOs*, 2007.
9. Michelle Young, George Peterson, and Paula Short, *The Complexity of Substantive Reform*, paper commissioned for the Meeting of the National Commission for the Advancement of Educational Leadership Preparation, 2001.
10. Gary Burnison, *The Twelve Absolutes of Leadership*, McGraw-Hill Education, 2012.
11. Edward Gerstner, *Elephants Can Dance*, Harper Collins, 2003.
12. Thomas Watson, Jr., *Father, Son and Co.*, Bantum Books, 1991.
13. Thomas Davenport, Brook Manville, and Laurence Prusak, *Judgment Calls: Twelve Stories of Big Decisions and the Teams That Got Them Right*, Harvard Business Press Books, 2012.
14. Alan Axelrod, *Elizabeth I, CEO: Strategic Lessons from the CEO who Built an Empire*, Prentice Hall Press, 2000.
15. Debra Nussbaum, *Calling All Superintendents*, New York Times, September, 2007.
16. Glenn Llopis, *The Most Successful CEOs Do 15 Things*, Forbes Magazine, 2013.
17. Thomas Glass, Lars Bjork, and Cryss Brunner, *The 2000 Study of the American Public School Superintendent*, American Association of School Administrators, 2000.
18. T.L. Asbury, *Superintendent and School Board Member Turnover*, Presentation, 2003.

19. *All in Favor: Cast your vote for student success*, publication of the Georgia School Boards Association, 2012.

20. Kerry Patterson, Joseph Grenny, David Maxfield, Ron McMillian, and Al Switzler, *Influencer: The Power to Change Anything*, McGraw-Hill, 2007.

21. John Clemens and Douglas Meyer, *The Classic Touch*, McGraw-Hill, 1987.

22. Kurt Lewin, Ronald Lippitt, and Ralph White, *Patterns of Aggressive Behavior*, Journal of Social Psychology, Volume 10, Issue 2, Heldref Publications, 1939.

23. Paul Houston and Doug Eadie, *The Board-Savvy Superintendent*, First Rowman & Littlefield, 2007.

24. Ken Blanchard, *One Minute Manager*, Harper Collins, 1982.

25. James Critin and Julie Hembrock, *You Need a CEO - Now What?*, Crown Business, 2011.

26. Antoinette E. LaBelle, *Transition to New Leadership*, The Bridgespan Group, 2012.

27. A. Gilmore, *In with the New: CEO Dos and Don'ts*, Talent Management, April 2008.

28. Marilu Goodyear and Cynthia Golden, *Leadership Transitions*, Professional Development, 2008.

Chapter 5

1. Kerry Patterson, Joseph Grenny, David Maxfield, Ron McMillian, and Al Switzler, *Influencer: The Power to Change Anything*, McGraw-Hill, 2007.

2. John Ivancevich, Andrew Szilagyi, and Marc Wallace, *Organizational Behavior and Performance*, Goodyear Publishing Company, 1977.

3. John Sheridan, John Slocum, and Max Richards, *Expectancy Theory as a Lead Indicator of Job Behavior*, Decision Sciences, Volume 5, Issue 3, 1974.

4. Tom Peter and Robert Waterman, *In Search of Excellence*, Harper Collins, 1982.

5. Jack Welch, *Winning*, Harper Collins, 2005.

6. *Campus Safety Survey*, Campus Safety Magazine, 2012.

7. *Workplace Bullying Survey*, Workplace Bullying Institute, Survey commissioned by Zogby International, 2010.

8. *No Work Place Bullies*, Civility Partners, LLC, San Diego, California.

9. Did Depression or an Alleged Bully Boss Prompt Editor's Suicide? ABC News, August 19, 2010.

10. *Dealing with Violence in the Workplace*, United States Office of Personnel Management, OWR-09, February, 1998.

11. *Tips for School Administrators for Reinforcing School Safety*, National Association of School Psychologists, NASP Resources, 2006.

12. *School Survey on Crime and Safety*, National Center for Education Statistics, 2011.

13. Dennis Kramer, *School Climate, Student Attendance and Discipline*, Georgia Department of Education, 2013.

Chapter 6

1. Jim Collins, *Good to Great*, Harper Business Essentials, 2001.

2. Daniel Goleman, *Leadership That Gets Results*, Harvard Business Review, 2000.

3. Center for Creative Leadership Survey, 2009.

4. Rick Piraino, *Leadership and Favoritism*, Ezine Articles, 2008.

5. Stephen Covey, *Speed of Trust*, Simon and Schuster, 2008.

6. Scott Edinger, *Three C's of Implementing Strategy*, Forbes Magazine, August 7, 2012.

7. Engaging the Employee – Motivation and Morale, Human Resources Brain Bank, resources.hrbrainbank.com, March 6, 2009.

8. Daisy McCarty, *The Role of Company CEOs in Change*, Employee Relations Articles, 2009.

9. *Six Traits of Great CEOs*, Inc. Online, March 22, 2012.

10. Daniel Pink, *The Surprising Truth About What Motivates Us*, Penguin Group, 2009.

11. Jeff Jarvis, *What Would Google Do?*, Harper Business, 2009.

12. Allen Cohen and David Bradford, *Influencing Up*, John Wiley and Sons, 2012.

13. Jack Welch, *Winning*, Harper Collins, 2005.

14. Henry Mintzberg, *The Nature of Managerial Work*, Prentice-Hall, 1983.

15. Albert Bandura, *Social Foundations of Thought and Action*, Prentice-Hall, 1985.

16. Rosabeth Moss Kanter, *Confidence: How Winning Streaks and Losing Streaks Begin and End*, Three Rivers Press, 2004.

17. Sara Weaver and George Yancey, *The Impact of Dark Leadership*

on Organizational Commitment, Leadership Review, Vol. 10, 2010.

18. Grady Bogue, *The Enemies of Leadership*, Phi Delta Kappa International, 1985.

19. Tom Peters and Robert Waterman, *In Search of Excellence*, Harper Collins, 1982.

Chapter 7

1. Matt Miller, *The Two Percent Solution*, Perseus Books Group, 2003.

2. Marc Joffe, Guardian Editorial, February 25, 2013.

3. Stephanie Lowell, Brain Treistad, and Bill Meehan, *The Rating Game*, Stanford Social Innovation Review, 2005.

Chapter 8

1. Michael Cohen and James March, *Leadership and Ambiguity*, Harvard Business Press, 1986.

2. John Baldoni, *How a Good CEO Reacts to a Crisis*, Harvard Business Review, January 4, 2011.

3. Helga Drummond, *Guide to Decision-Making: Getting it More Right than Wrong*, Wiley and Sons, 2012.

4. Michael Hyatt, *When Leadership Fails*, International Leadership, March 5, 2012.

5. Gene Klann, *Crisis Leadership*, Center for Creative Leadership, 2013.

6. Ken Sweeny, *Crisis Decision Theory*, Psychological Bulletin, January, 2008.

Chapter 9

1. Patrick Lencioni, *Death by Meeting: A Leadership Fable About Solving the Most Painful Problem in Business*, Jossey-Bass, 2004.

2. Stephen Covey, *Speed of Trust*, Simon and Schuster, 2008.

3. Jack Welch, *Winning*, Harper Collins, 2005.

4. Carly Florina, *Tough Choices*, Penguin Group, 2006.

5. Jon Katzenbach, *Teams at the Top*, McKinsey and Company, Inc., 1998.

6. Patrick Lencioni, *The Five Dysfunctions of a Team*, Jossey-Bass, 2002.
7. Marie McIntyre, *The Management Team Handbook*, Jossey-Bass, 1998.
8. Bradley Sugar, *Instant Team Building*, McGraw Hill, 2005.

Chapter 10

1. Garry McGiboney, *The Private Side of a Public Education*, Anaphora Literary Press, 2011.
2. Jack Welch, *Winning*, Harper Collins, 2005.
3. Antoinette LaBelle, *Transition to New Leadership: The First 1,000 Days*, BoardSource, 2011.
4. Michael Watkins, *The First 90 Days: Critical Success Strategies*, Harvard Business School Publishing, 2003.
5. John Maxwell, *Everyone Communicates Few Connect*, Thomas Nelson, Inc., 2010.
6. Jay Hall, *To Achieve or Not: The Manager's Choice*, California Management Review, Vol. XVIII, number 4, 1976.
7. Cindy Kraft, *Executive Transition,* Market Study, 2008.
8. *2008 Study on New Leadership*, Alexcel Group, Institute of Executive Development, 2009.
9. Mike Myatt, *15 Ways to Identify Bad CEOs*, Forbes Magazine, October 18, 2012.

Chapter 11

1. Carmen J. Lee, *Education 2000: Reforming Schools for a New Century*, Pittsburgh Post-Gazette, September 3, 2000.
2. Kathleen Cotton, *School Size, School Climate and School Performance*, Northwest Regional Education Lab, 1996.
3. Marshall Goldsmith, *What Got You Here Won't Get You There*, Hyperion, 2007.
4. Allan Kimmel, *Rumors and Rumor Control: Managers Guide to Understanding and Combating Rumors*, Prentice Hall Europe, 1995.
5. Alex Saez, *How Should Supervisors Handle Rumors*, Small Business, 2013.
6. Stephen Leigh, *Speaking Stones*, Harper Collins, 1999.
7. Susan Pendleton, *Rumor Research Revisited and Expanded,*

Language and Communication, January, 1998.

8. E.K. Fiske, *Research on Gossip: Taxonomy, Methods and Future Directions*, Review of General Psychology, June, 2004.

9. Prashant Borida and Nicholas DiFonzo, *Problem Solving in Social Interaction on the Internet: Rumors as Social Recognition*, Social Psychology Quarterly, Vol. 67, No. 1, 2004.

10. Colleen Mills, *Experiencing Gossip: The Foundations for a Theory of Embedded Organizational Gossip*, Group Organization Management, 2010.

11. Robert T. Whipple, *The Trust Factor*, Productivity Publications, 2003.

Chapter 12

1. Stephen Covey, *The Speed of Trust*, Simon and Schuster, 2008.

2. Mrunal Belvalkar, *Dangers of Misplaced Loyalty*, Buzzle, December 23, 2011.

3. Mark Buckingham, *The One Thing You Need to Know*, The Free Press, 2005.

4. Jack Welch, *Winning*, Harper Collins, 2005.

5. Stephen Covey, *The Seven Habits of Highly Effective People*, Simon and Schuster, 1989.

6. *Advantages and Disadvantages of Hiring Friends and Relatives*, BusinessKnowledgeSource.com, 2012.

7. Michael Farr and Edward Claflin, *The Arrogance Cycle*, Lyons Press, 2012.

8. Doug Blackie, *Obsequious Sycophants*, Real CEOs, 2012.

9. Warren Bennis, *On Becoming a CEO*, Alfred A. Knopf, Inc., 1989.

10. Celia Sandys, *We Shall Not Fail: Churchillian Principles*, Penguin Group, 2003.

11. Ira Chaleff, *The Courageous Follower*, Berrett-Koehler Publishers, 2009.

12. Peter Drucker, *The Effective Executive*, Harper Collins Publishers, Inc., 1967, 1985, 1996, 2002.

13. *Entrepreneur, Inc.*, Editorial, May 2013.

Chapter 13

1. Nate Silver, *The Signal and the Noise*, Penguin Group, 2012.

2. Bob Kaplan and David Norton, *Balanced Scorecard*, Harvard

Business Review, 1992.

3. Andrew Neely, *Does the Balanced Scorecard Work: An Empirical Investigation*, Cranfield CERES, January 2008.

4. Guido Schwerdt and Martin West, *The Impact of Alternative Grade Configurations on Student Outcomes through Middle and High School*, Harvard Institute for Economic Research, 2011.

5. Brian Christian, *The A/B Test: Inside the Technology That's Changing the Rules of Business*, Wired Magazine, April 25, 2012.

6. *The Problem with Data Driven Decisions*, Intercom, 2012.

7. Patricio Robles, *Five Rules for the Data-Driven Business*, E-Consultancy.com, November 22, 2010.

8. Kenneth Cukiers and Viktor Mayer-Schoenberger, Foreign Affairs, Vol. 92, Number 3, June 2013.

9. John Naisbitt, *Megatrends*, Avon Books, 1991.

OTHER ANAPHORA LITERARY PRESS TITLES

PLJ: Interviews with Best-Selling YA Writers
Editor: Anna Faktorovich

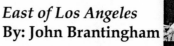 

East of Los Angeles
By: John Brantingham

Notes on the Road to Now
By: Paul Bellerive

Folk Concert
By: Janet Ruth Heller

100 Years of the Federal Reserve
By: Marie Bussing-Burks

River Bends in Time
By: Glen A. Mazis

Interviews with BFF Winners
Editor: Anna Faktorovich

An Adventurous Life
By: Robert Hauptman

CPSIA information can be obtained
at www.ICGtesting.com
Printed in the USA
LVOW12s1327310518
579121LV00001B/67/P